ESSENCE
Brings You
GREAT
COOKING

ESSENCE

Brings You

GREAT
COOKING

Jonell Nash

ESSENCE® **Magazine, Food Editor**

 **Amistad**

An Imprint of HarperCollinsPublishers

HarperCollins books may be purchased for educational, business, or sales promotional use. For information, please write: Special Markets Department, HarperCollins Publishers Inc., 10 East 53rd Street, New York, NY 10022.

Originally published in hardcover in 1994.

FIRST AMISTAD TRADE PAPERBACK EDITION 2001

Designed by Bonni Leon-Berman

Printed on acid-free paper

Library of Congress Cataloging-in-Publication Data

Nash, Jonell.
    Essence brings you great cooking / Jonell Nash.—1st ed.
        p. cm.
    Includes bibliographical references and index.
    ISBN 0-06-095813-8
      1. Afro-American cookery. 2. Menus. I. Essence. II. Title.
    TX715.N254 2001
    614.59'296073—dc21
                                              2001046088

01 02 03 04 05   10 9 8 7 6 5 4 3 2 1

To Mollie Nash

and Willie Nash, Sr. —

loving parents and great home cooks

who taught me that

the most important ingredient

that goes into the pot is

a measure of caring.

Acknowledgments

In ways large and small, tangible and intangible, many people helped in the creation of this book. I sincerely thank all who participated. There are some key individuals that I specifically would like to salute.

My family and a few close friends share in the credit for any of my accomplishments. They encouraged me throughout the writing of this book and understood why I could not be with them as much as we all wanted. Paul Butler, as always, provided invaluable suggestions and unwavering support.

My new friends at Amistad tenderly guided me through the maze of my first book-publishing venture. I am forever grateful to my deft and sure-footed editor, Malaika Adero; director of sales and marketing, and skilled troubleshooter, Sandy Summers Head; and to visionary publisher Charles Harris.

Literary agent Marie Brown championed the cause. Her early belief in the cookbook was instrumental in bringing it into existence.

Members of the Essence family, Edward Lewis, Clarence O. Smith, and James Forsythe, through this undertaking, once again broke new ground. Harry Dedyo and Bob Volepak kept the project operating smoothly. Stephanie Stokes Oliver and our editorial guiding light, Susan L. Taylor, contributed to the book's overall quality.

Venezuela Newborn, my predecessor and Essence food editor for thirteen years, laid a foundation of excellence. Vennie picked up the torch from the magazine's first food editor, Louise Prothro.

Many talented chefs and dedicated home cooks shared their recipes and love of cooking. Among them: Edna Lewis, my professional role model; Patrick Clark, with whom I am co-authoring a book featuring his recipes; and Leah Chase of the famed Dookie Chase in New Orleans.

The recipe squad of Cherella Cox, Tonya Adams, June Owens, and Charlotte Chorot was upbeat and diligent in their tedious job of transcribing. Rhonda Stieglitz applied caring and rigorous standards to recipe testing. Paula Sanchez served as test kitchen assistant. Celeste Bullock provided invaluable research that enriched the book and helped the pages sing. Barbara Hansen and Sherrill Clarke kept the copy in the right key.

The art team of photographer Judd Pilossof; food stylist Mariann Sauvion; book designer Bonni Leon-Berman; and art consultant LaVon Leak-Wilks made the book as beautiful as it is meaningful.

Last, yet far from least, were the Essence staffers and others who joined in the taste tests and took their roles seriously—even when tasting fun foods such as Slimline Chocolate Mousse and Sweet Potato Cheesecake!

ESSENCE BRINGS YOU
GREAT COOKING

Contents

From its inception, this cookbook took on a sense of celebration as a joyous tribute to our proud and brilliant African-American food tradition. Although this cookbook has been twenty-three years in the making, its actual development spans centuries and continents.

Enslaved Africans brought to this land okra, yams, peanuts, sesame seeds, wild greens, and hot peppers. Tucked deep inside their being, our ancestors also carried cooking formulas for meals with lively, earthy flavors. Our food story is deeply rooted and rich with culinary talent. These foods and cooking techniques became part of the foundation of Southern regional cookery—widely considered the most celebrated and distinctive American cuisine. Our dishes appeal to the senses—they are spicy, peppery, sweet, tangy, crispy, juicy, robust, and aromatic—and will please the most demanding palate.

Though many of our traditional foods are excellent sources of nutrients—sweet potatoes are rich in vitamin A, collard greens are loaded with vitamin C, dried beans brim with protein—the old methods of cooking and seasoning that include excessive fat, sodium, and sugar have contributed to the disproportionate health problems that African Americans suffer. Our challenge in updating some of the older recipes was to keep the rich, familiar taste and to lose the heaviness of the foods. We cut fat, salt, and sugar, and added more herbs, spices, and other seasonings to keep these dishes flavorful and satisfying.

It is my hope that this book will not be just collected, but actually used. If you are inexperienced or plain busy, cooking from scratch may appear to be too complicated and time consuming. You probably use packaged mixes, frozen dinners, and take-out from fast-food restaurants as your easy ways out. But what a price you pay! Convenience foods usually cost considerably more than homemade versions and they tend to offer much less nutritionally. Most noticeably, ready-to-eat and fabricated foods lack the flavor, taste, and all-around enjoyment of home-cooked foods. Give it a try, and you will see that homecooking is just a series of easy steps. Yet, truly great cooking is not just about skills—it's also a matter of the heart. Offering oneself and one's hospitality in a spirit of love and thankfulness can make the most humble meal a grand experience.

I have endeavored to write a cookbook for all time—one that reflects our history and our present awareness of the importance of good nutrition. I was also committed to preserving our "foodways" for the future.

Enthusiasm for African-American, Southern, and Caribbean cooking is spreading across the United States. Following centuries of oversight there's been a corresponding breakthrough in the food industry and in media recognition of today's African-American chefs and cooks of old. That which we have known and prized for so long has come of age.

Join the celebration.

How to Use This Book

First, read the recipe you are planning to make from beginning to end. Decide how you will improvise by substituting what's on hand, what's fresh at the market, or what you have a taste for. Before you begin, make sure that you have all the required equipment and ingredients, and that you understand the procedures and cooking techniques.

Use the cross references that are listed for dishes that require two recipes. For example, the recipe for Southern Corn Bread Dressing requires that you first make the basic Corn Bread recipe. Similarly, Creole Shrimp is found in the Seafood chapter and the recipe for its perfect accompaniment, Festive Rice Ring, is in the Grits and Other Great Grains chapter.

Recipe ingredients are listed in the order in which they are used. All measurements are based on standard measuring spoons and cups; all measurements are level.

In recipes that include salt, it is listed as an optional ingredient. The amount of salt suggested is minimal. If you are not sensitive to sodium, and care to use more, start with the amount stated, then adjust the seasonings to your taste. A tip: Salt is an acquired taste; as you use less, your desire and taste for salt tends to decrease.

Each recipe lists the amount of calories, protein, fat, carbohydrate, sodium, and cholesterol it contains. Optional garnishes are not included in the analysis. Although salt is listed in recipes as optional, it is included in the sodium count. If a recipe suggests an alternate ingredient (such as water instead of broth), the analysis is provided for the primary ingredient, not the alternative. For recipes that suggest a range of servings—for example: 4 to 6—analysis is provided for the smallest number of servings. See the section called Nutritional Analysis in Part One.

There's an old saying, "Talking 'bout fire doesn't boil the pot." Let's get started!

In Part Two, Chapter One: Vegetables, Chapter Two: Bountiful Beans, and Chapter Five: Eggs and Cheese, the nutritional analysis for sodium does not include the salt listed as an optional ingredient. If you add salt to a recipe from one of those chapters, calculate the sodium as follows: Divide the amount of sodium (one teaspoon of salt contains 2,200 milligrams of sodium) by the number of servings, then add that number to the amount of sodium listed for the recipe.

Be mindful that sodium occurs naturally in a wide variety of foods such as dairy products, eggs, meat, poultry, and vegetables. Sodium is added in surprisingly large amounts to a wide variety of convenience foods. Check nutritional labels routinely and tally amounts from all sources to gauge your sodium intake. For more information on salt and sodium, see page 6 in Part One.

S ETTING UP

We've come a long way to get back to the wisdom of our ancestors. Traditionally, root doctors, midwives, medicine men, herbalists, and mothers of sick children worked everyday healing miracles with common foods, plants, and herbs. Now, modern science, which once scoffed at the notion of the curative power of foods, proudly announces "new" conclusive findings linking food and eating habits with ailments and diseases ranging from incontinence to arthritis. We can now benefit from both of these worlds.

Some of the foods we love most are the best medicine against poor health and premature aging. Cabbage, mustard greens, collard greens, brussels sprouts, broccoli, and cauliflower are proven cancer fighters and belong to the lifesaving cruciferous vegetable family. Sweet potatoes with beta carotene and soluble fiber help lower blood cholesterol and remove toxins.

There is an abundance of fruits, vegetables, and whole grains with therapeutic benefits. Always include apples, dried beans, carrots, citrus fruits, cranberries, fish, garlic, oats, peppers, and prunes in your diet. **More trips to the produce section can mean fewer trips to the doctor.**

EATING FOR OPTIMUM HEALTH

The choices you make about diet and nutrition are vital to your, and your family's, well-being. Yet, the news reports that bombard us with what we should and should not eat can be contradictory and confusing. The following guidelines are reliable, easy-to-understand steps compiled by the United States Department of Agriculture—the USDA. Don't be put off if the list seems long. Do what you can. Consider starting with the third recommendation. Making small changes toward eating healthier can bring noticeable results.

NUTRITIONAL GUIDELINES

1. *Eat a wide variety of foods.*

Eating many different foods greatly improves your chances of receiving the full range of the 40 or more nutrients bodies need for optimum health.

2. *Maintain a healthy weight.*

If you eat more calories than you use, you will gain weight. By burning up more calories than you consume, you will lose weight. The most effective way to lose weight and keep it off is to lose weight slowly. Nutritionists recommend a loss of no more than one-half to one pound per week.

3. *Reduce fat, especially saturated fat.*

Fat intake should not exceed 30 percent of the day's calories, with less than ten percent of the calories coming from saturated fat. People who are overweight or have a heart problem may be advised to cut back to twenty five percent or less.

4. *Eat an abundance of vegetables, fruits, and grains.*

Adults should eat at least three servings of vegetables, two servings of fruit, and six servings of grain products—especially whole grains—every day.

5. *Use sugar only in moderation.*

Sweets offer little nutritional value and contain excessive calories that can lead to weight gain. Sweets have been shown to cause tooth decay.

6. *Use salt only in moderation.*

It is recommended that salt consumption from all sources should not exceed three grams (3,000 milligrams) per day. (See Nutritional Analysis section.)

7. *If you drink alcohol, do so in moderation.*

Not only does alcohol offer empty calories, but excessive use of it leads to ailments such as kidney and liver disease. A sound recommendation is to have no more than two small drinks a day. Because alcohol can cause birth defects, pregnant women are urged to abstain from all such beverages.

NUTRITIONAL ANALYSIS

Next to each recipe in this cookbook is a breakdown of the major nutrients that the prepared dish contains. Learn to look at your whole dietary picture. For example, if you are going to have a rich dessert such as cheesecake after dinner, enjoy it but make it your only sweet—other than fresh fruit—for the day. Also be sure that the other foods you eat will not take you over your daily calorie requirement, or exceed thirty percent of calories from fat.

CALORIES express the energy-producing value of food. To determine how many calories you need daily, multiply your weight by thirteen. For example, if you weigh 130 pounds, your calorie requirement would be 1,690. This number of calories represents the calorie needs of a moderately active person. If you are inactive, multiply your weight by eleven; if you are very active multiply by fifteen. If you are overweight, use the weight you would like to be as the gauge for multiplying. As everyone who has ever dieted to lose weight knows, if you burn up more calories than you take in, you lose weight; if you take in more than you use, you gain weight . . . simple.

PROTEIN is the body's main source for growth and tissue repair. It is made up of compounds called amino acids that build muscle and tissue and are crucial to the production of neurotransmitters—chemical elements in the brain related to essential functions such as memory and alertness. Ten to twenty percent of daily calories should come from protein.

FAT aids in the absorption of the fat-soluble vitamins A, D, E, and K. It also helps maintain cell membranes and stores extra energy in the body. The three types of fat are monounsaturated, polyunsaturated, and saturated. Although all fats are a mixture of the three types, one type usually predominates. Vegetable fats are mainly unsaturated and most animal fats are primarily saturated. The amount of fat needed by the body is minuscule—about one tablespoon of polyunsaturated fat per day. Fat, however, is a primary factor in making our food more palatable; it makes foods juicier, more flavorful, and satisfying. So we tend to overdo it.

ESSENCE BRINGS YOU
GREAT COOKING

The recommendation is that no more than thirty percent (preferably less) of daily calories come from fat; saturated fat should be limited to ten percent. Be aware that fat in the diet can be both visible and invisible. We tend to focus on the visible like butter and cooking oils, yet much of the fat we consume is not apparent—the fat in milk and cheese, in and under poultry skin, in french fries and other fried foods, and in baked goods such as oversized bran muffins.

WHY IS FAT FATTENING? One gram of fat contains nine calories, more than twice the four calories found in a gram of carbohydrate or protein.

CARBOHYDRATES convert into glucose, the body's main source of energy. There are two types of carbohydrates—simple and complex. Simple carbohydrates, also called simple sugars, are found in fruit, sugar, and sugary foods. These foods are quickly absorbed and converted into glucose, the result of which is a burst of energy that quickly dissipates. Complex carbohydrates, also called starches—pasta, bread, legumes, and grains, convert more slowly into glucose. As a result, they provide the body with a steadier flow of energy over a longer period of time. This group also supplies other needed nutrients. Fifty to sixty percent of the daily calories should come from carbohydrates.

SODIUM, in combination with chloride and potassium, regulates the amount and movement of body fluids, transports nutrients across intestinal membranes, controls blood volume, and transmits signals affecting nerves and muscles. Sodium can, however, be problematic when the intake is excessive. The average adult requires between two hundred and three hundred milligrams per day, or about one-tenth to one-eighth teaspoon of salt. Too much sodium can shift the balance of fluids in body cells and lead to a build up of water, which can cause swelling. Another possible result of excess sodium is the drawing of more water into the blood, which causes elevated pressure. Nutritionists recommend limiting sodium intake to between 1,100 and 3,300 milligrams per day.

CHOLESTEROL is a fatty substance present in every cell of the human body and in the fat of the animal foods we eat—meat, cheese, and egg yolks for example. Cholesterol performs important functions such as aiding digestion and helping produce hormones. Cholesterol and the lipoproteins that carry it, are produced by the liver. High-density lipoproteins (HDLs) move cholesterol safely between the liver and tissue cells; they are considered "good." Low-density lipoproteins—the "bad" ones—are not as efficient and lose cholesterol in the arteries, where it accumulates and forms fatty deposits called plaque. Cholesterol deposits eventually impede the flow of blood to the heart and lead to heart disease. The American Heart Association recommends limiting dietary cholesterol to 300 milligrams a day.

FIBER is any part of an edible plant that cannot be digested in the gastrointestinal tract. Although it provides no nutrients, fiber is essential to good health. There are two principal types—soluble and insoluble. Soluble fiber dissolves in water to form a gel in the intestine, which allows for greater absorption of glucose from the digestive tract and aids elimination by softening stools. Studies show that it may also reduce cholesterol. Insoluble fiber does not dissolve in water, but retains it instead, thus increasing stool volume and speeding elimination. Twenty to thirty grams of fiber each day are recommended for best results.

LET THEM REST IN PEACE

Though once a part of our food tradition, the following foods have not stood the test of time. Excessive saturated fat and/or sodium lay to rest any contribution these foods can offer. May they remain only in memory and as a part of history.

Crackling
Lard
Salt pork
Ham hocks
Salt-filled shakers

To help stay fit and well for a long time to come, in conjunction with your eating-for-good-health-plan, be sure to include a program of exercise.

Cooking with Herbs

Cooking with herbs is a simple way to create good-tasting, good-for-you meals. With just a sprinkle of flavor-packed herbs, otherwise bland-tasting low-salt or low-fat dishes take on a burst of flavor and aroma. Cooking with herbs may seem complicated to those who rely on just salt and pepper, yet it's almost as easy. A wider variety of fresh herbs is now available in supermarkets. Some come already potted and ready to go onto a window sill to snip as needed; or even better, grow your own.

Here are a handful of flavorful herbs for cooking and growing.

BASIL has a vegetable-like flavor that mixes especially well with tomato-based dishes and sauces and with pasta.

CHIVES are pungent-flavored herbs from the onion family. Chop them up and add to salads, sandwiches, and soups; or mix them with butter to make an herb butter.

DILL complements vegetable, egg, potato, and cheese dishes, as well as salmon. Especially tasty added to carrots, green beans, and brussels sprouts. Popularly used as a pickling herb.

MINT has a sweet and refreshing flavor that complements desserts. It is also an excellent seasoning for lamb dishes. Mint teas are known for settling the stomach.

PARSLEY is the all-purpose herb that goes so well with vegetables, meats, seafood, poultry, eggs, and cheeses. Add to soups, salads, stews, vegetables, pot roasts, omelets, and scrambled eggs. (Chew a sprig for fresh breath.)

THYME is pungent, aromatic, and my favorite herb. It is popularly used in gumbos and rice dishes. Use it to season seafood, poultry, potatoes, and eggs; add to soups, stews, and casseroles.

The Pot and the Kettle
and Other Cooking Essentials

Even if it's not the kitchen of your dreams, by having a few essential tools (plus maybe a few specialty items) and a bit of organization, cooking can become more of a breeze and a pleasure.

Select pots and pans that are heavyweight and have tight-fitting lids. Equip your kitchen with the following basics:

Dutch oven, sauce pot, or stock pot (6 quart or larger)

Saucepans—1-quart, 2-quart, and 3-quart

Skillets—7-inch (excellent for omelets), 10-inch (basic sautéeing and panfrying), and 12-inch (oversized for big batches, pancakes, etcetera.)

The following utensils are a step beyond basic yet will be very helpful as you expand your cooking repertoire.

Steamer pot—ideal for cooking vegetables, fish, and for reheating foods.

Wok—speed-cooking utensil designed by the Chinese. The rounded bottom allows foods to be stir-fried with a minimum of oil.

Pressure cooker—cooks food in a smaller amount of the time and liquid than it would take with regular cooking methods. Conveniently cooks dried beans or less tender cuts of meats. Good for nutrient retention during cooking.

Roasting pan—oversized pan for cooking large cuts of meat and poultry. Although it comes with a lid, the lid should not be used for actual roasting, as this causes the food to steam rather than roast.

Double boiler—for cooking heat-sensitive foods such as custards and delicate sauces; pans can be used separately.

BAKING PANS

General—13-by-9-by-2-inch pan and 8-inch square

Cake pans—two or three 9-inch round

Loaf pan—9-by-5-by-3-inch for cakes, meatloaf

Baking sheet—for baking cookies and general use

Muffin tin—one or two with twelve cups each ,

ESSENCE BRINGS YOU
GREAT COOKING

Consider Cast Iron

Cast iron cooking utensils are the oldest—dating back a few thousand years—and, to many, still the best! They are strong, hold heat well, conduct heat evenly, are excellent for long, slow cooking, and can actually add a dose of iron to the food cooked in them. Many dedicated cooks would not consider frying chicken or baking corn bread in anything but a cast iron skillet. Cast iron does, however, require special care. To prevent rust, the inside of the cookware should be occasionally treated with cooking oil. It should not be washed with strong detergents or scoured. To keep clean, wash with soapy water and a sponge or brush. Immediately after rinsing, dry thoroughly over heat using oven or burner.

Before cast iron cookware is used for the first time, it must be seasoned. Thoroughly coat inside and out with vegetable oil or shortening. Wipe off excess and heat in a 275° F. oven for about two hours. Cool and wipe with paper towel. Re-season as needed.

BAKING DISHES

Casseroles—1½-quart and 3-quart, preferably with lids
Pie plates—9- or 10-inch

KNIVES

Fine knives are your best helper in the kitchen. Buy the finest quality you can afford and, most important, keep them sharp. A dull knife takes more time to use and more pressure to cut, making it more likely to cut you than a sharp knife. Start with three basic knives (chef's, paring, and serrated).

CHEF'S KNIFE—an all-purpose knife for most slicing. It should be heavy and feel good in your hand.

PARING KNIFE—this small knife (two to four inches) is the all-purpose blade for peeling and fine slicing smaller items such as garlic and herbs.

SERRATED KNIFE—this scalloped blade is for slicing bread, tomatoes, and other items that require a sawing motion to avoid pressing down and squashing them.

CLEAVER—not an essential knife, but an excellent choice for cutting bulky items such as poultry and meat. Once you start to use this one, it will seem indispensable.

KNIFE RACK, CASE, OR MAGNETIZED BOARD—do not keep knives in a drawer because it is unsafe and does not protect the blade's cutting edge. A knife sharpener, sharpening stone, and a sharpening steel keeps blades in top shape.

CUTTING BOARD—two needed: one for cutting onions, garlic, and other foods with strong odors; another needed for general use.

HAND TOOLS

BRUSHES—one for pastry. Another for greasing pans and basting.

FORK—long-handled for turning and removing heavy foods from cooking vessel.

GRATER—four-sider for grating, shredding, and slicing. Great for coleslaw, carrots, zucchini, and cheese.

FAT SEPARATOR—cup that allows you to pour meat juices, stock, or soup through a spout without the fat, which remains in the cup.

LADLE—for serving soups, stews, and some sauces.

MEASURING CUPS—1-, 2-, and 4-cup glass measurers with spouts for measuring liquids. One or two sets of nesting metal or plastic cups for measuring dry ingredients. Sizes usually range from two tablespoons to two cups.

MEASURING SPOONS—two sets of nesting spoons. Spoons range from one-eighth teaspoon to one tablespoon.

NUTMEG GRATER—just one taste of freshly grated nutmeg will probably convert you to grating your own.

OPENERS—hand-held or wall-mounted; punch-type combination bottle and can opener. Corkscrew for wine bottles.

PASTRY BLENDER—this tool makes easy work of cutting in the fat when making biscuits, pie crusts, and similar doughs.

PASTA RAKE—ingenious device for stirring and serving pasta.

PEPPER MILL—freshly ground pepper is markedly superior to already ground. Mills allow you to adjust the coarseness of the pepper.

ROLLING PIN—for rolling biscuits, pie crusts, and making crumbs.

ROTARY BEATER—for mixing and whipping. Also known as an egg-beater.

SCISSORS—just for kitchen use. Use to cut string, snip herbs, trim pastry dough, cut up chicken. Use scissors instead of your good knives to open packages, cut string, and so forth.

SPATULAS—at least one rubber for scraping bowls. At least one narrow and one wide for turning food over and for lifting.

SPOONS—slotted for draining items being moved. Several wooden spoons for stirring while cooking and general mixing.

STRAINERS—at least two; one fine 2-to-3-inch sieve; one coarser large sieve.

THERMOMETERS—an oven thermometer is essential for checking the accuracy of the temperature for serious baking. Deep frying and meat thermometers are also helpful.

TIMER—there are many choices. Newer styles can time several procedures at once.

TONGS—for turning or removing food while cooking without piercing. Also handy for mixing and serving salads.

VEGETABLE PEELER—a versatile time-saver. Use it not only for potatoes, but for all kinds of vegetables and fruits.

WHISK—excellent for stirring and mixing; especially good for keeping sauces smooth.

OTHER EQUIPMENT

BLENDER OR FOOD PROCESSOR—excellent for pureeing, blending, chopping, and mixing foods.

BOWLS—the more the better, in sizes from two cups upward.

COLANDER—for draining pasta and canned foods; and for washing fruits and vegetables.

COOLING RACKS—at least two for cooling breads, cakes, and pies to prevent the bottoms from becoming soggy.

ELECTRIC MIXER—handy for beating, mixing, and whipping.

Cook's Parlance

The handing down of our recipes has long been an oral tradition. The formulas were most often passed from one generation to the next through hands-on lessons while helping in the kitchen. Experienced cooks used their senses as standards of measurement. This talent took time to develop. The pinch, smidgeon, dash, and handful were definite amounts. The color, aroma, texture, or touch defined when food was done and ready to be eaten.

Today, written recipes are saved, shared, and treasured. They make cooking much easier and preserve our food legacy. Recipes in general should be used as a jumping-off point for your own creativity, rather than as a strict dictate to be followed to the letter. If you are a novice, follow the recipes in this cookbook carefully and you are bound to get satisfactory results.

KEY COOKING TERMS FROM A TO Z

AL DENTE—An Italian term meaning "to the tooth," used to describe pasta cooked until tender but still firm.

AU GRATIN—A dish topped with bread crumbs and/or cheese and browned in the oven or broiler.

AU JUS—Meat served with its own natural juices, usually describes beef.

BAKE—To cook by dry oven heat.

BASTE—To spoon or brush pan juices, drippings, butter, or sauce over food as it cooks; adds flavor and prevents drying out.

BEAT—To stir in circular motion. Generally 100 strokes by hand equals about one minute by electric mixer.

BIND—To stir any of a variety of ingredients into a hot liquid, causing it to thicken. Also to hold moist ingredients together with dry ones as in meatloaf.

BISQUE—A thick, rich soup consisting of pureed seafood, poultry, or vegetables and cream.

BLANCH—To plunge food (usually vegetables) briefly into boiling water. This precooking is used to tenderize, loosen skin for peeling, or brighten color and flavor.

BOIL—To heat a liquid until bubbles break the surface (212° F for water at sea level). Also means to cook food in a boiling liquid.

BONE—To remove the bones from meat, fish, or poultry.

BOUILLON—Any broth made by cooking vegetables, poultry, meat or fish in water. The strained, or leftover, liquid can be used for soups, sauces, and poaching.

BOUQUET GARNI—A bunch of herbs (usually parsley, thyme, and bay leaf) tied together or placed in a cheesecloth bag, and used to flavor soups, stews, and broths.

BRAISING—cooking method by which food (usually meat or vegetables) is browned in fat, then cooked, in a small amount of liquid in a tightly covered vessel, at low heat until tender.

BREAD—To coat food with bread crumbs, cracker crumbs, or other crumbs.

BROCHETTE—French word for skewer.

BROIL—To cook food directly under or above the heat source. Usually in an oven directly under the gas or electric heat source.

CARMELIZE—To cook sugar or food with a natural or added high sugar content until the sugar liquefies and becomes a syrup, which ranges in color from golden to dark brown.

CASSEROLE—Refers to both the baking dish and the ingredients cooked in it. Usually the ingredients are baked and served in the same dish.

CHOP—To use a knife, cleaver, or food processor to cut food into bite-sized or smaller pieces.

CLARIFIED BUTTER—The clear liquid butter that is spooned or poured off after unsalted butter is melted and the milk solids settle on the bottom. Also known as drawn butter.

COAT—To cover food with an outer coating; to dip or roll food in seasoned bread crumbs or flour. Coating food in this manner usually precedes panfrying.

COMPOTE—A chilled dish of fresh or dried fruit that has been slowly cooked in a sugar syrup.

COURT BOUILLON—A seasoned broth used for poaching fish, seafood, or vegetables.

CREAM—To beat an ingredient or combination of ingredients until the mixture is soft and smooth. Often a recipe will call for creaming a mixture of butter and sugar.

CRIMP—To pinch or press two pastry edges together with fingers, fork, or other utensil thereby sealing the dough while forming a decorative edge.

CROQUETTES—A mixture of minced fish, meat, or vegetables breaded and deep-fried or panfried.

CROUTONS—Small pieces or cubes of bread that have been browned in an oven or skillet.

CRUDITE—Raw vegetables served as an appetizer with a dipping sauce.

CUBE—To cut food such as meat or cheese into cubes.

CUT IN—To mix a solid, chilled fat such as butter or shortening with ingredients such as a flour mixture, until the combination is in the form of small particles.

DEGLAZING—After food has been sautéed and the food and excess fat removed from the pan, a small amount of broth, wine, or other liquid is added to the pan then cooked and stirred to loosen any browned bits on the bottom of the pan. Deglazing creates a sauce to accompany the cooked food.

DEEP-FRYING—To cook in fat deep enough to completely cover the food being fried. The oil or fat used for deep-frying should have a high smoking point.

DEVILED—Mixed with hot or spicy seasoning such as mustard, red pepper, or hot pepper sauce.

DISSOLVE—To incorporate a dry ingredient such as sugar into a liquid so thoroughly that no grains of the dry ingredient are evident.

DOT—To scatter small bits of an ingredient (usually butter) over another food or mixture.

DREDGE—To lightly coat food to be fried with flour, cornmeal, or breadcrumbs. This coating helps the food brown.

DRESS—To prepare game, fowl, fish for cooking by plucking, scaling, gutting, and so forth.

DRIPPINGS—The melted fat and juices that gather in the bottom of a pan in which meat or other food is cooked. Drippings are used as a base for gravies and sauces.

DUST—To lightly coat food with a powdery ingredient such as flour or confectioners sugar.

ENTREE—In the United States this term refers to the main course of a meal.

FILLET/FILET—A boneless piece of meat or fish. Also to cut the bones from a piece of meat or fish.

FLAKE—To use a utensil (usually a fork) to break off small pieces or layers of food.

FLUTE—To press a decorative pattern into the raised edge of a pie crust.

FOLD—To gently combine a light, airy substance (such as beaten egg whites) with a heavier mixture. The light mixture is placed on top of the heavier one then carefully incorporated with a rubber spatula in a folding motion.

FRICASSEE—A dish of meat that has been sautéed and then stewed with vegetables or dumplings. The result is a thick, chunky stew.

GRATE—To reduce a piece of food into small particles by rubbing it against a coarse, serrated surface. Smaller in size than shredding.

GRILL—To prepare food on a grill over hot coals, wood, or other heat source.

JULIENNE—To cut into matchstick, or thicker, strips.

KNEAD—To mix and work a dough in order to form it into a cohesive mass.

LEAVEN/LEAVENER—Agents that are used to lighten the texture and increase the volume of baked goods such as cakes and breads. Baking powder, baking soda, and yeast are the most common leaveners.

MARINADE—A seasoned liquid in which foods such as meat, fish, and vegetables are soaked in order to absorb flavor and in some instances to be tenderized. Most marinades contain herbs and an acid such as lemon juice.

PAPILLOTE—Food cooked inside a wrapping of greased parchment paper. As the food bakes and lets off steam, the parchment puffs into a dome shape. At the table, the paper is slit and peeled back to reveal the food.

PARBOIL—To partially cook food by boiling it briefly in water.

PARE/PEEL—To remove the skin or peel from foods.

PIPE—To use a pastry bag or other tool to decoratively extrude one food onto another, such as when icing a frosted cake or placing masked potatoes back into potato shells.

PITH—The white bitter covering beneath the peel of citrus fruits.

PLUMP—To soak dehydrated foods in water or a seasoning liquid until they "plump" or rehydrate.

POACH—To cook food gently in liquid at or just below the boiling point. The amount and temperature of the liquid used depends on the food being poached. Meats and poultry are usually simmered in stock; fish in court bouillon; and eggs in lightly salted water, often with a little vinegar added. Fruit is often poached in a light sugar syrup.

PUREE—Any food, usually a fruit or vegetable, that is finely mashed to a smooth, thick consistency. Purees can be used as a garnish, served as a side dish, or added as thickener to sauces or soups.

REDUCE—To boil a liquid, usually stock, wine, or a sauce mixture, rapidly until volume is reduced by evaporation, thereby thickening the consistency and intensifying the flavor.

RENDER—To heat meat over low heat so that the fat melts and separates from the connective tissue.

ROAST—To oven-cook food in an uncovered pan—a method that usually produces a well-browned exterior and, ideally, a moist interior. Roasting requires reasonably tender pieces of meat or poultry. Tougher pieces of meat need moist cooking methods such as braising.

ROUX—A mixture of flour and fat slowly cooked over low heat until it ranges in color from light brown to rich mahogany. It is used to thicken mixtures such as soups and sauces. Roux is a foundation of many famed Creole dishes.

SAUTÉ—To cook food quickly in a small amount of oil in a skillet or sauté pan over direct heat.

SCALD—To heat a liquid to just below the boiling point. Often used to prevent milk from separating during cooking.

SCALLOP—To prepare a food, most notably potatoes, by layering slices of it with cream or a creamy sauce in a casserole. Scalloped foods are often topped with bread or cracker crumbs before being baked. Also, to form a decorative edge on the raised rim of pie dough; also referred to as crimp or flute.

SCORE—To make shallow cuts, usually in a diamond pattern, in the surface of certain foods, such as meat or fish. This is done for several reasons: as a decoration on some foods (breads and meats); as a means of assisting flavor absorption (as with marinated foods); to tenderize tougher cuts of meat; and to allow excess fat to drain during cooking.

SEAR—To brown meat quickly by subjecting it to very high heat either in a skillet, under a broiler, or in a very hot oven. The object of searing is to seal in the meat's juices.

SEASON—To flavor foods in order to improve their taste. To age meat, which helps both to tenderize it and to improve its flavor.

SIFT—To pass dry ingredients through a fine-mesh sifter so any large pieces can be removed or dissolved. Sifting also incorporates air to make ingredients, such as confectioners sugar or flour lighter.

ESSENCE BRINGS YOU
GREAT COOKING

SIMMER—To cook food gently in liquid at a temperature of about 185° F, which is the point at which tiny bubbles just begin to break the surface.

SKIM—To remove the top layer from a liquid, such as cream from milk or foam and fat from stock, soups, and sauces.

STEAMING—A method of cooking whereby food is placed on a rack or in a special steamer basket over boiling or simmering water in a covered pan. Steaming does a better job than boiling or poaching of retaining a food's flavor, shape, texture, and many of the vitamins and minerals.

STEEP—To soak dry ingredients such as tea leaves, ground coffee, herbs, and spices in liquid (usually hot) until the flavor is infused into the liquid.

STEW—Any dish that is prepared by stewing. The term is most often applied to dishes that contain meat, vegetables, and a thick soup-like broth resulting from a combination of the stewing liquid and the natural juices of the food being stewed. Also, a method of cooking by which food is barely covered with liquid and simmered slowly for a long period of time in a tightly covered pot. Stewing not only tenderizes tough pieces of meat but also allows the flavors of the ingredients to blend deliciously.

STIR-FRY—To quickly fry small pieces of food in a large pan over very high heat while constantly and briskly stirring the food. This cooking technique, which is associated with oriental cooking and the wok, requires a minimum amount of fat and results in food that is crisp-tender.

STOCK—In the most basic terms, stock is the strained liquid that is the result of cooking vegetables, meat, or fish and other seasoning ingredients in water.

TOSS—To turn pieces of food over multiple times, thereby mixing the ingredients together. The term is most often applied to salad, where various ingredients and the salad dressing are combined.

TRUSS—To secure poultry or other food (usually meat) with string, pins, or skewers so the food maintains a compact shape during cooking.

WHIP—To beat ingredients, such as egg whites, cream, etcetera, thereby incorporating air into them and increasing their volume until they are light and fluffy.

ZEST—The perfumy outermost skin layer of citrus fruit (usually oranges or lemons), which is removed with the aid of a citrus zester, paring knife, or vegetable peeler. Only the colored portion of the skin (not the white pith) is considered the zest.

PART TWO

RECIPES

Vegetables—
Back to Our Roots

Recipes

MIXED GREENS

JOHN'S COLLARD GREENS WITH TOMATOES

HOT-AND-SPICY COLLARDS

KIELBASA AND CABBAGE

SPLENDID AND CHEAP CABBAGE ROLLS

VEGETARIAN CABBAGE ROLLS

POTATO-STUFFED CABBAGE LEAVES

BRAISED KALE AND LEEKS

EDNA LEWIS'S SENSATIONAL SPINACH

BRUSSELS SPROUTS WITH WALNUTS

GRILLED CORN WITH HERB BUTTER

CARIBBEAN RATATOUILLE

EGGPLANT ROLLANTINE

CREOLE OKRA AND TOMATOES

PICKLED OKRA

ROASTED BELL PEPPERS

REAL MASHED POTATOES

GOLDEN ROASTED POTATOES

CHRISTOPHENE AU GRATIN CASSEROLE

ACORN SQUASH STUFFED WITH APPLE DRESSING

Recipes

BAKED YAM CASSEROLE

SWEET POTATO DINNER SOUFFLÉ

HOLIDAY HONEYED YAMS

SWEET POTATO FRIES

FRIED GREEN TOMATOES

EASY ALL-PURPOSE TOMATO SAUCE

MOLLIE NASH'S CHOW-CHOW

SOUTHERN TURNIPS AND RUTABAGA

ALI'S VEGETABLE CURRY

ISLAND PUMPKIN FRITTERS

BAGIA (MIXED VEGETABLE FRITTERS)

FRESH CORN CHOWDER

CREAM OF CAULIFLOWER SOUP

BROCCOLI-POTATO SOUP

LO-CAL CREAMY POTATO SALAD

DORIS'S POTATO SALAD

GRANDMA'S COLESLAW

RUBY'S RAISIN COLESLAW

NEW CARROT–RAISIN SALAD

AVOCADO-ORANGE SALAD

Recipes in this chapter do not include nutritional analysis for sodium content
when salt is listed as an optional ingredient.

PEOPLE of the African diaspora have traditionally lived close to nature—near gardens and fields. In the early South, life and food preparation revolved around the seasons—sowing, tending, harvesting, and eating according to the calendar. Just-picked vegetables vibrated with life. In spring, there were small, red-skinned new potatoes. Early summer brought vines laden with ripe tomatoes. Late summer yielded corn, and the first frost brought prime collards. In winter, it was time to uproot sweet potatoes, as well as to enjoy the summer bounty that had been canned, dried, or otherwise put away.

This cycle of eating local, often homegrown, produce was repeated with little variation until recent times. Food technology and supermarkets now provide us with an amazing year-round assortment of vegetables—many from halfway around the world. Instead of being covered with fresh dew, many of today's vegetables come wrapped in cellophane, packed in cans, or frozen in boil-and-serve pouches. It's not only important that we base our meals around produce and grains, but that we also choose the most healthful forms available. All of us have those busy, pressure-filled times when it's smart to opt for the timesaving features of frozen and canned vegetables. Yet what could be easier to prepare or better tasting than a naturally syrupy baked sweet potato? Eating fresh-picked vegetables simply prepared is one of life's pleasures. It seems that the less you do to fresh vegetables the better the taste and the better they are for you!

BREAKING WITH TRADITION

The down-home style of cooking vegetables has been to add salted, fatty meats to the pot, then cook them almost to a pulp. This method of cooking strips away the vegetable's natural flavor, color, and nutrients and, at the same time, adds ingredients that can contribute to poor health. I am not advocating that we abandon adding meat to vegetables or that we only steam them until crisp-tender. We can retain our flavorful tradition by seasoning with bouillon or broth, restricting rather than eliminating salt, adding turkey and other lowfat meats (being mindful of sodium and nitrates), and using herbs and seasonings such as onion and garlic. See the Cooking with Herbs guide in Part I on page 8.

GREAT GREENS

"Of all the vegetables leafy and green,
Collards are definitely the queen."

In her ode to collards, poet Coleen Bunting expresses the sentiments of so many of us. Their phenomenal flavor, remarkable nutritional value, and overall prominence in our food tradition place greens—particularly collards—at the top of our vegetable list.

Collard greens are a variety of cabbage that does not form a head, instead the leaves fan out in a loose rosette at the top of a tall stem. A sturdy field green, collards are easy and quick to grow. Their blue-green leaves are a common sight in urban gardens as well as on farmland. (Be sure not to let the leaves grow too large; and don't purchase large greens because they are likely to be tough.)

Even among the members of this nutritionally powerful cabbage family (which includes brussels sprouts, cauliflower, kale, kohlrabi, mustard greens, turnip greens, and the various other types of cabbage), collards stand out as an excellent source of vitamins A and C, calcium, iron, and potassium. Cruciferous vegetables is another name for this group. They are now well known as cancer fighters. The anticancer agent in these vegetables helps to detoxify and remove harmful molecules from the body. (Mamas who relentlessly urged us to eat our greens somehow knew all of this.) Nutritionists recommend that we eat three servings of vegetables daily and that at least one serving should come from the cruciferous group.

SELECT THE BEST

Look for bright green leaves that are unblemished and crisp. Smaller leaves are more tender and milder tasting. Greens that are wilted and yellow have lost both flavor and nutrients.

Store raw greens loosely packed in a plastic bag in the refrigerator crisper; they will stay fresh three or four days. Frozen collards, mustards, and turnips, now readily available in most supermarkets, are a good choice when fresh greens or time are unavailable. Just add seasonings to frozen greens (see following recipes for suggestions) to liven them up and provide home-cooked flavor.

ESSENCE BRINGS YOU
GREAT COOKING

Field of Greens

Here's a quick guide to greens commonly available at vegetable stands, farmers' markets, and supermarkets across the country.

BOK CHOY Similar to Chinese cabbage, this popular choice for stir-frying and soups is readily available at Asian markets and large supermarkets.

CHARD Often called Swiss chard. This soft-textured green, like spinach, cooks quickly and should not be boiled.

COLLARD High in vitamin C. Collards are delicious cooked with scallions and hot chilies.

DANDELION These "wild" greens are best picked or purchased with the roots still attached. Tasty when added raw to salads.

KALE A nutritional bonaza—high in vitamin A, calcium, and potassium. A winter green, now available year-round.

MUSTARD Tame these sharp-tasting greens by blanching before actual cooking.

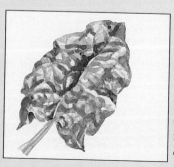

SPINACH Leaves are crinkled or smooth. Fresh is markedly superior in taste and texture to canned and frozen forms. Eat raw or cook.

TURNIP This rather bitter-tasting vegetable is tasty cooked in combination with other greens.

MIXED GREENS

Collards and cabbage are a great-tasting duo. Combine any of your favorite greens by adding those that require less cooking to the pot toward the end.

3 pounds fresh collard greens
1 cup water
1 2-pound green cabbage
2 tablespoons margarine
1 teaspoon salt *(optional)*
½ teaspoon ground black pepper

Makes 6 servings.

PER SERVING:

95 calories
4 g protein
4 g fat
15 g carbohydrate
115 mg sodium
0 mg cholesterol

   Discard any discolored or wilted collard leaves; remove and discard stems. Rinse greens in at least 3 changes of water, swishing, then lifting from water to remove all traces of grit. Stack bunch of leaves; fold lengthwise, then slice crosswise into strips. Repeat with remaining greens. To Dutch oven or kettle, add collards and water. Cover and simmer about 30 minutes. Meanwhile, remove and discard any tough or discolored outer leaves from cabbage. Rinse with cold water. Using long, sharp knife, halve cabbage, then halve again; cut core from each wedge. Cut each wedge crosswise into strips. To same Dutch oven, add cabbage, margarine, salt (if desired), and pepper. Cover and simmer, stirring occasionally, 15 to 20 additional minutes.

ESSENCE BRINGS YOU
GREAT COOKING

JOHN'S COLLARD GREENS WITH TOMATOES

This recipe by photographer and talented cook John Pinderhughes is from his cookbook Family of the Spirit *(Simon & Schuster). The flavor is so pleasing, we did not miss the slab bacon we omitted from the original recipe.*

Makes 6 servings.

PER SERVING:

97 calories
6 g protein
4 g fat
11 g carbohydrate
114 mg sodium
0 mg cholesterol

- 2 pounds fresh collard greens
- 3 cups water
- 2 tablespoons vegetable oil
- 1 large onion, chopped
- 3 garlic cloves, minced
- 1 16-ounce can whole tomatoes, chopped
- ½ teaspoon red pepper flakes
- 1 teaspoon salt *(optional)*
- Freshly ground black pepper to taste

Check greens, discarding yellow leaves and thick stems; rinse thoroughly. In small bunches, roll leaves into cigar shape; slice crosswise. Place in covered stockpot or large kettle with 3 cups water; bring to boil; reduce heat and simmer 15 minutes. Remove cover; simmer 30 minutes. Meanwhile, in large cast-iron skillet, over medium heat, heat oil; add onion and garlic. Sauté until onion wilts. Add tomatoes, pepper flakes, salt (if desired), and black pepper; mix well. Simmer 10 to 15 minutes. When greens are almost tender and liquid is reduced, stir in tomato mixture. Simmer uncovered 15 minutes or until greens are done.

HOT-AND-SPICY COLLARDS

Fresh greens are always a potluck crowd pleaser. This batch by Treneta Burns of Simi Valley, California, is especially tasty.

5 pounds fresh collard greens
2 tablespoons vegetable oil
1 large onion, chopped
3 garlic cloves, minced
2 to 3 cups water
½ pound turkey ham, shredded or diced
4 pickled jalapeño peppers, stems removed, sliced
2 tablespoons sugar

Soak greens in several changes of cold water to remove all grit (Mrs. Burns scrubs each leaf). Remove and discard tough stems. In bunches, stack, roll, and slice crosswise into 1-inch-wide strips. In large pot, heat oil; sauté onion and garlic. Stir in water, turkey, jalapeño peppers, and sugar; simmer about 5 minutes. Add greens; cover and cook over low heat until of desired tenderness, about 1 to 1½ hours. Serve with pepper relish (see note at right).

Makes 12 servings.

PER SERVING:

152 calories
13 g protein
5 g fat
19 g carbohydrate
243 mg sodium
11 mg cholesterol

NOTE

For even more flavor, Mrs. Burns often serves greens with a homemade pepper relish of chopped fresh tomato, onion, and banana peppers.

KIELBASA AND CABBAGE

Makes 4 servings.

PER SERVING:

414 calories
19 g protein
35 g fat
6 g carbohydrate
910 mg sodium
10 mg cholesterol

1 medium-size head green cabbage
1 pound kielbasa (smoked Polish sausage) cut into 2-inch pieces
2 tablespoons butter or margarine
1 small onion, sliced

Remove and discard tough outer leaves from cabbage. Quarter and core cabbage head. Coarsely chop cabbage; set aside. In large skillet over medium heat, cook kielbasa until lightly browned; remove from skillet. Melt butter in same skillet; add cabbage and onion. Stir to cook cabbage several minutes. Add meat; cover and cook about 15 minutes. Serve with sautéed apple rings.

Picking mustard greens in the early South.

ESSENCE BRINGS YOU
GREAT COOKING

SPLENDID AND CHEAP CABBAGE ROLLS

1 medium-size head green cabbage
Water
1 pound ground chuck
½ teaspoon salt *(optional)*
¼ teaspoon ground black pepper
1 small onion, finely chopped
1 garlic clove, minced
½ cup uncooked long-grain or brown rice
1 large egg, slightly beaten
1 28-ounce can stewed tomatoes
1 tablespoon brown sugar
Optional garnish: bell pepper rings, parsley sprigs, scallion tops

Makes 6 servings.

PER SERVING:

340 calories
22 g protein
18 g fat
25 g carbohydrate
85 mg sodium
114 mg cholesterol

Discard tough outer leaves of cabbage; with sharp knife remove core. Fill 8-quart saucepot ¾ full with water; bring to boil. Place cabbage in pot; cook over medium heat. Carefully remove 8 to 12 leaves as they soften and separate from head; drain on paper towels. Trim thick rib from each leaf; set leaf aside. Remove remaining cabbage from pot; drain, then coarsely chop. Place chopped cabbage in greased, shallow 3-quart baking dish or casserole. Heat oven to 350° F. In medium bowl, combine ground chuck, salt (if desired), pepper, onion, garlic, rice, and egg; mix well. Place an equal amount of meat mixture on center of each leaf. Fold sides over stuffing; roll from the thick end to form packet. Place cabbage rolls seam-side down on chopped cabbage in dish. Mix tomatoes and sugar; pour over cabbage. Loosely cover with a sheet of foil; bake 50 minutes. Uncover and cook 10 additional minutes. Garnish with bell pepper rings and parsley, if desired. Serve with carrot sticks and corn muffins.

ESSENCE BRINGS YOU
GREAT COOKING

VEGETARIAN CABBAGE ROLLS

Makes 4 servings.

PER SERVING:

349 calories
11 g protein
17 g fat
47 g carbohydrate
348 mg sodium
0 mg cholesterol

1 medium-size green cabbage
2 cups water
1 tablespoon canola oil
1 medium-size onion, chopped
1 medium-size rib celery, chopped
1 small green bell pepper, seeded, chopped
1 carrot, shredded
⅓ cup unsalted sunflower kernels
2 cups cooked brown rice
1 28-ounce can peeled tomatoes (with juice), chopped
1 tablespoon lemon juice or vinegar
1 tablespoon honey
¼ teaspoon salt *(optional)*
¼ teaspoon cayenne pepper

Discard coarse or yellowed outer cabbage leaves. Using small sharp knife, core cabbage. In large pot, bring about 2 cups water to boil; add whole cabbage. Steam, covered, about 7 minutes; remove and drain. Carefully remove 8 leaves; cover and set aside. Coarsely chop remaining cabbage; arrange in even layer in medium-size baking dish. Heat oven to 350° F. In medium-size nonstick skillet, heat oil; sauté onion, celery, bell pepper, carrot and sunflower kernels until lightly browned, about 8 minutes. Stir in rice and about ⅛ cup juice from tomatoes, mixing well; remove from heat. To prepare rolls: At stem end of each reserved leaf, place about ⅓ cup rice mixture; fold sides of leaf over stuffing, then roll. Place rolls seam side down on cabbage in baking dish. In bowl, mix tomatoes with remaining juice, lemon juice, honey, salt (if desired), and pepper; pour over cabbage rolls. Cover dish with foil; bake about 45 minutes. Uncover; bake 15 additional minutes, basting frequently with pan juices.

POTATO-STUFFED CABBAGE LEAVES

Cabbage is a vegetable of international acclaim. This spicy, exotic-tasting recipe is from noted Indian cookbook author, Madhur Jaffrey. Use this lively blend of seasonings to add exciting flavor to other dishes.

5 medium-size potatoes
4 medium-size onions, sliced
6 tablespoons vegetable oil
2 teaspoons whole fennel seeds
1 teaspoon whole cumin seeds
1 teaspoon garam masala* *(optional)*
1¾ teaspoon salt *(optional)*
¼ teaspoon cayenne pepper
1 tablespoon lemon juice
1 medium-size head cabbage
Water
Optional garnish: tomato wedges, cilantro

Makes 8 servings.

PER SERVING:

215 calories
4 g protein
11 g fat
29 g carbohydrate
14 mg sodium
0 mg cholesterol

*Garam masala, a mixture of many spices frequently used in East Indian dishes, is available at international food stores.

Boil potatoes in skins; peel, then dice into ¼-inch pieces. Peel onion, cut in half lengthwise; slice into fine half circles. In large skillet, heat 4 tablespoons oil over medium heat; add onions and sauté about 7 minutes. Add fennel and cumin; cook another 7 minutes over low heat. Onions should look reddish brown. Add potatoes to onion mixture and continue cooking, mashing potatoes with back of slotted spoon or potato masher. Add garam masala and ¾ teaspoon salt (if desired), pepper, and lemon juice. Stir to mix well. In large saucepot, bring to boil enough water to cover cabbage. Place cabbage in water; add remaining salt (if desired), cover and boil 5 minutes. Lift cabbage from water; run under cold water and carefully remove each leaf, taking care not to break them. Dry leaves thoroughly with paper towels. Spread out leaves one at a time. Cut or snip out hard core of each leaf. Place 2 tablespoons potato mixture in center of leaf, then fold edges over. Squeeze with paper towels to remove excess moisture and to seal. In 10-inch skillet, heat remaining 2 tablespoons oil over medium heat. Fry a few cabbage rolls at a time for several minutes until browned; arrange all roles in skillet in tight layer. Add about 1 tablespoon water, cover, and cook over low heat about 12 minutes. Arrange on platter; garnish with tomato wedges and cilantro.

ESSENCE BRINGS YOU GREAT COOKING

33

BRAISED KALE AND LEEKS

Makes 6 servings.

PER SERVING:

160 calories
7 g protein
12 g fat
11 g carbohydrate
201 mg sodium
31 mg cholesterol

1½ pounds kale
2 medium-size leeks
6 tablespoons butter or margarine
1 teaspoon salt *(optional)*
¼ teaspoon ground black pepper
3 tablespoons balsamic vinegar

Thoroughly rinse kale in several changes of cold water to remove grit. Remove and discard coarse stems; coarsely chop leaves. Trim leeks to about 6 inches in length; make lengthwise slit, halfway through each. Under cold running water, rinse leeks to remove grit; slice crosswise. In Dutch oven, heat butter; add leeks. Sauté about 5 minutes. Add kale; cover and cook until wilted, about 8 minutes or until of desired tenderness. Sprinkle with salt (if desired), pepper, and vinegar; toss to mix.

EDNA LEWIS'S SENSATIONAL SPINACH

Taking simple ingredients and bringing out their inherently wonderful flavors is Ms. Lewis's way with food.

½ cup sun-dried tomato pieces
1 cup hot water
1 tablespoon olive oil
1 garlic clove, minced
2 pounds fresh smooth-leaf spinach (preferably unpackaged)
2 tablespoons butter or margarine

In small bowl, place tomatoes and water; let stand about 2 minutes, until tomatoes are reconstituted. Drain. Combine tomatoes with olive oil and garlic; set aside. Remove spinach stems. Rinse leaves thoroughly in cold running water to remove grit. Shake and dry thoroughly. In large skillet, heat butter until it foams; add spinach. Increase heat to medium-high. With 2 spoons, toss spinach until wilted and cooked (about 5 minutes). Sprinkle spinach with tomatoes.

Makes 4 servings.

PER SERVING:

167 calories
9 g protein
13 g fat
11 g carbohydrate
334 mg sodium
16 mg cholesterol

ESSENCE BRINGS YOU
GREAT COOKING

BRUSSELS SPROUTS WITH WALNUTS

This vegetable side dish by chef extraordinaire Patrick Clark makes any meal more of a celebration.

Make 10 servings.

PER SERVING:

136 calories
5 g protein
10 g fat
8 g carbohydrate
31 mg sodium
5 mg cholesterol

1 cup fresh walnut meats
2 pounds fresh brussels sprouts
Water
1 teaspoon kosher salt
2 tablespoons walnut oil
2 tablespoons unsalted butter

Heat oven to 325° F. In shallow baking pan, spread walnuts in single layer; toast in oven until lightly browned and fragrant, about 5 to 7 minutes. Trim stem ends from brussels sprouts and rinse with cold water. In Dutch oven or large pot ⅔ filled with water, bring water and salt (if desired) to boil. Add sprouts; blanch until crisp-tender, about 5 minutes. Drain immediately; transfer to container filled with ice water to prevent further cooking and to set color. Cut sprouts lengthwise into halves. In same Dutch oven, heat oil and butter; add sprouts. Sauté 3 to 4 minutes. Gently stir in toasted walnuts. Transfer to serving bowl.

Corn

THOUGH we think of it as a vegetable, corn (maize) is actually a cereal. It is America's only indigenous grain. Today's corn descended from the wild corn that Native Americans carefully cultivated over hundreds of years. Because it was a food staple and life sustainer, corn was a part of their celebrations and ceremonies. (Grits, which are made from ground corn kernels, are discussed in the Grits and Other Great Grains chapter on page 101.)

The delicious new strains of sweet corn are nothing short of extraordinary! Its flavor is fragile, so the sooner you buy it, and eat it after picking the better. Shop for corn at local farm stands or from stores with high-volume shopping.

SELECT THE BEST

Look for ears with tight, green husks; dark brown silks; and shiny, plump kernels. Avoid corn with spaces between the kernels, limp husks, and worm damage. Bursting a kernel should produce a stream of thin, milky juice. Medium-size ears are more tender than large ears. If the corn is not being prepared right away, do not remove the husks. Place it in plastic bags with several holes, then refrigerate.

TO CUT CORN FROM COB

Using a sharp knife, starting at the top of the ear, cut straight down to the stem end. Do not cut into the cob—just remove the kernels. Use whole kernel corn in salads, casseroles, soups, and relishes.

Corn on the Cob

Remove husks. Using a vegetable brush makes removing the silk easier. Snap or cut off the stem end. Rinse ears in cold water. In rapidly boiling water, cook corn, uncovered, 3 to 7 minutes. To enhance flavor, a small amount of sugar or milk can be added to boiling water. Avoid adding salt, it tends to toughen the kernels. When cooked, a sprinkle of pepper and salt, if desired, and a smear of butter is all that's required for excellent eating.

GRILLED CORN WITH HERB BUTTER

Roasting fresh ears of corn in their husks helps lock in flavor and moisture.

Makes 16 servings.

PER SERVING:

135 calories
3 g protein
7 g fat
19 g carbohydrate
71 mg sodium
15 mg cholesterol

- 16 fresh ears of corn in husks
- ½ cup (1 stick) margarine or butter
- 1 teaspoon paprika or ground cumin
- ½ teaspoon salt *(optional)*
- ½ teaspoon ground black, white, or cayenne pepper
- 1 tablespoon fresh or 1 teaspoon dried parsley, oregano, or marjoram

Soak unshucked ears of corn in cold water about 1 hour to moisten kernels and prevent husks from catching fire. Prepare grill; place grill grid 4 inches above hot coals. Meanwhile, in small bowl, blend margarine and seasonings; set aside. Carefully peel back husks; remove and discard silks. Rub or brush kernels with seasoned margarine. Pull leaves back into place, covering kernels; to secure leaves, tie at end with wet kitchen twine. Arrange corn on the greased grid; roast, turning frequently, about 20 minutes; or place directly on coals and roast about 15 minutes.

Tip: Add rounds of corn to vegetable kabobs.

CARIBBEAN RATATOUILLE

Vegetable lovers take delight.

2 tablespoons olive oil
2 medium-size onions, coarsely chopped
1 garlic clove, minced
¼ pound okra, tops removed, cut into 1-inch rounds
1 large eggplant, unpeeled, cubed
1 cup quartered fresh mushrooms
1 medium-size green bell pepper, coarsely chopped
1 medium-size red bell pepper, coarsely chopped
3 large ripe tomatoes, peeled, seeded, coarsely chopped
½ teaspoon dried oregano
½ teaspoon crumbled dried thyme or 2 teaspoons fresh thyme
½ teaspoon salt *(optional)*
Freshly ground black pepper to taste

In large heavy saucepan, heat oil; sauté onions and garlic until soft, about 5 minutes. Stir in remaining ingredients. Reduce heat to low; cover and simmer, stirring occasionally, until vegetables are tender but not mushy, about 30 minutes. Add more seasonings to taste.

Caribbean Ratatouille, Bean Fritters (see page 94), and raw christophene on salad greens.

Makes 6 to 8 servings.

PER EACH OF 6
SERVINGS:

91 calories
3 g protein
5 g fat
12 g carbohydrate
9 mg sodium
0 mg cholesterol

EGGPLANT ROLLANTINE

This flavorful vegetarian dish was created by caterer Dee Dee Dailey of Brooklyn, New York. DeeDee specializes in Caribbean and South American cookery.

Makes 5 servings

PER SERVING:
566 calories
31 g protein
43 g fat
18 g carbohydrate
725 mg sodium
148 mg cholesterol

SAUCE:
1 tablespoon olive oil
1 small onion, peeled, chopped
2 medium-size garlic cloves, chopped
1 tablespoon chopped flat-leaf parsley
1 teaspoon crushed, dried oregano
1 teaspoon crushed, dried basil
¼ teaspoon salt (optional)
1 28-ounce can crushed tomatoes with puree
¼ teaspoon ground black pepper
2 tablespoons dry red wine *(optional)*

CHEESE FILLING:
1 large egg
1 pound ricotta cheese
½ pound mozzarella cheese
½ cup grated Romano or Parmesan cheese
3 tablespoons chopped flat-leaf parsley
⅛ teaspoon ground white pepper
¼ teaspoon grated nutmeg
1 large eggplant (1 to 1½ pounds)
¼ cup unbleached all-purpose flour
2 egg whites
2 tablespoons water
4 tablespoons vegetable oil
¼ cup grated Romano or Parmesan cheese

In medium-size non-stick saucepan, heat olive oil; tilt and rotate pan to spread oil over bottom. Add onion and garlic; sauté until onion is tender, about 5 minutes. Stir in parsley, oregano, basil, and salt (if desired). Stir in tomatoes with puree, pepper, and wine. Simmer over medium-low heat 20 minutes. Meanwhile, prepare filling. In medium-size mixing bowl, beat egg lightly. Stir in cheeses and seasonings; mix well. Set aside. To prepare eggplant, rinse well; peel or leave skin intact. Slice crosswise into ¼-inch-thick slices. Dredge eggplant slices with flour. In large shallow dish, beat egg whites and water. Dip eggplant into egg mixture. In large non-stick skillet, heat 1 tablespoon oil; tilt and rotate pan to coat bottom. Without overlapping, add a single layer of eggplant to the skillet. Cook about 5 minutes on each side, or until lightly browned; transfer eggplant to paper towels as cooked. Add oil as needed, to cook remaining eggplant. Heat oven to 375° F. In bottom of large shallow baking pan (about 13-by-8 inches), spread about half of tomato sauce. Spread each eggplant slice with filling; fold in half, placing filled slices in single layer in baking pan. Pour remaining sauce over eggplant; sprinkle with grated cheese. Bake until sauce is bubbly, about 30 minutes.

Okra

Okra is uniquely rooted in our history. Enslaved Africans stripped of their possessions, family, and even language, managed to bring okra seeds with them to these shores. The seeds were first planted in the fertile soil of Louisana, and, as is often said—the rest is history! The name of the most distinctive and prized dish of the region—gumbo—is a derivative of an African word for okra—*ki-ngombo*. Okra was a thickener and the base upon which the rich seafood soups of early nineteenth-century New Orleans were made. Later, filé powder (ground sassafras leaves concocted by the local Native Americans), became a common thickener. Today, gumbo purists contend there are two types of gumbo—those made with okra and those made with filé powder, never with both.

SELECT THE BEST

Look for blemish-free pods that are no longer than 3 inches. Black or brown spots are signs of bruising and age. Do not wash until time to cook. Store in refrigerator; use within 3 days.

Eggplant

The rich, meaty flavor of eggplant makes it a popular choice in vegetarian dishes. Select satiny-smooth eggplant that are heavy for their size. To tenderize and rid eggplant of some of its liquid, this vegetable is often "salted." First, peel the eggplant, then cut it into slices and place the slices in a single layer. Sprinkle the eggplant very lightly with salt. Place the eggplant in a colander; put a plate on top as a weight. Let the eggplant drain for about an hour. Rinse gently, then blot dry with paper towels.

CREOLE OKRA AND TOMATOES

Makes 4 servings.

PER SERVING:

122 calories
5 g protein
6 g fat
16 g carbohydrate
64 mg sodium
16 mg cholesterol

2 tablespoons butter or margarine
1 large onion, chopped
1 pound small okra pods, caps trimmed, whole or sliced
1 tablespoon water
2 medium-size, firm tomatoes, cut into wedges
1 teaspoon brown sugar
¼ teaspoon salt *(optional)*
½ teaspoon hot pepper sauce or ⅛ teaspoon cayenne pepper

In large skillet (not iron or aluminum, which darkens okra), heat butter; sauté onion and okra. Cook, turning occasionally with a wide spatula, about 5 minutes. Add 1 to 2 tablespoons water if mixture is somewhat dry or sticky. Add tomatoes, sugar, salt (if desired), and pepper sauce; gently stir to combine. Cover and cook over low heat just until tomatoes are heated through, about one minute. Serve warm as a side dish or over rice.

PICKLED OKRA

Select young, tender, blemish-free pods for best results.

3 dozen (about 2 pounds) medium-size okra pods
⅓ cup cider or red wine vinegar
¼ cup vegetable oil
2 large garlic cloves, split
1 teaspoon red pepper flakes
1 teaspoon sugar
½ teaspoon salt *(optional)*
1 small red onion, sliced crosswise, separated into rings

Makes 36 appetizers.

PER POD:

23 calories
1 g protein
2 g fat
2 g carbohydrate
2 mg sodium
0 mg cholesterol

Rinse okra thoroughly in cold water. With small sharp knife, trim tip of stem ends (to avoid sliminess, don't cut off cap or cut into pod). In large, non-aluminum skillet, heat vinegar, oil, garlic, pepper, sugar, and salt (if desired). Add okra, reduce heat to low; simmer until okra is crisp-tender, about 3 minutes. Remove from heat. Transfer okra and pickling liquid to large shallow baking dish; stir in onion rings. Let cool; wrap and refrigerate, turning occasionally, at least 4 hours, preferably overnight. Transfer okra and onion from marinade to serving platter.

ESSENCE BRINGS YOU
GREAT COOKING

Peppers

There are two main types of peppers—sweet and hot. Sweet peppers are commonly called "bell" peppers because of their characteristic shape. These peppers are most commonly green, but through ripening many varieties turn yellow, orange, and ultimately red. The more they ripen, the sweeter they become. Bell peppers can be very flavorful and far more versatile than just being chopped and added to season other dishes. Stuffing, roasting, or pureeing bring out new flavor dimensions in bell peppers. Sweet peppers are rich in vitamins A, C, and E. They are available year-round, but are most abundant from June through October. When selecting bell peppers, look for well-shaped peppers with glossy, tight, thick skins. They should be firm to the touch with no soft spots. Italian frying peppers are also sweet peppers; they are elongated and come in pea green, reddish green, and yellow (often called banana peppers).

Hot peppers come in a variety of shapes and heat intensities. The pick of peppers include: ancho, habanera, jalapeño, pequin, serrano, and Scotch bonnets. These members of the capsicum family are also known as chiles.

Be careful not to touch your face or eyes when handling chiles, the pain can be excrutiating. (People with sensitive skin should wear rubber gloves.) After handling the chiles, wash hands and cutting equipment thoroughly. To beat the heat or diminish the fire of hot peppers, remove and discard the seeds, stems, and veins.

There are claims that hot peppers protect against conditions that range from colds to being a "cold fish." They are guaranteed, however, to add delightful flavor.

ROASTED BELL PEPPERS

6 medium-size bell peppers (use a mix of colors)
¼ cup olive oil
2 garlic cloves, halved
½ teaspoon ground black pepper

Heat broiler as directed by manufacturer. Halve peppers lengthwise; remove ribs and seeds. On broiler-pan rack, place peppers skin side up (cut side down). Broil 2 to 3 inches from heat and watch carefully. Turn peppers until skins are black all over, about 5 minutes. Using tongs, transfer peppers to paper bag or wrap in dampened paper towels; seal completely. Let peppers steam in bag 15 to 20 minutes. Meanwhile, in shallow dish or medium-size bowl, combine oil, garlic, and black pepper; mix well. Working with one pepper half at a time (leaving the remainder in the bag to stay warm), peel off charred skin and cut away any stubborn bits of skin. Cut into long, thin strips. Add to oil mixture. Repeat with remaining peppers. Stir peppers, coating well with seasoned oil. Peppers can be eaten right away or stored up to 5 days in refrigerator. Discard garlic before serving.

Makes 6 servings.

PER SERVING:

99 calories
1 g protein
9 g fat
4 g carbohydrate
2 mg sodium
0 mg cholesterol

The Truth About Potatoes

Potatoes have an image problem. Many people feel they are just starchy and fattening. So potatoes are typically one of the first foods given up when a person starts a weight-loss diet. The real facts are, on its own, a medium-size potato that has been baked, broiled, or steamed contains almost no fat and only about 100 calories. It's when potatoes are fried, slathered with butter, topped with sour cream, or mashed with butter that the calories soar. Potatoes topped with plain yogurt mixed with scallions or fresh herbs, or grated Parmesan cheese can be a dieter's delight.

TYPES OF POTATOES

Russets, also called Idahos, have reddish-brown skin and a mealy texture; they are excellent for baking and French-frying.

Long Whites, also called all-purpose, have tan, smooth skin.

Round Whites, also called all-purpose, have beige, smooth skin.

Red-Skinned have pinkish-red skin and firm white flesh; best for steaming and boiling. These are often called "new" potatoes; however, the term actually applies to any early-in-the-season, young, thin-skinned potato.

BAKING POTATOES

Potatoes do not require a specific temperature for baking. They can be baked right alongside a roast, meatloaf, casserole, or other dish at an oven setting of 325° to 450° F. As a cooking gauge, at 400° F a medium-size potato will bake in about 40 to 45 minutes. Lower temperatures will, of course, require longer baking.

REAL MASHED POTATOES

2 cups water
3 medium-size potatoes, peeled and quartered
¼ cup skim milk, warmed
1 tablespoon butter or margarine
½ teaspoon salt *(optional)*
¼ teaspoon pepper *(optional)*
Optional garnish: ⅓ teaspoon paprika or freshly chopped parsley

In 1-quart saucepan, bring water to boil. Add potatoes. Cover and boil until potatoes are tender when pierced with knife, about 20 minutes; drain. Over low heat, shake pan for several minutes to further dry potatoes; mash. Add milk and margarine a little at a time, beating after each addition until potatoes are fluffy. Add ½ teaspoon salt (if desired) and pepper. Garnish with paprika or freshly chopped parsley.

Makes 4 servings.

PER SERVING:

108 calories
3 g protein
1 g fat
21 g carbohydrate
266 mg sodium
trace cholesterol

ESSENCE BRINGS YOU
GREAT COOKING

GOLDEN ROASTED POTATOES

Makes 12 servings.

6 medium-size baking potatoes
½ cup (1 stick) butter or margarine, melted
¾ teaspoon salt *(optional)*
½ teaspoon freshly ground black pepper

PER SERVING:

177 calories
3 g protein
8 g fat
25 g carbohydrate
38 mg sodium
20 mg cholesterol

Heat oven to 425° F. Scrub potatoes in cold water. With vegetable peeler, remove peels and eyes. Cut potatoes in half lengthwise; cut halves diagonally into thick slices. In large bowl combine potatoes, butter, salt (if desired), and pepper; toss to coat well. In large baking pan arrange potatoes in single layer. Roast in oven 45 minutes (occasionally shake pan and turn potatoes), until potatoes are cooked through and are golden brown.

ESSENCE BRINGS YOU
GREAT COOKING

Squash

There's an incredible variety of squash, but they are simply divided into two types—summer and winter. Summer squash include pattypan (disc-shaped with scalloped edge), yellow crookneck, zucchini, and christophene.

Christophene is known by several names, but the crisp, refreshing flavor is the same.

- Mirliton—in the southern states
- Chayote—in Spanish-speaking areas
- Cho-Cho—in the Caribbean

To prepare the summer variety, simply wash well, trim stem and blossom ends, cut into slices, chunks, or spears; then cook in a steamer or small amount of simmering water.

Winter squash include acorn, banana, buttercup, butternut, golden nugget, pumpkin, spaghetti squash, and hubbard. Hubbards are huge in size and are usually sold by the chunk. Bake winter squash whole or in halves. Or peel, remove seeds, then cut into chunks and steam or simmer.

Looking for a dish that's tasty, new, and interesting? Try spaghetti squash. After baking or boiling, the inner strands of the squash can be pulled apart to resemble spaghetti; top it with your pasta sauce of choice.

Gourds

Gourds and squash are close kin. Throughout Sub-Saharan Africa, gourds in their vast range of shapes and sizes are hollowed, then the extremely hard, watertight shells are carved into bowls, bottles, ladles, and spoons. Other diverse uses include musical instruments, smoking pipes, and wash basins. Hollowed gourds are not just used for utilitarian purposes; there is, especially in Nigeria, a highly developed art of the intricate engraving and decorating of the vegetable.

In the States, small whole ornamental squash are used to dress up our Thanksgiving tables and herald the coming of fall and winter.

CHRISTOPHENE AU GRATIN CASSEROLE

Highly popular on the Caribbean islands, this crisp, tasty squash is increasingly available at produce stands and supermarkets across the country. Look for mirliton in the South and chayote in Latin neighborhoods.

Makes 6 servings.

PER SERVING:

117 calories
5 g protein
8 g fat
6 g carbohydrate
302 mg sodium
23 mg cholesterol

4 medium-size christophenes
1 quart water
2 tablespoons butter or margarine
2 tablespoons unbleached all-purpose flour
¼ teaspoon salt *(optional)*
¼ teaspoon ground black pepper
1 cup milk
1 small onion, grated
½ cup grated Parmesan or cheddar cheese

Rinse and peel christophenes. Cut into 1-inch cubes. In large saucepan, bring about 1 quart water to boil. Add christophenes; reduce heat and simmer until tender, about 25 minutes. Meanwhile, heat oven to 350° F. In heavy 1-quart saucepan over low heat, melt butter. Add flour, salt (if desired), and pepper; stir until smooth. Gradually add milk, stirring constantly, until thickened and smooth. Stir in onion. Drain christophenes. In 1½-quart baking dish, combine christophenes and white sauce. Sprinkle with cheese. Bake until sauce bubbles, about 15 minutes.

ACORN SQUASH STUFFED WITH APPLE DRESSING

1 cup seedless raisins
½ cup rum, brandy, or apple cider
2½ cups vegetable bouillon or chicken broth
½ cup (1 stick) unsalted butter or margarine
1 large onion, minced
5 ribs celery, chopped
3 Golden Delicious apples, peeled, cored, and cut into ½-inch cubes
1 pound herb-seasoned stuffing crumbs
1 cup coarsely chopped walnuts
2 teaspoons ground coriander
2 teaspoons dried thyme leaves
¼ teaspoon salt *(optional)*
¼ teaspoon freshly ground pepper
Water
6 acorn squash, halved crosswise, seeded
½ cup maple syrup
Optional garnishes: fresh herb leaves, (such as parsley, rosemary, or thyme), dried cranberries

Makes 12 servings.

PER SERVING:

448 calories
8 g protein
16 g fat
75 g carbohydrate
783 mg sodium
21 mg cholesterol

In medium-size saucepan, combine raisins, rum, and bouillon; bring to boil. Reduce heat; simmer 10 minutes. In large skillet over medium-high heat, melt butter; add onion and celery. Sauté until vegetables are soft, about 10 minutes. Add apples; cook 3 additional minutes. Transfer mixture to large mixing bowl; stir in stuffing crumbs, until well mixed. Pour raisins and liquid over ingredients in bowl. Stir in walnuts, coriander, thyme, salt (if desired), and pepper. Cover dressing and store in refrigerator until time to stuff and bake squash. Heat oven to 375° F. Trim bottom of each squash so it will sit level. Fill 2 large baking pans (13 by 11 inches) with about ½ inch water; add squash halves cut side down. Bake 20 minutes; turn squash halves upright in dish. Brush insides with maple syrup. Spoon apple dressing into hollows, mounding slightly in center. (Any extra dressing can be baked at same time in separate buttered casserole dish.) Drizzle remaining maple syrup over tops of squash. Cover pan with foil; bake 25 minutes. Uncover and bake until squash are tender and dressing is crusty brown, about 20 additional minutes. Arrange squash on platter; garnish as desired.

ESSENCE BRINGS YOU
GREAT COOKING

FAR DOWN AT the corner, I saw an old man warming his hands against the sides of an odd-looking wagon, from which a stovepipe reeled off a thin spiral of smoke that drifted the odor of baking yams slowly to me, bringing a stab of swift nostalgia. . . .

At home we'd bake them in the hot coals of the fireplace, had carried them cold to school for lunch, munched them secretly, squeezing the sweet pulp from the soft peel as we hid from the teacher behind the largest book, the World's Geography. Yes, and we'd loved them candied, or baked in a cobbler, deep-fat fried in a pocket of dough, or roasted with pork and glazed with the well-browned fat; had chewed them raw—yams and years ago.

"Get yo hot, baked Car'lina yam," he called. . . . "How much are your yams?" I said, suddenly hungry. "They ten cents and they sweet," he said, his voice quavering with age. "These ain't none of them binding ones neither. These here is real sweet, yaller yams. How many?" "One," I said. "If they're that good, one should be enough."

The yams, some bubbling with syrup, lay on a wire rack above glowing coals that leaped to a low blue flame when struck by the draft of air. He took the dime, "If that ain't a sweet one, I'll give you another one free of charge. . . ." I knew that it was sweet before I broke it: bubbles of brown syrup had burst the skin. . . . I broke it, seeing the sugary pulp steaming in the cold. I held it watching him pour a spoonful of melted butter over the yam and the butter seeping in. I took a bite, finding it as sweet and hot as any I'd ever had, and was overcome with such a surge of homesickness that I turned away to keep my control. . . ."

—Ralph Ellison, *Invisible Man*

BAKED YAM CASSEROLE

2 pounds (about 6 medium-size) yams or sweet potatoes, cooked, peeled, chopped
2 tablespoons melted butter or margarine
4 tablespoons firmly packed light brown sugar
Grated rind of 1 orange
3 to 4 tablespoons cognac
½ teaspoon salt *(optional)*

TOPPING:
3 slices whole wheat bread, crusts removed, cut into ¼-inch cubes
2 tablespoons firmly packed light brown sugar
1 teaspoon cinnamon
2 tablespoons melted butter or margarine

Heat oven to 325° F. Grease 2-quart baking dish. In large bowl, combine yams, butter, sugar, orange rind, cognac, and salt (if desired). Beat with large whisk or electric mixer on low setting until light and fluffy. Spoon mixture into baking dish. To prepare topping, in small mixing bowl, combine bread, sugar, and cinnamon; toss until well mixed. Spoon topping over yams. Pour melted margarine over casserole. Bake 1 hour. Serve warm.

Makes 6 servings.

PER SERVING:

277 calories
4 g protein
8 g fat
35 g carbohydrate
154 mg sodium
0 mg cholesterol

ESSENCE BRINGS YOU
GREAT COOKING

SWEET POTATO DINNER SOUFFLÉ

Makes 6 servings.

PER SERVING:

200 calories
5 g protein
9 g fat
25 g carbohydrate
110 mg sodium
197 mg cholesterol

3 tablespoons packed brown sugar
1 tablespoon cornstarch
½ teaspoon ground nutmeg
⅛ teaspoon ground ginger
1 teaspoon grated lemon peel
⅛ teaspoon salt *(optional)*
¾ cup milk
4 large eggs, separated
2 tablespoons melted butter or margarine
1 teaspoon vanilla extract
2 cups cooked, mashed sweet potatoes or yams

Grease bottom of 1½-quart soufflé dish or straight-sided casserole; set aside. In medium saucepan, mix sugar, cornstarch, nutmeg, ginger, lemon peel, and salt (if desired). Gradually stir in milk until blended. Over medium heat, cook mixture, stirring constantly, until thickened; remove from heat. Heat oven to 375° F. In small bowl, using fork, beat egg yolks well. Add small amount of hot milk mixture; mix well. Mix yolk mixture with remaining hot milk mixture. Stir in butter, vanilla, and sweet potatoes. In small bowl, beat egg whites with rotary or electric mixer until stiff peaks form; carefully fold into sweet potato mixture. Pour into soufflé dish. Bake 35 minutes. Serve immediately.

HOLIDAY HONEYED YAMS

6 large yams
Water
1 tablespoon cornstarch
2 tablespoons cold water
¾ cup honey
¼ cup orange juice
4 tablespoons butter

In 8-quart Dutch oven, place yams and enough water to cover. Bring to boil over medium-high heat; reduce heat and simmer about 45 minutes or until tender. Remove yams; let cool until they can be handled. Peel yams and remove any eyes. Heat oven to 350° F. Slice yams diagonally into ¼-inch slices; arrange in 2-quart casserole dish. In small bowl blend cornstarch and cold water; set aside. In small saucepan, combine honey and orange juice; heat until honey melts. Stir in cornstarch mixture; cook over medium heat, stirring constantly for several minutes until mixture thickens. Remove from heat; stir in butter. Pour mixture over yams. Bake 40 minutes, basting yams occasionally with sauce from dish.

Makes 12 servings.

PER SERVING:

183 calories
1 g protein
6 g fat
34 g carbohydrate
65 mg sodium
16 mg cholesterol

SWEET POTATO FRIES

Makes 4 servings.

PER SERVING:

231 calories
2 g protein
14 g fat
26 g carbohydrate
10 mg sodium
0 mg cholesterol

3 medium-size sweet potatoes or yams
½ cup oil
Salt *(optional)*

Panfry Method: Peel potatoes (if desired); cut lengthwise into ½-inch-thick French-fry strips. In large skillet over medium heat, heat oil; pan-fry (in batches if necessary) until cooked 6 to 7 minutes. Using slotted metal spoon or spatula, transfer French fries as cooked to absorbent paper to drain. Sprinkle with salt (if desired).

Oven Method: Heat oven to 400° F. In large bowl, toss cut potatoes with ¼ cup oil to coat evenly. On 1 or 2 baking sheets, arrange in single layer; bake until golden on bottom, about 15 minutes. Using spatula or pancake turner, turn potatoes and bake until golden all over, about 15 additional minutes. Remove from oven; transfer to absorbent paper to drain. Sprinkle with salt (if desired).

Tomatoes

The lady with the red dress on. Bright, juicy, and full of life—vine-ripened tomatoes are one of summer's splendid treats. Tomatoes are one of our most versatile vegetables (although technically a fruit). Delicious when perfectly ripe and eaten raw, tomatoes can also be baked, broiled, fried, and stuffed. Add them to salads, sandwiches, sauces, soups, stews, and jams.

DO RIGHT BY FRESH TOMATOES

Tomatoes should always be stored right side up—that is, stem end up. The hilly tops of the stem end are the tomato's tenderest part and can bruise simply from it's own weight. So sit a tomato on its smooth bottom.

Make it a rule not to eat pale-pink, over-firm tomatoes raw. Just allow them to ripen at room temperature. Never put unripe tomatoes in the refrigerator—cool temperatures halt ripening and kill the flavor.

FRIED GREEN TOMATOES

4 large green tomatoes (may use firm pink tomatoes)
¼ cup cornmeal or unbleached all-purpose flour
1 tablespoon sugar
1 teaspoon salt *(optional)*
¼ teaspoon ground black pepper
2 tablespoons vegetable oil or olive oil

Makes 6 servings.

PER SERVING:

79 calories
1 g protein
5 g fat
8 g carbohydrate
96 mg sodium
0 mg cholesterol

Cut tomatoes into ½-inch thick slices; set aside. In shallow bowl, or on waxed paper, combine cornmeal, sugar, salt (if desired), and pepper; mix well. Dredge tomato slices in mixture until coated lightly. In large skillet, heat oil. Add tomatoes in single layer. Using wide spatula to turn, fry until browned on both sides. Transfer as cooked to paper towels to drain; keep warm in oven. Cook remaining tomatoes, adding oil as needed.

ESSENCE BRINGS YOU
GREAT COOKING

EASY ALL-PURPOSE TOMATO SAUCE

Perfect for topping any pasta shape, this sauce can also be used for baked pasta dishes.

Makes about 4 cups, 8 servings.

PER ½ CUP SERVING:

80 calories
2 g protein
4 g fat
11 g carbohydrate
194 mg sodium
0 mg cholesterol

> **TOMATO SAUCE is one of those dishes that's "even better the next day."**

2 tablespoons olive or vegetable oil
1 medium-size onion, chopped
1 small green bell pepper, seeded, cut into strips or chopped
2 garlic cloves, minced
1 28-ounce can whole tomatoes, cut up
1 6-ounce can tomato paste
1 cup water
1 teaspoon dried oregano leaves or 2 tablespoons chopped fresh oregano
½ teaspoon ground black pepper
½ teaspoon sugar *(optional)*
¼ teaspoon salt *(optional)*
1 large bay leaf

In Dutch oven or large saucepan, heat oil. Add onion, bell pepper, and garlic; sauté until tender, about 5 minutes. Stir in remaining ingredients; simmer until thickened, about 30 minutes. Remove bay leaf.

ESSENCE BRINGS YOU GREAT COOKING

MOLLIE NASH'S CHOW-CHOW

As a child I never fully appreciated the know-how and effort that Momma put into canning her green tomato relish; I was only aware of how good it made the greens taste. Now that salsa has put relishes back on the table in a big way, it's time to dust off this classic recipe. Enjoy it with fish, roasts, and egg dishes, and as a topping on burgers, hot dogs, and other sandwiches. A pint of chow-chow makes a thoughtful gift.

2 quarts (about 8 large) green tomatoes, chopped
1 medium-size head green cabbage, chopped (about 2 quarts)
4 medium-size onions, chopped
3 green bell peppers, seeded, chopped
3 red bell peppers, seeded, chopped
¼ cup coarse salt
Water
6 cups cider vinegar
2 cups sugar
2 tablespoons dry mustard
2 tablespoons mustard seeds
2 tablespoons mixed whole pickling spices
1 teaspoon ground ginger
½ teaspoon cayenne pepper

Makes about 8 pints. See following instructions for preparing jars.

PER 2 TABLESPOONS:

21 calories
0 protein
0 g fat
5 g carbohydrate
140 mg sodium
0 mg cholesterol

In large, deep bowl, place all vegetables. Add salt and enough cold water to cover; loosely cover and refrigerate or let stand in cool place overnight. Next morning drain off all liquid. In large, deep stainless steel or enamel pan, combine vinegar, sugar, and spices; mix well. Over medium heat, bring mixture to boil. Reduce heat; simmer until sugar dissolves and flavors blend, about 5 minutes. Add drained vegetables; cook, stirring constantly, about 5 minutes. Into hot, sterilized canning jars, spoon chow-chow to ¼ inch from top. Seal at once or cool and refrigerate. To store at room temperature, it is necessary to process in boiling water bath. To process, place jars in canning rack; lower into canning pot or any deep kettle with enough boiling water to cover jars by 2 inches. (If canning rack is not available, a folded towel can be placed on bottom of pot.) Boil 8 minutes.

ESSENCE BRINGS YOU
GREAT COOKING

59

To Sterilize Jars

Check jars to be sure there are no nicks or cracks. Make sure screw bands are not bent; use new lids. Wash jars, lids, and bands with hot soapy water; rinse. In canning pot or other large pot, place jars, lid parts, and large spoon on rack. Cover jars with water; cover pot with lid. Bring to boil; boil 15 minutes. Leave jars and equipment in this pot until ready to use.

Turnips and Rutabagas

Called turnip roots or bottoms, these slightly sweet, yet sharp-tasting vegetables can be eaten raw as well as cooked. Peel the white and purple skin before preparing. Available year round. Choose roots free of cracks and scars. An excellent source of potassium.

Though they are often called yellow turnips, rutabagas are an entirely different vegetable from their botanical cousin. Much larger than the turnip, rutabagas are yellow-fleshed and the pale-orange skin must be peeled before eating. Rutabagas are often sold waxed to preserve their moisture. A southern favorite, rutabagas are delicious boiled, steamed, or mashed as a side dish, or cubed and added to soups and stews. Available year round. Just 60 calories in a cup of cooked cubes.

SOUTHERN TURNIPS AND RUTABAGA

2 pounds turnip bottoms, peeled, cubed
1 medium-size rutabaga (about 1 pound)
1 bay leaf
4 cups water
2 tablespoons butter or margarine
2 scallions, sliced
½ teaspoon salt *(optional)*
¼ teaspoon ground black pepper
½ teaspoon crushed red pepper
4 cups cooked turnip greens

In Dutch oven, combine turnips, rutabaga, bay leaf, and water. Bring to boil; reduce heat and simmer until vegetables are fork-tender, about 20 minutes. Meanwhile, in large skillet, melt butter; sauté scallions about 4 minutes. Add drained turnips and rutabaga; sprinkle with salt (if desired) and peppers. Add turnip greens; gently toss vegetables to mix. Transfer to large serving dish.

Makes 6 servings.

PER SERVING:

139 calories
3 g protein
4 g fat
21 g carbohydrate
151 mg sodium
110 mg cholesterol

ESSENCE BRINGS YOU
GREAT COOKING

61

ALI'S VEGETABLE CURRY

This spicy stew of mixed vegetables is from Ruth Ali, owner/chef of the Bombay Indian Restaurant in Harlem. This is one of the dishes most frequently requested by her customers.

Makes 8 servings.

PER SERVING:

221 calories
8 g protein
8 g fat
31 g carbohydrate
297 mg sodium
0 mg cholesterol

- ¼ cup vegetable oil
- 3 garlic cloves, minced
- 2 medium-size yellow onions, chopped
- 1 tablespoon grated fresh ginger
- 1 teaspoon whole cloves
- 2 bay leaves
- 1 stick cinnamon, broken up
- 3 teaspoons turmeric
- 2 teaspoons paprika
- 1½ teaspoons ground coriander
- 1½ teaspoons cumin
- 1 teaspoon salt *(optional)*
- ¼ teaspoon cayenne pepper
- ¼ teaspoon ground black pepper
- 3 carrots, thinly sliced crosswise
- 2 medium-size white potatoes, diced
- 2 stalks celery, thinly sliced
- ½ pound fresh string beans, cut into 2-inch pieces
- 1 10-ounce package frozen lima beans
- 2½ cups water
- 1 8-ounce can garbanzo beans, drained

In heavy Dutch oven or saucepot, heat oil. Add garlic and cook about 30 seconds. Add onion, ginger, cloves, bay leaves, and cinnamon. Sauté about 5 minutes. Stir in turmeric, paprika, coriander, cumin, salt (if desired), and peppers; blend well. Add carrots, potatoes, celery, string beans, lima beans, and water. Stir to blend liquid and mix vegetables. Bring liquid to boil; reduce heat and simmer 15 minutes, stirring occasionally. Add garbanzo beans and cook about 5 additional minutes until all vegetables are cooked through. Discard bay leaves.

ISLAND PUMPKIN FRITTERS

1 cup cooked mashed pumpkin (butternut squash may be substituted)
½ cup milk
1 large egg
1 cup unbleached all-purpose flour
1 teaspoon ground nutmeg
1 teaspoon ground cinnamon
½ teaspoon cayenne pepper
⅓ cup granulated sugar
¼ teaspoon salt *(optional)*
1 cup vegetable oil

In large mixing bowl, combine all ingredients except oil; stir until well mixed and smooth. In deep fryer or heavy deep skillet, heat vegetable oil to 375° F (or until 1-inch cube of bread dropped into oil browns in 1 minute). Using greased tablespoon, drop balls of batter, 6 to 8 at a time, into hot oil; cook until golden brown and crisp, about 4 minutes. As they are cooked, using slotted spoon, transfer fritters to paper towels to drain; keep warm in oven while cooking remaining fritters. Delicious plain or with dipping sauce.

Makes 15 to 20 appetizers.

PER FRITTER:

127 calories
1 g protein
7 g fat
11 g carbohydrate
46 mg sodium
19 mg cholesterol

BAGIA

(Mixed Vegetable Fritters)

Also by Ruth Ali, these savory vegetable fritters make a tasty side-dish or hors d'oeuvres.

Makes 4 servings.

PER SERVING:

304 calories
8 g protein
19 g fat
28 g carbohydrate
87 mg sodium
0 mg cholesterol

- ¾ cup all-purpose flour
- ¼ cup whole wheat flour
- ⅛ teaspoon baking powder
- ½ teaspoon turmeric
- ½ teaspoon salt *(optional)*
- ⅛ teaspoon cayenne pepper
- 1 small carrot, finely chopped
- 1 small onion, finely chopped
- ½ celery stalk, finely chopped
- ½ small bell pepper, chopped
- ½ cup water
- 1 cup vegetable oil

In medium-size bowl combine flours, baking powder, turmeric, salt (if desired), and cayenne. Mix until well blended. Add chopped vegetables; mix well. Stir in water until all flour is moistened and mixture is somewhat pasty. In 9-inch skillet, heat oil. Add batter to hot oil by rounded tablespoons spaced at least 1 inch apart. (It will be necessary to cook fritters in batches.) After cooking about 30 seconds, turn balls to other side, then flatten with fork to form pancake-like shape. Cook about 5 minutes, turning twice. Drain on paper towels. Keep completed fritters warm while cooking remaining batter.

Fragrant, full-flavored vegetable soups are ideal as an elegant first course, to go along with a sandwich, or as a filling main dish.

FRESH CORN CHOWDER

2 tablespoons butter or margarine
1 large onion, chopped (about 1 cup)
½ cup sliced celery
2 tablespoons unbleached all-purpose flour
1½ cups low-fat milk
1 cup chicken broth
½ cup water
2 medium-size potatoes, peeled, cut into small cubes
1½ cups corn kernels, freshly cut (or frozen or canned corn)
½ teaspoon salt *(optional)*
¼ teaspoon ground white pepper, or to taste
⅛ teaspoon paprika
2 tablespoons chopped parsley

Makes 6 servings.

PER SERVING:

173 calories
5 g protein
5 g fat
27 g carbohydrate
216 mg sodium
14 mg cholesterol

In 3-quart saucepan, melt margarine; add onion and celery and cook about 6 minutes until vegetables are tender. Stir in flour; cook over low heat, stirring occasionally, until mixture is blended and thickened. Remove from heat. Stir in milk and broth until blended. Return to heat; bring to boil. Add potatoes, corn, salt (if desired), and pepper. Partially cover pan and cook over low heat; simmer about 20 minutes or until potatoes are tender. Ladle soup into warm tureen or soup bowls. Sprinkle with paprika and parsley.

ESSENCE BRINGS YOU
GREAT COOKING

CREAM OF CAULIFLOWER SOUP

Makes 4 servings

PER SERVING:

75 calories
5 g protein
1 g fat
13 g carbohydrate
274 mg sodium
.30 mg cholesterol

1 large cauliflower
2 cups water
1 leek, chopped
1 cup chopped celery
¼ cup chopped onion
2 cups fresh or canned chicken broth
¼ cup skim milk
½ teaspoon salt *(optional)*
¼ teaspoon ground white pepper
Optional garnish: chopped parsley, pinch freshly grated nutmeg

Cut cauliflower into florets. Discard hard stem and green leaves. In medium-size saucepan, combine cauliflower and water. Cover and bring to boil. Reduce heat to low; simmer exactly 2 minutes; drain. Add leek, celery, onion, and broth. Simmer uncovered until vegetables become tender. Pour soup through strainer; return liquid to saucepan. In blender or food processor, in batches as needed to prevent overfilling, puree cooked vegetables. Return puree to saucepan. Stir in milk, salt (if desired), and pepper. Garnish, if desired, with chopped parsley and nutmeg.

BROCCOLI-POTATO SOUP

2 medium-size white potatoes, scrubbed
Water
1 small bunch broccoli
1 tablespoon butter or margarine
1 small yellow onion, chopped
1 small rib celery, thinly sliced
1 garlic clove, minced
2 tablespoons unbleached all-purpose flour
½ teaspoon salt *(optional)*
¼ teaspoon ground black or white pepper
1 cup skim milk
½ cup chicken broth
2 teaspoons lemon juice

Makes 4 servings.

PER SERVING:

255 calories
14 g protein
9 g fat
42 g carbohydrate
18 mg sodium
17 mg cholesterol

In large saucepan, cover potatoes with cold water; over high heat, bring to boil. Reduce heat to low; cover and simmer about 30 minutes or until tender. Meanwhile, prepare broccoli. Remove any large leaves and cut off tough stalk ends; split stalks lengthwise. To another large saucepan, add 1 inch water; bring to boil. Add broccoli; reduce heat to low. Cover and simmer about 10 minutes until crisp-tender. Remove broccoli, reserving cooking liquid; set both aside. In same saucepan, over medium heat, melt margarine; sauté onion, celery, and garlic until tender, about 5 minutes. Stir in flour, salt (if desired), and pepper. Cook 1 minute, stirring constantly until blended and bubbly. Gradually stir in milk and broth. Cook, stirring constantly, about 2 to 4 minutes, until slightly thickened; do not boil. Drain potatoes, peel, and cube. Chop broccoli; add, with reserved cooking liquid, to creamy mixture in saucepan. Mash some potatoes against sides of pan to thicken soup. Heat thoroughly (do not boil); stir in lemon juice.

ESSENCE BRINGS YOU
GREAT COOKING

Potato salad has become so entrenched in our food tradition, it's hard to image a picnic, reunion, or potluck supper without the creamy, well-seasoned spuds. Contrasting flavors, textures, and colors make vegetable salads a lively addition to any meal. A salad's leading drawback is fatty dressing. Cut back on fat by reducing the amount of dressing or by substituting low-fat yogurt, creamed cottage cheese, buttermilk, broth, or juice for some of the oil or standard mayonnaise.

LOW-CAL CREAMY POTATO SALAD

This weight-conscious version of the ever-popular salad goes well with grilled poultry and fish.

Makes 6 servings:

PER SERVING
(without egg):

169 calories
4 g protein
.5 g fat
37 g carbohydrate
397 mg sodium
.37 mg cholesterol

- 8 to 12 new potatoes or small red-skinned potatoes
- Water
- 1 teaspoon salt *(optional)*
- 2 hard-cooked eggs, chopped *(optional)*
- 2 scallions, sliced or chopped
- 2 stalks celery, chopped
- 1/4 cup chopped pickle or pickle relish
- 1/2 cup low-fat mayonaise
- 1/2 cup low-fat plain yogurt
- 1 tablespoon prepared mustard
- 1 tablespoon chopped fresh dill
- 1/4 teaspoon ground white, black, or cayenne pepper
- Several lettuce leaves
- *Optional garnish:* fresh dill sprigs

Scrub potatoes thoroughly; cut away eyes. Peel potatoes only if desired. In large pot, combine potatoes with enough water to cover, add salt (if desired) ; bring to boil. Cook on high heat until tender, about 20 to 30 minutes (do not overcook); drain. When cool enough to handle quarter potatoes. In large bowl, while potatoes are still warm, combine with eggs, scallions, celery, and pickle. In small bowl, blend mayonaise, yogurt, mustard, dill, and pepper. Stir dressing into potato salad. Serve on lettuce leaves; garnish with dill. Serve chilled or at room temperature.

DORIS'S POTATO SALAD

This lightly dressed salad by Doris Cole of Baltimore, allows the aroma and flavor of the potatoes to dominate. This is a basic recipe to which you can add your own creative touches. Mrs. Cole is the mother of our fashion editor, Harriette Cole.

6 medium-size white potatoes, peeled
Water
1 cup mayonnaise or salad dressing
1 tablespoon vinegar
1 teaspoon salt *(optional)*
½ teaspoon celery seeds
¼ teaspoon ground pepper
2 medium-size ribs celery, chopped
1 medium-size onion, chopped
1 medium-size bell pepper, chopped
Optional garnish: lettuce leaves

Makes 10 servings.

PER SERVING:

240 calories
1 g protein
18 g fat
17 g carbohydrate
249 mg sodium
13 mg cholesterol

Place potatoes in Dutch oven or kettle with 2 inches cold water. Bring to boil; reduce heat. Simmer until tender but still firm, about 25 minutes. Meanwhile, in large bowl, combine mayonnaise, vinegar, salt, celery seed, and pepper; stir. Drain potatoes; when cool, cube or slice. To dressing, add potatoes, celery, onion, and bell pepper. Lightly stir to mix and coat. Line salad bowl or platter with lettuce leaves; top with potato salad.

GRANDMA'S COLESLAW

This slaw is made the old-fashioned way—with boiled dressing. Its taste is markedly superior to quicker methods.

Makes 6 servings.

1 small head green cabbage
2 carrots
1 small onion, minced
1 small green pepper, cut into thin rings for garnish; finely chop remainder for coleslaw
1 teaspoon salt or to taste
¼ cup (½ stick) butter or margarine
1 tablespoon unbleached all-purpose flour
1 cup sugar
1 cup vinegar
1 teaspoon dry mustard
1 teaspoon celery seed
¼ teaspoon cayenne pepper
2 large eggs
Optional garnish: green pepper rings

Remove, rinse, and reserve outer cabbage leaves to line salad bowl, if desired. Coarsely shred remaining cabbage; rinse well, pat dry; place in large bowl. Shred carrots; add to cabbage with onion, chopped green pepper, and ½ teaspoon salt. Toss well to combine; set aside. In small saucepan, melt butter over medium heat; stir in flour until blended. Add sugar, vinegar, mustard, celery seed, pepper, and remaining salt. When hot but not quite boiling, remove from heat; set aside. In small bowl, beat eggs. Briskly stir about 4 tablespoons of vinegar mixture into eggs, adding one tablespoon at a time. Stir egg mixture into vinegar mixture in saucepan. Over medium heat, cook, stirring constantly, until mixture thickens. Pour desired amount of dressing over cabbage mixture in bowl; toss to coat well. Chill. Serve in cabbage-leaf-lined salad bowl; garnish with pepper rings. Any remaining dressing may be served in separate bowl.

RUBY'S RAISIN COLESLAW

Looking for an easy way to make an impressive showing? Serve, or carry to a potluck, this gourmet-quality salad by Ruby Pitts of Detroit. Ruby, a friend of mine since childhood, has a flair for creating healthful dishes that are also flavorful and eye-catching.

1 small head red cabbage
1 small head green cabbage
4 medium-size carrots
1½ cups golden raisins
2 tablespoons chopped fresh dill or 2 teaspoons dried dill
½ cup bottled coleslaw dressing, or blend ½ cup whipped salad dressing, 1 tablespoon milk, 1 tablespoon vinegar, 1 teaspoon sugar, ¼ teaspoon salt *(optional),* and dash of paprika
2 medium-size cooking apples, preferably Granny Smith or Rome Beauty

Remove and discard coarse or blemished outer leaves from cabbages; carefully remove and set aside several whole leaves to use as garnish, if desired. Quarter cabbages, remove cores; finely shred cabbage and carrots. In large salad bowl, toss cabbage, carrots, raisins, dill, and dressing. Peel, core, and shred apples into coleslaw; toss to coat and mix well. Cover and chill until ready to serve.

Makes 8 servings.

PER SERVING:

181 calories
3 g protein
5 g fat
35 g carbohydrate
191 mg sodium
8 mg cholesterol

ESSENCE BRINGS YOU
GREAT COOKING

NEW CARROT–RAISIN SALAD

A ½-cup serving of raw carrots supplies the entire adult recommended daily allowance of beta carotene, an anti-cancer nutrient and source of vitamin A.

Makes 2 servings.

PER SERVING:

235 calories
2 g protein
11 g fat
35 g carbohydrate
109 g sodium
8 mg cholesterol

2 medium-size carrots
Ice cubes
2 tablespoons mayonnaise
1 tablespoon honey
1 teaspoon grated lemon peel
1 teaspoon lemon juice
¼ teaspoon ground ginger
⅓ cup raisins

In large bowl, place carrots on ice for 30 to 60 minutes. Meanwhile, in medium-size bowl, blend mayonnaise, honey, lemon peel, lemon juice, and ginger. Grate carrots into bowl; add raisins. Stir and toss to coat and mix well. Cover and store in refrigerator.

AVOCADO-ORANGE
SALAD

An avocado is ripe and ready to eat when its flesh yields to pressure gently applied by the fingers.

SALAD:
2 ripe avocados, peeled, pitted, sliced, or cut into chunks
2 tablespoons freshly squeezed lemon juice
2 medium-size navel oranges
Iceberg, leaf, Bibb, or other lettuce leaves

DRESSING:
¼ cup olive oil
2 tablespoons freshly squeezed lemon or lime juice
1 scallion, sliced
1 clove garlic, chopped
¼ teaspoon cayenne pepper

Makes 4 servings.

PER SERVING:

306 calories
4 g protein
24 g fat
25 g carbohydrate
10 mg sodium
0 mg cholesterol

   Sprinkle avocado with lemon juice; gently stir to coat. Peel oranges; slice crosswise or cut into segments. On platter or 4 salad plates, arrange bed of lettuce; top with avocados and oranges. In jar with tight-fitting lid or small bowl, combine dressing ingredients; shake or whisk vigorously to blend. Drizzle salad with dressing.

ESSENCE BRINGS YOU
GREAT COOKING

Bountiful Beans

Recipes

CREOLE RED BEANS AND RICE

KING OF RED BEANS

CARIBBEAN PEAS AND RICE

FRESH BLACK-EYED PEAS AND OKRA

VEGETABLE BEAN CHILI IN TORTILLA BASKETS

CUBAN BLACK BEANS AND YELLOW RICE

SAVORY HERBED LENTILS

QUICK CASSOULET

BARBECUED BEANS AND TOFU

TWO-BEAN CASSEROLE

BEAN FRITTERS (*Akara*)

BLACK-EYED PEA SALAD

WHITE BEAN SALAD

BLACK BEAN SOUP

NAVY BEAN SOUP

SPLIT PEA SOUP

WHITE BEAN AND COLLARD GREEN SOUP

Recipes in this chapter do not include nutritional analysis for sodium content when salt is listed as an optional ingredient.

was the warm and familiar autograph of famed trumpeter and first son of New Orleans, Louis Armstrong. During the 1920s in Louisiana, where red beans were an important crop and a favorite among its legendary dishes, Armstrong and youngsters of his era literally grew up on beans. And rightly so—second only to meat, dried beans and peas are the highest source of protein and contain appreciable amounts of calcium, iron, and B vitamins.

There's more Louisiana tradition tied to using the old bean. Mondays were laundry and "red and white" day. Washing clothes on a scrubboard was a laborious task that routinely took all day. Those doing the laundry were usually in charge of cooking. Red beans and rice became the ideal meal for Mondays because beans could be put on early, then left to simmer and develop their rich, earthy flavor without much pot watching. Today, even in the age of push-button washers and dryers, Mondays remain red-beans-and-rice day in New Orleans!

The legacy of beans spans the ages and the globe. Looking back even further in time, beans were highly valued because they could be dried and stored as a source of food for the winter. There's evidence that the early Egyptians actually worshiped dried beans. But due to their wide availability and relative low cost, beans subsequently fell from glory and became known as "the poor man's meat." As our elders sometimes remind us, it's been that pot of beans on the stove that has kept many a family eating during tough times.

Fortunately, dried beans and peas (also called legumes) have again come into their own. In addition to their thoroughly satisfying flavors, legumes fit the profile of a modern-day health food: no cholesterol, low in calories, fat, and sodium, and high in complex carbohydrates and dietary fiber.

So how does slow-cooking dried beans and peas fit into today's fast-paced lifestyle? Easily! It's easy to cook beans on the weekend or when time permits. You can place them into tightly sealed containers, in meal-size quantities, and freeze them for up to a year, or store them in the refrigerator to enjoy within four days. Right before dinnertime, heat the pre-cooked beans while cooking or reheating rice, fixing a salad, and slicing a loaf of crusty bread for a well-balanced, soul-satisfying meal.

ESSENCE BRINGS YOU
GREAT COOKING

GENERAL METHOD OF PREPARATION

For better results, all varieties of legumes except split peas and lentils require soaking before cooking. Soaking cuts cooking time in half and saves nutrients that would be destroyed by lengthier cooking. First, rinse beans thoroughly, picking through and removing debris and any damaged beans. In a large mixing bowl or the pot in which they will cook, cover beans with about four times their volume of water. Let soak overnight or for a minimum of four hours. Drain soaking water, then rinse beans with fresh water. Cover beans with fresh water. Add desired seasonings such as bay leaves, celery, cumin, garlic, herbs, onions, and peppers. To avoid toughening and extended cooking, do not add salt or acidic ingredients such as lemon juice, vinegar, tomatoes, or molasses to the beans before they are tender. Over low heat, partially cover pot and slowly simmer beans. (Boiling can toughen the skins.) Cook until tender, about 1 to 1½ hours, depending on the type of bean. To test for doneness, bite a bean, or press it with a fork against a hard surface.

> Dried beans and peas are also called legumes. It's a French word—pronounced lehg-yooms. In French, however, legumes means vegetables.
>
> Beans e-x-p-a-n-d when cooked. Two cups of dried beans (about 1 pound) become 5 to 7 cups of cooked beans, depending on size of beans.

SOAKING WATER VERSUS FRESH WATER

There is a debate as to whether beans should be cooked in their soaking water, or if they should be drained and cooked in fresh water. Though some nutrients are lost when the soaking water is discarded, there's good riddance to some of the notorious gas-producing agents, pesticide residue, and sourness.

Here are timesaving ways to get delicious, versatile, healthful beans on the table faster.

QUICK-SOAK METHOD

Carefully rinse and pick through beans; place in pot. Add cold water to measure 2 inches above beans. Bring water to boil. Cover pot; cook 2 minutes. Remove from heat; let stand, covered, 1 hour.

ESSENCE BRINGS YOU
GREAT COOKING

PRESSURE-COOKING

Pressure-cooking makes cooking dried beans from-scratch a practical choice for weekday meals. Cooking under pressure can cut cooking time seventy five percent or more. For example, soaked black beans cooked on top of the range are ready in about an hour and 15 minutes; cooking time in a pressure cooker is only 15 minutes! Be sure not to fill the cooker, including cooking liquid, to more than half its volume. Carefully follow manufacturer's directions for use, cooking times, and care of the pressure cooker.

CANNED BEANS

Though the qualities of flavor and texture are not as high as those of home-cooked beans, canned beans are tasty and—perhaps their most redeeming quality—they're instant! Always pour off the canning liquid, rinse if desired, then add fresh seasonings. In addition to a wide range of main and side dishes, canned beans can be added to soups, stews, casseroles, and salads; mashed for sandwich spreads and party dips; and refried for tacos, burritos, tostadas, and other Tex-Mex favorites.

Dried Beans as Baking Weights

To keep unfilled piecrusts from shrinking or puffing during baking, uncooked dried beans can be used as an alternative to metal or ceramic baking weights.

BLACK BEAN: Also called TURTLE BEAN—small, oval, black skin; meaty, earthy flavor. Available dried and canned. Widely used in Latin-American cooking. Makes delicious soup; great tasting with rice.

BLACK-EYED PEA: Also called BLACK-EYED SUZIES—small, kidney-shaped, beige with black dot in center; mild, pealike flavor. Sold fresh, frozen, canned, and dried. Southern classic.

BUTTER BEAN: Also called LARGE LIMA BEAN—cream colored or light green, flat, slightly sweet taste. Especially delicious in soups.

CHICK-PEA: Also called GARBANZO BEAN—medium-size, round, light tan; nutty flavor. Widely available canned or dried. Popular in Mediterranean and Mexican cooking. Puree to make hummus—a bean dip or sandwich filling.

CROWDER PEA: Small, medium to dark brown; soaking required. Popular in Southern cooking.

GREAT NORTHERN BEAN: Large, oval, white bean; mealy texture. Excellent for soups and salads.

KIDNEY BEAN: Large, dark red, kidney-shaped. Popular in southern and Mexican cooking.

LENTIL: Small, round, flat legume. Brown is most popular variety; also available in green, orange, and other colors. No soaking necessary.

NAVY BEAN: White bean, smaller than Great Northern Bean. Often used in soups and "baked beans."

PIGEON PEA: Also called CONGO PEA—small, round, beige speckled with brown; available canned or dried. Popular Caribbean side dish.

PINK BEAN: Medium-size, pale red color; related to Kidney Bean.

DRY BEANS AND PEAS

are a rich source of protein. Because they lack one or two of the eight "essential" amino acids—protein building blocks—vegetable sources of protein are considered incomplete. But eaten with other types of plant protein, such as grains, or with small amounts of animal protein, such as eggs, cheese, or milk, the proteins "complement" one another and complete the protein chain. This concept of complementary protein may seem complicated, but our ancestors figured it out naturally. Traditional combinations such as red beans and rice, black-eyed peas and cornbread, and bean and cheese enchiladas exemplify this principle.

ESSENCE BRINGS YOU
GREAT COOKING

PINTO BEAN: Medium-size, speckled pink and brown; popular in chili and refried beans.

RED BEAN: Smaller relative of the kidney bean, dark red. A favorite in southern cooking.

SOY BEAN: Small, round, hard; requires long cooking.

SPLIT PEA: Small green or yellow dried pea that is split in half. No soaking required. Used primarily in soups.

Peanuts are actually a legume, not a nut.

Girl with peanut crop in Richmond, Virginia, circa 1870.

ESSENCE BRINGS YOU
GREAT COOKING

CREOLE RED BEANS AND RICE

This is a meatless version of the New Orleans classic "red and white."

1 pound dried red kidney beans or small red beans
Water
2 tablespoons olive oil
1 large onion, chopped
2 ribs celery, sliced
1 green bell pepper, seeded, chopped
2 cloves garlic, minced
6 cups water or vegetable broth or combination
1 teaspoon dried thyme
1 teaspoon crushed red pepper flakes
½ teaspoon ground black pepper
2 bay leaves
1 teaspoon salt *(optional)*

Makes 6 main-dish or
8 side-dish servings.

PER MAIN
DISH SERVING:

432 calories
19 g protein
6 g fat
76 g carbohydrate
199 mg sodium
0 mg cholesterol

Rinse beans carefully and pick through. In large bowl or pot, cover beans with water; soak at least 8 hours or overnight. Drain soaked beans and rinse with cold running water. In Dutch oven, heat oil; add onion, celery, bell pepper, and garlic. Sauté until vegetables are tender, about 5 minutes. Add beans, 6 cups water, thyme, pepper flakes, black pepper, and bay leaves. Cover pot; over low heat, simmer 1½ hours. Stir in salt (if desired); simmer about 30 to 60 minutes or until tender. Remove bay leaves. Serve over rice.

ESSENCE BRINGS YOU
GREAT COOKING

KING OF RED BEANS

This recipe by the late Louis Evans, who was an executive chef of the Pontchartrain Hotel in New Orleans and cookbook author, won him the title in a local red-bean cookoff. It is especially rich. To reduce saturated fat, omit the sausage and add 2 tablespoons olive oil.

Makes 6 servings.

PER SERVING:

388 calories
24 g protein
9 g fat
53 g carbohydrate
734 mg sodium
12 mg cholesterol

- ¼ pound bulk sausage
- 1 large onion, finely chopped
- 1 medium-size green bell pepper, seeded, finely chopped
- 1 medium-size rib celery, finely chopped
- 3 bay leaves
- 1 teaspoon salt *(optional)*
- 1 teaspoon white pepper
- 1 medium-size ham bone
- ¼ pound cooked ham scraped from bone, chopped
- 1 pound dried red beans
- 1 tablespoon sugar
- 1 gallon cold water

Elder vendor with red beans.

Heat oven to 450° F. In 12-inch cast-iron skillet or other oven-proof skillet, place all ingredients except beans, sugar, and water. Place in oven, roast, stirring occasionally, until bone is brown. Meanwhile, rinse and pick through beans. In large saucepot or Dutch oven, place beans, sugar, and water; stir in cooked seasonings (drain seasonings before adding to reduce fat). Over high heat, bring to boil; reduce heat. Cover and simmer about 2 hours or until beans are tender and the liquid creamy. Remove bone and bay leaves.

ESSENCE BRINGS YOU
GREAT COOKING

CARIBBEAN PEAS AND RICE

This famous West Indian dish is served throughout the Caribbean. The subtle taste of coconut makes the flavor unique. Black-eyed peas may be used as an alternative to the red beans.

1 cup dried small red beans or red kidney beans
Water
1 teaspoon salt *(optional)*
¼ cup coconut cream
1 scallion, thinly sliced
1 tablespoon chopped fresh thyme or 1 teaspoon dried thyme
½ teaspoon ground black pepper
2 cups uncooked rice

Rinse beans thoroughly. Pick over and discard any debris or beans that are broken or shriveled. In large bowl, cover beans with 3 cups water; soak 8 hours or overnight. Drain beans; transfer to large saucepan. Add 3 cups fresh water. Over medium-low heat, simmer beans until tender, about 1 hour; add ½ teaspoon salt (if desired) during last 15 minutes cooking time. Meanwhile, in Dutch oven, bring 1 quart water to boil, stir in coconut cream, scallion, thyme, remaining ½ teaspoon salt (if desired), pepper, and rice. Reduce heat to low; cover and simmer until rice is tender, about 15 minutes. Using fork, stir rice from bottom to fluff; stir in beans and liquid. Over low heat, cover and cook 1 to 2 additional minutes. Remove from heat, let sit, covered, until all liquid is absorbed, about 5 minutes.

Makes 10 side-dish servings.

PER SERVING:

214 calories
8 g protein
2 g fat
42 g carbohydrate
10 mg sodium
0 mg cholesterol

ESSENCE BRINGS YOU GREAT COOKING

FRESH BLACK-EYED PEAS AND OKRA

*Green black-eyes are a refreshing and quick cooking alternative
to the dried version.*

Makes 6 servings.

PER SERVING:

160 calories
8 g protein
5 g fat
22 g carbohydrate
360 mg sodium
0 mg cholesterol

2 tablespoons olive oil or vegetable oil
1 medium-size onion, finely chopped
1 large garlic clove, minced
Water
2 small bay leaves
1 teaspoon salt *(optional)*
½ teaspoon ground black pepper
1 pound fresh or frozen black-eyed peas
1 pound fresh okra, tops trimmed

In large saucepan, heat oil; sauté onion and garlic until tender, about 5 minutes. Add three cups of water, bay leaves, salt (if desired), and pepper. Bring to boil; stir in peas. Reduce heat; simmer 20 minutes. Add okra; cook until of desired tenderness, about 5 to 10 additional minutes (do not overcook). Remove bay leaves.

VEGETABLE BEAN CHILI IN TORTILLA BASKETS

This vegetarian chili is hearty and satisfying. Serving it in shaped tortillas (which are optional) adds fun as well as flavor.

1 tablespoon vegetable oil

1 onion, chopped

1 small green bell pepper, seeded, chopped

2 garlic cloves, minced

1 16-ounce can tomatoes, chopped, or 2 cups chopped fresh
tomatoes

1 8-ounce can tomato sauce

2 tablespoons chili powder

2 teaspoons ground cumin

1 teaspoon red pepper flakes

½ teaspoon salt *(optional)*

2 medium-size carrots, sliced

2 medium-size zucchini, sliced

1 cup corn, fresh, canned, or frozen

2 cups cooked red kidney beans; or 1 16-ounce can kidney beans,
drained, rinsed

4 tortilla baskets (see following recipe)

Makes 4 servings.

PER SERVING:

252 calories
12 g protein
5 g fat
46 g carbohydrate
783 mg sodium
0 mg cholesterol

In Dutch oven over medium-high heat, heat oil; add onion, bell pepper, and garlic. Cook, stirring occasionally, until tender, about 5 minutes. Add tomatoes, tomato sauce, chili powder, cumin, pepper flakes, and salt (if desired). Reduce heat to low; simmer 20 minutes. Add carrots and zucchini; simmer 15 additional minutes, adding corn and beans during last 5 minutes cooking time. Place tortilla baskets on plates; ladle chili into shells.

Tortilla Baskets

These edible bowls are ideal containers for Tex-Mex-style dishes such as chili, salads, and Huevos Rancheros.

Makes 4 baskets.

PER TORTILLA
BASKET:

127 calories
2 g protein
8 g fat
13 g carbohydrate
1 mg sodium
0 mg cholesterol

2 tablespoons vegetable oil
4 8-inch flour or corn tortillas

Heat oven to 400° F. On baking sheet place, bottoms up, 4 small oven-proof bowls or 4-inch balls of aluminum foil; set aside. In large skillet over high heat, heat oil. One at a time, cook tortillas about 5 seconds on each side until soft and pliable; transfer to paper towels to drain. Center a tortilla over each bowl or ball of foil. Bake until golden, about 5 minutes. Remove from oven; let cool slightly before filling.

CUBAN BLACK BEANS AND YELLOW RICE

It's the dash of rum that adds the exciting flavor of island cooking to this quick-fix dish. Heat evaporates most of the alcohol, leaving just the spirited flavor.

1 tablespoon olive oil
1 small onion, diced
½ medium-size green bell pepper, seeded, diced
2 garlic cloves, minced
2 16-ounce cans black beans, drained
¼ cup rum or dry red wine
2 teaspoons crushed oregano
1 large bay leaf
Yellow Rice (see recipe on page 115)
Optional garnish: chopped parsley

Makes 6 servings.

PER SERVING:

134 calories
7 g protein
2 g fat
19 g carbohydrate
322 mg sodium
0 mg cholesterol

In large, heavy-bottom saucepan, heat oil; sauté onion, bell pepper, and garlic until garlic is golden. Stir in beans and rum; add oregano and bay leaf. Cook over medium heat, about 10 minutes, until beans are heated through and flavors have blended; discard bay leaf. Garnish with parsley. Serve over yellow rice.

ESSENCE BRINGS YOU
GREAT COOKING

SAVORY HERBED LENTILS

No soaking is required for these quick-cooking legumes. Serve over brown rice for a hearty and satisfying low-fat main dish.

Makes 6 servings.

PER SERVING:

292 calories
21 g protein
1 g fat
51 g carbohydrate
291 mg sodium
0 mg cholesterol

1 pound dried lentils
Water
Vegetable cooking spray
1 medium-size onion, chopped
2 medium-size garlic cloves, minced
1 medium-size stalk celery, including leaves, chopped
½ small green bell pepper, seeded, chopped
½ small red bell pepper, seeded, chopped
2 cups fat-reduced chicken broth
1 cup water
1 teaspoon dried thyme
1 teaspoon dried oregano
1 bay leaf

In colander, sort through and remove any debris or discolored or broken lentils; rinse well with cold water. Over low heat, heat Dutch oven coated with cooking spray. Add onion, garlic, celery, and bell peppers; sauté until crisp-tender, about 5 minutes. Stir in broth and remaining ingredients; bring to low simmer. Cover and simmer gently until tender, about 30 minutes. Discard bay leaf before serving.

QUICK CASSOULET

Though it retains the rich, savory flavor of the classic French bean stew, this updated version slashes time and fat.

½ pound fat-reduced kielbasa or other garlicky sausage, cut into 2-inch slices
6 chicken thighs or drumsticks, skin removed
1 large onion, chopped
2 garlic cloves, minced
1 cup tomato sauce
½ teaspoon salt *(optional)*
1 teaspoon crumbled dried thyme
½ teaspoon ground black pepper
1 bay leaf
2 large carrots, cut into 1-inch-thick pieces
2 16-ounce cans white beans, drained; or 4 cups cooked white beans, drained, rinsed

Makes 6 servings.

PER SERVING:

333 calories
31 g protein
8 g fat
33 g carbohydrate
584 mg sodium
80 mg cholesterol

In unheated Dutch oven, arrange sausage slices. Over low heat, slowly render enough fat from meat to prevent sticking. Increase heat to medium; cook sausage until lightly browned. Remove meat and set aside. To remaining fat in Dutch oven, add chicken, onion, and garlic. Cook, turning chicken occasionally until browned, about 10 minutes. Heat oven to 350° F. Into Dutch oven, stir tomato sauce, salt (if desired), thyme, pepper, bay leaf, and carrots; mix well. Over medium-low heat, bring liquid to simmer, cook about 5 minutes. Into 3-quart bean pot or casserole with lid, transfer chicken and sauce, alternating with beans and sausage. Cover; bake 30 minutes. Delicious served with crisp green salad, crusty bread, and hearty red wine.

ESSENCE BRINGS YOU
GREAT COOKING

BARBECUED BEANS AND TOFU

Mild-tasting, nutritious tofu takes on a bold and inviting new flavor in this saucy vegetarian casserole.

Makes 5 main-dish servings or 8 side-dish servings.

PER MAIN DISH SERVING:

245 calories
14 g protein
9 g fat
31 g carbohydrate
670 mg sodium
0 mg cholesterol

1 pound firm tofu
2 tablespoons vegetable oil
1 small onion, chopped
1 small green bell pepper, seeded, chopped
1 garlic clove, minced
3 cups cooked kidney beans; or 2 16-ounce cans kidney beans, drained, rinsed
1 large tomato, diced
¾ cup prepared barbecue sauce
1 tablespoon packed brown sugar *(optional)*

Heat oven to 350° F. Cut tofu into 1-inch cubes. In large non-stick skillet, heat 1 tablespoon oil; sauté tofu about 2 minutes. Remove tofu from skillet. Add remaining oil to skillet and heat. Sauté onion, bell pepper, and garlic until tender, about 5 minutes. Stir in remaining ingredients; mix well. Transfer mixture into greased 2-quart casserole or bean pot. Bake about 20 minutes or until hot and bubbly.

Tofu

In a process similar to making cheese, soybean curd is made into blocks of tofu. (Soybeans are considered to have the highest quality of protein in the bean family and the vegetable kingdom.) Almost tasteless on its own, tofu takes on the flavor of the ingredients it is cooked with. Tofu is popularly made into mock dishes such as scrambled "eggs," curried "chicken," and "cheesecake." Firm tofu is best for slicing and cubing.

Until recently, buying tofu required a trip to a health-food store or Asian market; it can now be found in supermarkets across the United States.

TWO-BEAN CASSEROLE

Canned beans combined with fresh vegetables make this a hearty, wholesome, delicious dish.

1 tablespoon butter or margarine
½ cup diced onion
½ cup diced red bell pepper
1 garlic clove, minced
1 16-ounce can pinto beans, drained
1 16-ounce can red kidney beans, drained
2 cups broccoli florets, blanched
1 large ripe tomato, chopped
1 teaspoon dried oregano
⅛ teaspoon cayenne pepper
½ cup shredded cheddar cheese
Optional garnish: red bell-pepper rings, parsley sprigs

Heat oven to 350° F. In large saucepan heat butter; sauté onion, bell pepper, and garlic. Stir in beans, broccoli, tomato, oregano, pepper, and half of the cheese. Pour mixture into greased 1½-quart baking dish; sprinkle with remaining cheese. Bake about 20 minutes or until cheese is melted. Garnish with pepper rings and parsley.

Makes 6 servings.

PER SERVING:

264 calories
14 g protein
5 g fat
39 g carbohydrate
379 mg sodium
10 mg cholesterol

ESSENCE BRINGS YOU
GREAT COOKING

BEAN FRITTERS
(Akara)

These crisp fritters with tender insides from Benin make a delicious appetizer, side dish, or snack.

Makes 6 servings.

PER SERVING:

332 calories
8 g protein
22 g fat
28 g carbohydrate
7 mg sodium
0 mg cholesterol

1½ cups dried white beans; or 3 cups canned white beans, drained and rinsed
¼ cup water
1 teaspoon salt *(optional)*
½ cup unbleached all-purpose flour
2 tablespoons finely chopped onion
Ground cayenne pepper to taste
About 1 cup peanut oil for frying

Rinse, soak, and cook dried beans according to package directions; drain. In blender container, combine water and salt (if desired); add beans. Blend on low speed until thick, doughlike paste forms (add more water if necessary). Add flour, onion, and pepper; mix well. In deep, heavy skillet or deep fryer, heat oil to a temperature between 350° and 375° F. By rounded teaspoonfuls, drop mixture into hot oil; fry until golden brown, about 3 minutes on each side. As cooked, transfer to paper towels to drain; serve hot.

BLACK-EYED PEA SALAD

Bean salads are ideal for summertime eating that's filling, yet light. Salads are also a tasty way to recycle leftover beans.

4 cups cooked black-eyed peas, drained
2 scallions, sliced
1 small green bell pepper, seeded, chopped
1 large tomato, seeded, chopped
1 rib celery, thinly sliced
4 large basil leaves, chopped; or 2 teaspoons dried basil or thyme
⅓ cup olive oil or vegetable oil
2 tablespoons red wine vinegar or cider vinegar
1 large garlic clove, minced
½ teaspoon ground black pepper
½ teaspoon hot pepper sauce
½ teaspoon salt *(optional)*
Salad greens

Makes 8 side-dish servings.

PER SERVING:

241 calories
9 g protein
13 g fat
25 g carbohydrate
199 mg sodium
0 mg cholesterol

In large bowl, combine peas, scallions, bell pepper, tomato, celery, and basil. In small bowl or jar with tight-fitting lid, combine oil, vinegar, garlic, black pepper, pepper sauce, and salt (if desired); shake to blend. Pour dressing over vegetable mixture. Gently toss to coat and mix. Cover and refrigerate at least 2 hours. Arrange bed of salad greens in salad bowl or on plates; add marinated vegetable mixture.

ESSENCE BRINGS YOU
GREAT COOKING

WHITE BEAN SALAD

Makes 4 servings.

PER SERVING:

150 calories
8 g protein
5 g fat
23 g carbohydrate
26 mg sodium
0 mg cholesterol

2 cups cooked northern beans or other white beans
1 cup water
½ cup thinly sliced celery
½ cup diced green bell pepper
½ cup chopped pimiento
2 scallions, thinly sliced
2 tablespoons white wine vinegar or cider vinegar
2 tablespoons water
1 tablespoon lemon juice
1 tablespoon vegetable oil
¼ teaspoon ground white pepper
8 Bibb lettuce leaves
8 spinach leaves
2 tomatoes, cut into wedges

In a colander, drain beans; rinse with about 1 cup of cold water. Drain well. In large bowl, combine beans, celery, bell pepper, pimiento, and scallions. In small bowl, combine vinegar, water, lemon juice, oil, and pepper; using whisk, beat mixture until blended and thickened into dressing. Pour dressing over bean mixture; toss gently to coat. Cover and refrigerate until thoroughly chilled or let marinate for 8 hours, stirring occasionally. To serve, line dinner plates with lettuce and spinach leaves; top with bean salad. Add tomato wedges.

BLACK BEAN SOUP

This hearty, savory soup can surely take the chill off a fall or winter night.
Though this recipe does not call for meat, cooked spicy sausage can
be added if desired.

2 cups dried black beans
Water
2 tablespoons olive oil
1 large onion, chopped
1 green bell pepper, seeded, diced
3 medium-size garlic cloves, minced
2 teaspoons dried thyme
2 teaspoons ground cumin
2 teaspoons chili powder
1 teaspoon salt *(optional)*
½ teaspoon cayenne pepper
2 medium-size tomatoes, seeded, diced
¼ cup water
2 bay leaves
Optional garnishes: chopped hard-
    cooked egg, chopped raw onion or
    scallions, sour cream, cilantro

Makes 5 main-dish
servings, 10 first-course
servings.

PER EACH OF 5
SERVINGS:

433 calories
25 g protein
11 g fat
52 g carbohydrate
32 mg sodium
0 mg cholesterol

Rinse beans thoroughly with cold water, sorting through and discarding shriveled, discolored, or broken beans and debris. In large bowl, cover beans with water; soak 8 hours or overnight. Pour off soaking water. In Dutch oven or kettle, combine beans and 8 cups fresh water or broth or combination. Over low heat, simmer until very tender, about 2½ hours. Meanwhile, in medium-size skillet, heat oil; sauté onion and bell pepper, about 5 minutes. Stir in garlic, thyme, cumin, chili powder, salt (if desired), pepper, tomatoes, water, and bay leaves; simmer about 10 minutes. Stir tomato mixture into beans, mixing well; simmer to thicken and blend flavors, about 10 additional minutes. Transfer to tureen or soup bowls; add garnishes.

ESSENCE BRINGS YOU
GREAT COOKING

NAVY BEAN SOUP

A favorite around Washington, D.C., this flavorful, stick-to-the-ribs soup is traditionally made with Michigan navy beans.

Makes 6 servings.

PER SERVING:

196 calories
13 g protein
6 g fat
24 g carbohydrate
592 mg sodium
14 mg cholesterol

1 cup dried navy beans
6 cups water
2 cloves garlic, minced
3 sprigs parsley
1 teaspoon crushed thyme
1 bay leaf
2 whole cloves
1 cup diced cooked ham *(optional)*
1 large carrot, diced
1 large onion, chopped
1 large stalk celery, chopped
½ teaspoon salt *(optional)*
½ teaspoon freshly ground black pepper
2 tablespoons chopped fresh parsley

Place beans in colander and rinse with cold running water, picking through to remove any stones or foreign particles. In Dutch oven or 5-quart saucepot, cover beans with cold water; let soak overnight. Or, to quick-soak, bring beans and water to boil for 2 minutes; remove pot from heat, cover tightly and let stand 1 hour. Drain soaked beans; cover with 6 cups fresh water. Add garlic. In small cheesecloth bag, combine and tie parsley, thyme, bay leaf, and cloves. Simmer, partially covered, about 1½ hours or until beans are tender; add to pot. Skim any froth from top. Discard bag with seasonings. With back of wooden spoon, mash some beans against side of pot to thicken liquid. Add water for thinner consistency. Add ham (if desired), carrot, onion, celery, salt (if desired), and black pepper; cook an additional 20 minutes or until vegetables are tender. Sprinkle with chopped parsley.

SPLIT PEA SOUP

Along with steaming bowls of soup, serve slices of crusty bread and a raw vegetable salad for a satisfying meal.

2 tablespoons butter or margarine
2 medium-size carrots, thinly sliced or chopped
1 medium-size onion, chopped
½ teaspoon whole allspice
½ teaspoon whole peppercorns
1 or 2 sprigs of fresh thyme, chopped
1 bay leaf
7 cups chicken broth, water, or combination
1 16-ounce package dried green split peas
½ teaspoon salt *(optional; delete if using broth)*
Optional garnish: chopped parsley

Makes 6 servings.

PER SERVING:

312 calories
21 g protein
4 g fat
51 g carbohydrate
977 mg sodium
trace mg cholesterol

In Dutch oven or 4-quart saucepan over medium heat, melt butter. Stir in carrots and onion; cook, stirring occasionally, until soft but not brown, about 5 minutes. Meanwhile, in cheesecloth square, tie together allspice, peppercorns, thyme, and bay leaf; add to pot. Slowly stir in broth; bring to simmer. Cook, partially covered, about 10 minutes. Meanwhile, rinse and sort through peas. Add peas to pot; reduce heat to medium-low. Simmer gently, partially covered, until peas are tender, about 1 hour. Stir in salt (if desired); taste and correct seasonings. Discard herbs in cheesecloth bundle. Ladle soup into warmed tureen or soup bowls; garnish with chopped parsley.

ESSENCE BRINGS YOU
GREAT COOKING

WHITE BEAN AND COLLARD GREEN SOUP

Once this soup is ready, all that's needed is warm cornbread and a hearty appetite.

Makes 6 servings.

1 pound dried small white beans
4 to 5 cups water
2 chorizo sausages
¼ pound turkey bacon, cut in bite-size pieces
1 large onion, chopped
1 large green pepper, seeded and chopped
3 large garlic cloves, smashed or minced
Salt *(optional)*
¼ teaspoon black pepper
1 teaspoon dried thyme *(optional)*
1 teaspoon dried oregano *(optional)*
1 small bunch collard greens

Rinse beans in cold water; remove any stones or foreign matter. In 5-quart Dutch oven or large bowl, cover beans with water; soak overnight. Drain; transfer to or let remain in Dutch oven. Add water. Bring to boil over medium heat; add sausage, bacon, onion, green pepper, garlic, salt (if desired), pepper, and herbs. Cover; reduce heat. Slowly simmer about 1¼ hours or until beans are soft. Meanwhile, thoroughly rinse greens, remove thick stems, and chop coarsely. When beans are ready, mash some of them against side of pot with wooden spoon. Add greens; simmer 30 additional minutes. Adjust seasonings and serve.

CHAPTER THREE

Grits and Other Great Grains

Aris's Kush Tabuleh.

Recipes

BAKED CHEESE GRITS

ORANGE-BLOSSOM GRITS

GRITS SOUFFLÉ

TUNA AND GRITS CASSEROLE

HUSH PUPPIES

CORNMEAL COO COO

POLENTA WITH CHUNKY TOMATO SAUCE

YELLOW RICE

BROWN RICE ROYAL PILAF

CONFETTI RICE

RICE RING

PEANUT RICE

MEXICAN RICE

RICE PILAF WITH PINE NUTS

DIRTY RICE

WILD RICE AND SCALLIONS

WILD RICE AND MUSHROOM DRESSING

NEW TRADITION JOLLOF RICE

SHRIMP FRIED RICE

THAI CRABMEAT FRIED RICE

Recipes

CREOLE CHICKEN AND RICE SALAD

LEMON RICE SOUP

CARROT BARLEY SOUP

COPPER'S CURRIED COUSCOUS

COUSCOUS SEAFOOD SALAD

ARIS'S KUSH TABULEH

BULGUR PILAF

BULGUR HEALTH SALAD

OATMEAL WITH WARM FRUIT COMPOTE

HOMEMADE GRANOLA

LIGHT MACARONI AND CHEESE

OLD-FASHIONED BAKED MACARONI

NOODLES WITH SPICY PEANUT SAUCE

LINGUINE PRIMAVERA

NEW SPAGHETTI AND MEATBALLS

LIGHT LASAGNA

SLIM-LINE FETTUCCINE ALFREDO

LINGUINE GEECHEE ROSA

WARM PASTA SALAD

SEA AND SHELLS SALAD

GRAINS were the first foods cultivated by humankind. These seeds of grasses are also called cereals. Wheat, rice, barley, corn, oats, and millet are the world's major grains. All grains have the same basic construction—a germ at the core. The germ, similar in function to the yolk of an egg, is designed as a rich source of nourishment for the new plant. This germ is an important source of nutrients for people as well.

All too often, the germ is stripped away in the "refinement" process. When possible, select unrefined, or whole, grains for their valuable supply of plant proteins and minerals. Rich in complex carbohydrates and dietary fiber, grains are an excellent choice for disease prevention, overall good health, energy, and weight control. Fiber allows you to fill up without filling out. For lasting energy, athletes load up on these complex carbohydrates before competitions.

Grains are team players—from the sidelines they bring out the best in accompanying vegetables, fish, and meats. To reach the recommended daily requirement of 35 to 50 grams of dietary fiber, it's smart to go with grains. Get acquainted with lesser-known types such as bulgur (cracked wheat), couscous, kasha (buckwheat grains), and millet. Millet, a nutritionally superior grain and long a staple in Africa, is just coming to America.

GRITS

In days past in many Southern states, grits with breakfast was as certain as the sunrise. Mornings have now become less leisurely, and breakfast is a more rushed meal. But with the growing popularity of more relaxed weekend breakfasts and brunches, grits are back and all gussied up with cheese, garlic, chives, and other flavorings. Grits are also moving into a later time slot and being enjoyed as side dishes for dinner.

WHAT EXACTLY ARE GRITS?

Grits begin as whole kernels of corn. First, the hulls are removed, then the kernels are soaked; this process turns the corn into hominy.

Grits are hominy that is dried, then coarsely ground. Cornmeal is grits more finely ground. Corn flour is cornmeal ground even finer.

Packaged grits come in three forms: regular—takes about 20 to 30 minutes to cook; quick—takes about 5 minutes to cook; and instant—mix with boiling water and eat. The consistency of grits is all important. When spooned onto a plate, grits should softly hold their shape—not run or sit stiffly. A small pat of butter adds surprising richness to their otherwise mild flavor. Leftover grits are commonly recycled by slicing them when cold, then panfrying the slices.

PASTA

Though not itself a grain, pasta's primary ingredient is a grain—wheat. Very simply, wheat flour and water are mixed to form a dough that's kneaded, then forced through perforations to make it into one of more than a hundred shapes. Choices of pasta range from rice-size orzo to large tubes of manicotti, from thin strands of spaghetti to broad strips of lasagna, and shapes from sea shells to butterflies. There's a new, wide selection of flavors that includes whole wheat, buckwheat, spinach, tomato, black pepper, and squid ink (black pasta). Now, if you consider the variations of sauces you can add, pasta possibilities are endless!

FRESH VERSUS DRIED PASTA

Fresh pasta is now widely available in supermarkets across the nation. If you have the time and inclination, it is relatively easy to make fresh pasta at home. Recipes are easy to find in the newer all-purpose cook-books. Fresh pasta has a lighter texture and slightly richer taste than its dried counterpart. Fresh pasta keeps in the refrigerator for about four days, but it's best when prepared the day it's made or purchased.

Dried pasta is made with harder flour than fresh pasta. The texture is firmer (more bite). A shelf life of a full year makes dried pasta excellent to keep on hand for quick and impromptu meals.

BAKED CHEESE GRITS

Sized for a crowd, this is an ideal dish for a big breakfast or brunch.

Makes 12 servings.

PER SERVING:

239 calories
7 g protein
14 g fat
21 g carbohydrate
270 mg sodium
89 mg cholesterol

- 8 cups water
- ½ teaspoon salt *(optional)*
- 2 cups uncooked regular grits
- ½ cup butter or margarine
- 3 large eggs, at room temperature
- 2 cups shredded cheddar cheese
- ¼ teaspoon cayenne pepper

Heat oven to 350° F. In Dutch oven, bring water and salt (if desired) to boil. Using wooden spoon, gradually stir in grits; cook just until mixture begins to thicken. Cover pot. Over low heat, cook 25 minutes. Grease 2 ½-quart baking dish; set aside. Remove pan from heat; stir butter into grits. In medium-size bowl, beat eggs until fluffy; stir in cheese and pepper. Stir cheese mixture into grits; spoon into prepared baking dish. Bake 40 minutes.

ORANGE-BLOSSOM GRITS

Serving grits as a sweetened, hot breakfast cereal is common in the South; this delightful recipe could make grits a tradition in your home.

1 cup water
½ cup orange juice
⅓ cup uncooked quick-cooking grits
½ teaspoon grated orange peel *(optional)*
⅛ teaspoon salt *(optional)*
2 tablespoons packed brown sugar

In medium-size saucepan, over medium-high heat, bring water and orange juice to boil. Slowly stir in grits, orange peel, and salt (if desired). Reduce heat; simmer, stirring occasionally, 3 to 4 minutes or until thickened. Pour into serving dishes; sprinkle with brown sugar. Let stand until sugar melts, about 2 minutes.

Makes 3 servings.

PER SERVING:

149 calories
3 g protein
.34 g fat
34 g carbohydrate
92 mg sodium
0 mg cholesterol

ESSENCE BRINGS YOU
GREAT COOKING

GRITS SOUFFLÉ

Grits have gone gourmet! This is a particulary tasty and impressive side dish.

Makes 8 servings.

PER SERVING:

249 calories
10 g protein
15 g fat
18 g carbohydrate
480 mg sodium
118 mg cholesterol

4 cups water
1 teaspoon salt *(optional)*
1 cup uncooked quick grits
6 tablespoons butter
3 tablespoons flour
2 teaspoons dry mustard
3 egg yolks, beaten
2 cups grated cheddar cheese
3 egg whites

In 2-quart saucepan, combine water and salt (if desired); bring to boil. Using wooden spoon, slowly stir in grits. Cook, stirring constantly, until mixture begins to thicken. Cover and continue cooking 20 additional minutes. While grits are cooking, in small saucepan, melt butter. Stir in flour and mustard; cook 5 minutes. When grits are done, vigorously stir in egg yolks. Add butter mixture and cheese; stir well to blend. Beat egg whites until stiff; fold into grits. Into well-greased 2-quart casserole, pour mixture. Bake 45 minutes.

SONG TO GRITS

When my mind's unsettled,
When I don't feel spruce,
When my nerves get frazzled,
when my flesh gets loose—
What knits
Me back together's grits.
Grits with gravy,
Grits with cheese,
Grits with bacon,
Grits with peas.
Grits with a minimum
Of two over-medium eggs
   mixed in 'em: um!
Grits, grits, it's
Grits I sing—
Grits fits
in with anything.
Rich and poor, black and white,
Lutheran and Campbellite,
Jews and Southern Jesuits,
All acknowledge buttered grits.
      —Roy Blount, Jr.
      One Fell Soup, 1982

TUNA AND GRITS CASSEROLE

The ingredients in this main dish may not be a familiar combination, but the dish drew raves from our staff when it was served at a tasting.

Vegetable oil or cooking spray
1⅔ cups water
½ teaspoon salt *(optional)*
½ cup uncooked quick grits
3 tablespoons butter or margarine
⅓ cup finely chopped celery
2 tablespoons minced onion
1 6½-ounce can tuna or 1 cup canned salmon, drained, flaked
1 large egg
2 tablespoons milk
¼ teaspoon cayenne pepper
½ cup dry or fresh bread crumbs

Makes 4 servings.

PER SERVING:

256 calories
18 g protein
8 g fat
26 g carbohydrate
608 mg sodium
62 mg cholesterol

Heat oven to 325° F. Grease 1-quart baking dish with vegetable oil or cooking spray; set aside. In heavy medium-size saucepan, bring water and salt (if desired) to boil; slowly stir in grits. Return to boil; reduce heat. Cook, stirring occasionally, 3 to 5 minutes. Meanwhile, in small skillet, heat 1 tablespoon butter; add celery and onion. Sauté until tender, about 5 minutes. Stir celery mixture and tuna into grits; mix well. In small bowl, lightly beat egg; stir in small amount of grits mixture. Stir egg mixture, milk, and pepper into grits. Spoon into prepared baking dish. Melt remaining butter. Evenly sprinkle casserole with crumbs; drizzle with butter. Bake 25 to 30 minutes.

HUSH PUPPIES

The story goes: At fish fries, the cook would resort to shaping and frying little cakes of cornmeal (used for coating the fish) and tossing them to the barking dogs, with the command "Hush, puppies!"

Makes about 20 hush puppies.

PER HUSH PUPPY:

110 calories
2 g protein
6 g fat
11 g carbohydrate
116 mg sodium
12 mg cholesterol

2 cups white or yellow cornmeal
1 teaspoon baking powder
1 teaspoon salt *(optional)*
1 small scallion, finely chopped
1 cup milk
1 large egg, slightly beaten
¼ cup vegetable oil
Peanut or corn oil for frying

In medium-size bowl, combine cornmeal, baking powder, salt (if desired), and scallion; stir to mix well. Add milk, egg, and oil; mix well. Stir only enough to blend ingredients. Fill deep skillet or fryer with about 2 inches oil; heat oil to 370° F. Meanwhile, shape batter into 1-inch balls (or drop by tablespoonfuls); adding a few at a time, fry hush puppies until golden brown, about 2 to 3 minutes. As cooked, transfer to paper towels to drain.

CORNMEAL COO COO

This surprisingly tasty side dish of boiled cornmeal is a popular Caribbean classic that accompanies boiled, steamed, or panfried fish. It is also known as fungi and can be made without okra.

About 12 fresh okra pods
4 pints water
4 tablespoons butter or margarine
1 teaspoon salt *(optional)*
¼ teaspoon ground black pepper
1 pound yellow cornmeal

In cold water, rinse okra; remove stems and slice into rounds. In large saucepan, combine okra and water; bring to boil. Stir in butter, salt (if desired), and pepper. Remove pan from heat. Using whisk or fork, stir in cornmeal until all lumps are dissolved and mixture is smooth. Return to heat. Using wooden spoon, stir until mixture is well blended, slightly stiff, and comes away from the sides of the pan. Spoon into lightly buttered bowl; let sit about 30 minutes until set. Cover top of bowl with platter and invert to transfer coo coo to serving platter.

Makes 8 servings.

PER SERVING:
261 calories
5 g protein
7 g fat
45 g carbohydrate
327 mg sodium
15 mg cholesterol

ESSENCE BRINGS YOU
GREAT COOKING

POLENTA WITH CHUNKY TOMATO SAUCE

Polenta is a cornmeal dish that's a specialty of northern Italy; it is a first cousin of the Caribbean coo coo and of the corn pone of the American South.

Makes 6 to 8 servings.

PER SERVING:

332 calories
6 g protein
9 g fat
56 g carbohydrate
682 mg sodium
20 mg cholesterol

7½ cups water
1 teaspoon salt *(optional)*
3 cups yellow cornmeal
¼ cup butter or margarine
1 cup chunky tomato sauce

In Dutch oven, bring water and salt (if desired) to boil. Lower to medium heat; slowly add cornmeal ½ cup at a time, stirring constantly with whisk or flat wooden spoon to prevent lumps. Continue cooking and frequently stirring (stir constantly for best results) until polenta is very thick, about 35 to 45 minutes. Add butter; stir until melted. Spoon cornmeal mixture into buttered 2-quart baking or serving dish; gently press to pack. Allow polenta to set several minutes; slice or cut into squares and top with chunky tomato sauce.

Rice

The early history of rice in the Unites States is bound to slavery. Beginning off the coast of South Carolina about 300 years ago, enslaved Africans supplied the knowledge and intensive labor to cultivate a grain—the fabled Carolina Gold—and an industry that would reach around the world. Karen Hess, a culinary historian, describes her book, *The Carolina Rice Kitchen*, as "a hymn of praise for the African men and women torn from their homelands so long ago who made it all possible." Hess's book celebrates the role of the Black cook in America and is a must read.

THE LONG AND SHORT OF GRAIN SIZE

Choosing rice by length is a matter of taste preference and recipe needs. Here's how they differ.
- Long: Four to five times as long as it is wide. When cooked, it is separate and fluffy; good for pilafs.
- Medium: Shorter and plumper than long grain. More moist and tender; greater tendency to cling.
- Short: Short and rounded, the most moist and tender; sticky texture. Popular in Caribbean and Asian cooking.

TIPS FOR COOKING PERFECT RICE

- Use a heavy-bottomed saucepan so the rice at the bottom doesn't stick and scorch.
- Measure the amounts of rice and liquid.
- Add a tablespoon of butter or oil to the water for flavor and to help keep grains separate.
- Time cooking accurately.
- Keep lid on tight during cooking to prevent steam from escaping. No peeking!

Making Rice Nice

Try these flavor enhancers.

COOKING LIQUID: Instead of water, or in combination with water to equal required amount of liquid, add vegetable, chicken, fish, or beef broth; apple, orange, or pineapple juice; coconut milk.

COOK WITH RICE: Sautéed onion, garlic, celery, bell pepper, or mushrooms; grated orange peel, lemon peel, or coconut; raisins or chopped apples; grated Parmesan cheese; thyme, curry powder, turmeric, or saffron.

ADD DURING COVERED STANDING TIME: Chopped nuts, chopped fresh parsley, or other herbs.

Rice as Rite

Since ancient times and in cultures around the world, rice has been associated with fertility. Showering the bridal couple with rice is a custom that continues to this day.

YELLOW RICE

This dressed-up rice goes well with bean, curry, or Creole dishes.

2 cups water

½ teaspoon turmeric or ⅛ teaspoon saffron

¼ teaspoon ground ginger

¼ teaspoon dry mustard

½ teaspoon cayenne pepper

1 teaspoon salt *(optional)*

2 teaspoons granulated sugar

1 cup uncooked long-grain rice

In 3-quart saucepan with tight-fitting lid, over medium-high heat, combine all ingredients; bring to boil. Reduce heat to low simmer. Using fork, stir mixture 1 or 2 times. Cover pan and simmer, without stirring or lifting the lid, until rice is tender and all liquid is absorbed, about 14 minutes.

Makes 4 servings.

PER SERVING:

182 calories
3 g protein
.39 g fat
40 g carbohydrate
536 mg sodium
0 mg cholesterol

ESSENCE BRINGS YOU
GREAT COOKING

BROWN RICE ROYAL PILAF

Makes 4 servings.

PER SERVING:

247 calories
4 g protein
8 g fat
40 g carbohydrate
4 mg sodium
0 mg cholesterol

2 tablespoons olive oil
1 small onion, diced
1 cup chopped mushrooms
1 bay leaf
1 cup uncooked brown rice
2 cups water or vegetable or chicken broth, heated to boiling

In heavy-bottomed large saucepan, heat oil. Add onion, mushrooms, and bay leaf; sauté until vegetables are tender, about 5 minutes. Add rice; sauté additional 5 minutes. Add hot water or broth; briefly stir to mix. Bring to boil; lower heat, cover pan, and simmer until liquid is absorbed, about 45 minutes.

BROWN RICE is more nutritious than white rice. It has more protein, calcium, phosphorus, potassium, niacin, fiber, and vitamin E than enriched white rice. The bran layers are still intact, giving the rice its characteristic tan color, nutlike flavor, and chewy texture. Brown rice requires a longer cooking time and slightly more liquid than white. There are now quick-cooking and instant brown rice products on the market. Because brown rice is the least processed type of rice, store it uncooked in the refrigerator to help retain freshness.

ESSENCE BRINGS YOU
GREAT COOKING

CONFETTI RICE

1 14-ounce can chicken broth
Water
2 tablespoons olive or vegetable oil
1 cup uncooked converted rice
1 medium-size onion, coarsely chopped
2 garlic cloves, minced
½ teaspoon crushed oregano
2 cups chopped bell peppers, any combination of red, green, and
   yellow
⅛ teaspoon ground black pepper
⅓ cup grated Parmesan cheese, or to taste

Combine broth with enough water to total 2¼ cups liquid; set aside. In large saucepan, heat oil; add rice, onion, and garlic. Over medium heat, cook, stirring constantly, 3 to 4 minutes. Add oregano and broth; bring to boil. Reduce heat, cover tightly, and simmer 20 minutes. Remove from heat; stir in bell peppers. Let stand covered until all liquid is absorbed, about 5 minutes. Sprinkle with pepper and cheese.

> CONVERTED OR PARBOILED RICE has been treated to remove the outer hull. The processing also makes the grain harder; this firmness results in grains that are separate and fluffy. This is why converted rice is such a popular choice today. Do not mistake parboiled for precooked (instant-type) rice.

Makes 6 servings.

PER SERVING:

209 calories
6 g protein
7 g fat
30 g carbohydrate
332 mg sodium
4 mg cholesterol.

ESSENCE BRINGS YOU
GREAT COOKING

117

RICE RING

For dinner-party looks, fill the hollow of this ring (it can overflow slightly) with the dish it is to accompany—beans, curries, shrimp creole, and so on.

Makes 6 to 8 servings.

PER 6 SERVINGS:

210 calories
6 g protein
3 g fat
39 g carbohydrate
410 mg sodium
5 mg cholesterol

1½ cups uncooked converted rice
3 cups chicken broth
1 tablespoon butter or margarine
½ small red bell pepper, seeded, diced
½ small green bell pepper, seeded, diced

In medium-size saucepan, combine rice, broth, and butter. Bring to boil; reduce heat to medium low. Cover and simmer 20 minutes. Remove rice from heat; let stand covered about 5 minutes. Stir in bell pepper. Into a buttered 6- or 7-cup ring mold, pack rice mixture. Cover tightly with foil; let stand 10 minutes. Using tip of knife, loosen edge of rice from mold. Place serving platter, top side down, over mold; invert rice mold onto serving plate. Spoon filling into center of mold.

PEANUT RICE

2 cups water
1 cup uncooked, converted rice
¼ cup chopped peanuts
½ teaspoon salt *(optional)*
½ teaspoon cumin
⅛ teaspoon turmeric

In medium-size saucepan, bring water to boil. Stir in rice; cover tightly, and simmer for 10 minutes. Gently stir in peanuts and seasonings. Cover tightly and continue cooking for about 10 minutes. Remove saucepan from heat. Let stand, covered, until all water is absorbed, about 5 minutes.

Makes 4 servings.

PER SERVING:

224 calories
6 g protein
5 g fat
40 g carbohydrate
308 mg sodium
0 mg cholesterol

MEXICAN RICE

Makes 8 servings.

PER SERVING:

229 calories
5 g protein
4 g fat
43 g carbohydrate
419 mg sodium
0 mg cholesterol

2 tablespoons olive oil
1 large onion, chopped
½ cup diced green bell pepper
1 8-ounce can tomato sauce
½ teaspoon salt *(optional)*
½ teaspoon ground cumin
¼ teaspoon cayenne pepper
1½ cups water
1 cup chicken broth
2 cups uncooked converted rice
Optional garnish: cilantro sprigs, ripe olives

In large (4-quart) heavy-bottomed saucepan, heat oil. Add onion and bell pepper; cook until tender, about 5 minutes. Stir in tomato sauce, salt (if desired), cumin, and cayenne. Add water and broth, stirring to mix well; bring to boil. Add rice; using fork, gently stir rice to distribute evenly. Reduce heat to simmer; cover and cook 15 minutes, fluffing rice once with fork. Remove from heat and let rice sit tightly covered about 5 minutes, or until tender and liquid is absorbed. Garnish with cilantro and olives. Serve immediately.

RICE PILAF WITH PINE NUTS

¼ cup minced onion

1 garlic clove, minced

½ cup (1 stick) butter or margarine

3 cups uncooked long-grain rice

½ cup golden raisins

1 cup water

4 cups (or more) chicken broth

2 tablespoons grated Parmesan cheese

1 cup thinly sliced onions, halved

½ cup pine nuts

1 cup thinly sliced mushrooms

2 tablespoons minced parsley

¼ teaspoon ground white pepper

Heat oven to 350° F. In ovenproof, 5-quart saucepan or Dutch oven, sauté minced onion and garlic in 3 tablespoons butter. Add rice, stirring until well coated. Add raisins, water, and enough chicken broth to cover rice by ¾ inch. Bring to boil over high heat. Cover and place in oven; bake 20 to 25 minutes. Transfer rice to large bowl. Add 3 tablespoons butter and cheese; gently fluff with fork to coat and mix. Keep warm. In medium-size skillet, sauté onions in remaining butter. Using slotted spoon, transfer to bowl with rice. In same skillet, sauté pine nuts, stirring until golden. Using slotted spoon, remove to paper towels to drain. In same skillet, sauté mushrooms. Add pine nuts, mushrooms, parsley, and pepper to rice. Toss gently to combine.

Makes 8 servings.

PER SERVING:

425 calories

11 g protein

12 g fat

69 g carbohydrate

482 mg sodium

17 mg cholesterol

ESSENCE BRINGS YOU
GREAT COOKING

DIRTY RICE

Makes 4 main-dish
servings.

PER SERVING:

431 calories
35 g protein
10 g fat
48 g carbohydrate
624 mg sodium
446 mg cholesterol

1 tablespoon vegetable oil
1 tablespoon flour
1 small onion, finely chopped
1 stalk celery, finely chopped
½ medium-size green bell pepper, chopped
1 pound chicken giblets, chopped
¾ teaspoon salt *(optional)*
¼ teaspoon ground black pepper
⅛ teaspoon cayenne pepper
¾ cup chicken broth
3 cups hot cooked rice
¼ cup sliced scallions tops

    In Dutch oven or large (preferably iron) skillet, heat oil. Add flour, onion, celery, and green pepper; cook and stir until vegetables are tender. Stir in giblets and seasonings; cook until meat loses its red color. Blend in broth; cover and simmer until meat is tender, about 20 minutes. Stir in rice and scallion tops. Cook 5 minutes longer. Mixture should be slightly moist.

WILD RICE AND SCALLIONS

¼ cup uncooked wild rice

1 cup hot water

1 tablespoon butter or margarine

1 scallion, thinly sliced

1 cup water or broth (chicken, beef, or vegetable)

¼ cup uncooked brown rice

In medium bowl, cover wild rice with hot water; soak 30 minutes. Drain well. In heavy-bottom, 3-quart saucepan, heat butter. Sauté scallion in butter, about 2 minutes, until just tender. Stir in water; bring to boil. Stir in wild rice and brown rice; reduce heat to low. Cover and simmer 40 to 45 minutes, until rice is tender and all liquid absorbed.

Makes 2 servings.

PER SERVING:

208 calories

5 g protein

7 g fat

33 g carbohydrate

61 mg sodium

15 mg cholesterol

WILD RICE

Not actually a rice, this rice look-alike is a dark, richly flavored type of grain from a different kind of grass.

WILD RICE AND MUSHROOM DRESSING

Makes 4 cups;
8 servings.

PER SERVING:

164 calories
5 g protein
7 g fat
22 g carbohydrate
522 mg sodium
0 mg cholesterol

1 4-ounce package (¾ cup) wild rice
Water
½ cup butter or margarine
4 shallots, minced or 1 medium-size onion, chopped
1 cup chopped celery
½ pound mushrooms, sliced
4 cups dried bread cubes
1 teaspoon dried oregano
1 teaspoon dried sage
1 teaspoon ground black pepper
1 teaspoon salt *(optional)*
1 cup turkey broth or chicken broth
Optional garnishes: sliced mushrooms, fresh herbs, celery leaves

Rinse wild rice thoroughly under running water. In large saucepan ¾-filled with water, bring water to boil. Add rice; boil until tender but still a little chewy, about 45 minutes. Drain at once; transfer to large bowl. Heat oven to 350° F. In medium-size skillet, over medium heat, heat 2 tablespoons butter; add shallots and celery. Sauté until the vegetables are tender (do not brown), about 8 minutes. Add the remaining butter and mushrooms; sauté about 5 minutes. To rice, add the sautéed vegetables, bread cubes, seasonings, and broth; toss until well mixed. Into lightly greased 2-quart baking dish, spoon dressing; partially cover and bake for 15 to 20 minutes. Garnish as desired.

ESSENCE BRINGS YOU
GREAT COOKING

NEW TRADITION JOLLOF RICE

This classic West African dish can take on infinite variations—add shrimp or meat or serve as is for an excellent vegetarian main dish.

1 cup dried black-eyed peas
Water
⅓ cup vegetable oil
3 tablespoons grated fresh ginger
2 large onions, chopped
4 garlic cloves: 1 whole, 3 minced
1 3-pound chicken, cut into 8 serving pieces, rinsed, dried
3 to 4 ripe large tomatoes or 1½ cups crushed canned tomatoes
1½ tablespoons tomato paste
4 cups liquid from cooked peas (supplement with water or chicken broth if necessary to equal 4 cups), reserve peas
1 tablespoon curry powder
2 tablespoons cayenne pepper, or to taste
2½ cups long-grain brown rice
1 pound carrots, peeled, diced
½ pound string beans, ends trimmed, cut into 1-to-2-inch pieces
1 teaspoon sea salt *(optional)*

Makes 8 servings.

PER SERVING:

528 calories
29 g protein
16 fat
68 g carbohydrate
362 mg sodium
66 mg cholesterol

Clean and soak peas overnight; drain and discard liquid. In 6-quart saucepan, cover peas with 3 quarts water; over low heat, bring to simmer. Cook covered 15 minutes; set aside. In oven-proof Dutch oven or iron kettle, heat oil; add 1 tablespoon ginger, 3 tablespoons onion, whole garlic clove, and chicken pieces. Brown chicken on all sides, about 5 minutes. Using slotted spoon, remove chicken to plate; set aside. Add remaining ginger, onion, and garlic to pot; sauté until wilted. Stir in tomatoes, paste, liquid from peas, curry, and cayenne; bring to simmer. Stir in rice, peas, and carrots; over low heat, simmer 10 minutes. Add chicken, string beans, and sea salt; simmer 15 additional minutes. Meanwhile, heat oven to 400° F. Cover and transfer to oven; bake 25 to 30 minutes. Let stand 15 minutes before serving.

ESSENCE BRINGS YOU
GREAT COOKING

SHRIMP FRIED RICE

Better than take out. Cook rice ahead of time, or this recipe can be a great way to use leftovers.

Makes 4 servings.

PER SERVING:

323 calories
14 g protein
6 g fat
52 g carbohydrate
592 mg sodium
109 mg cholesterol

1 tablespoon vegetable oil
1 small onion, chopped
½ medium-size green pepper, chopped
3 cups cold cooked rice
1 to 2 cups cooked shrimp
1 5-ounce can sliced water chestnuts, drained
1 large egg, slightly beaten
2 tablespoons soy sauce
1 tablespoon chopped pimiento
⅛ teaspoon cayenne pepper
Optional garnish: sliced scallion tops

In Dutch oven or large skillet, heat oil. Add onion and green pepper; cook until onion is slightly browned around the edges. Add rice, shrimp, and water chestnuts; heat thoroughly, stirring occasionally. Stir in egg, soy sauce, pimiento, and pepper; cook, stirring, about 3 minutes, or until egg is set. Garnish with scallion tops. Serve with snow peas and fried Oriental noodles.

THAI CRABMEAT FRIED RICE

2 tablespoons vegetable oil
2 tablespoons minced garlic
1 medium-size onion, halved, sliced lengthwise into strips
3 tablespoons fish sauce
2 tablespoons granulated sugar
3 large eggs
8 ounces cooked crabmeat
4 cups cooked rice, chilled
3 scallions, sliced crosswise
1 cucumber, scored, sliced
2 tomatoes, cut into wedges

In wok or large skillet, heat oil; add garlic and stir-fry until light golden. Add onions and stir-fry until slices are barely translucent. Add fish sauce and sugar; mix thoroughly. Stir in eggs one at a time; continue to stir until eggs are scrambled and set. Add crabmeat and rice. Stir until well combined. Stir in scallions. Transfer to warm serving platter; serve with cucumber and tomato.

Makes 4 servings.

PER SERVING:

514 calories
23 g protein
13 g fat
75 g carbohydrate
1,342 mg sodium
190 mg cholesterol

ESSENCE BRINGS YOU
GREAT COOKING

CREOLE CHICKEN AND RICE SALAD

Makes 6 to 8 servings.

PER EACH OF 6
SERVINGS:

393 calories
16 g protein
28 g fat
20 g carbohydrate
604 mg sodium
57 mg cholesterol

2 cups cooked brown rice
2 cups diced cooked chicken
¾ teaspoon salt
1 tablespoon fresh lemon juice
½ cup sliced scallion
½ cup diced green pepper
1 tablespoon chopped olives
¾ cup coarsely grated cauliflower
4 tablespoons bottled French dressing
⅛ teaspoon cayenne pepper
⅔ cup mayonnaise
½ cup chopped fresh parsley

In large mixing bowl, combine rice, chicken, salt, lemon juice, scallions, green pepper, olives, and cauliflower; toss lightly to blend. In small mixing bowl, combine French dressing, cayenne, mayonnaise, and parsley; stir well. Spoon over chicken mixture; toss to coat ingredients. Cover and chill thoroughly. Serve on lettuce leaves.

LEMON RICE SOUP

2 tablespoons olive oil
1 medium-size onion, finely chopped
1 cup cooked brown rice
Dash of cayenne pepper
2 cups vegetable stock
½ cup freshly squeezed lemon juice
4 thin lemon slices
1 tablespoon finely chopped fresh mint or finely chopped chives

In large saucepan, heat oil. Add onion; sauté until tender, about 5 minutes. Stir in rice, pepper, vegetable stock, and lemon juice. Over medium-low heat, bring to gentle boil. Remove from heat; add lemon slices and mint.

Makes 4 servings.

PER SERVING:

154 calories
3 g protein
8 g fat
18 g carbohydrate
45 mg sodium
4 mg cholesterol

CARROT BARLEY SOUP

Don't throw away that turkey carcass—here's one last recipe.
Barley is a wholesome grain that's especially tasty in soup. Hulled or whole
grain barley has only the outer husk removed; pearl is more refined and
cooks quicker.

Makes 6 main dish
servings.

PER SERVING:

265 calories
13 g protein
6 g fat
40 g carbohydrate
738 mg sodium
28 mg cholesterol

2 tablespoons butter or margarine
1 cup coarsely chopped onion
1 turkey skeleton, broken into pieces or about 1 cup of chopped
  cooked turkey
4 cups chicken broth
4 cups water
1 cup pearl barley
½ teaspoon salt *(optional)*
½ teaspoon ground black pepper
4 carrots, peeled, cut in 1-inch slices
2 parsnips, peeled, cut in ½-inch slices
2 tablespoons chopped fresh parsley

In large Dutch oven, heat butter; sauté onion 5 minutes (do not brown). Add turkey bones, chicken broth, barley, water, salt (if desired), and pepper; cover and bring to boil. Lower heat; simmer 1 hour, stirring occasionally. Add carrots and parsnips; cover and cook 30 minutes longer. Sprinkle with parsley.

COPPER'S CURRIED COUSCOUS

This exotically flavored side dish was created by Copper Cunningham, a popular New York City photographer. Copper's picnics, which brought together hundreds of her friends from the arts and other walks of life, are local legend. This is one of the dishes that helped to make her events so special.

¼ cup hot water
½ cup raisins
2 tablespoons Grand Marnier liqueur *(optional)*
3 tablespoons olive oil
1 medium onion, finely chopped
2½ cups chicken, lamb, or beef broth
2 garlic cloves, minced
2 teaspoons curry powder or to taste
⅛ teaspoon black pepper
½ teaspoon crushed red-pepper flakes
1-pound box couscous (2½ cups)*

Makes 16 servings.

PER SERVING:

151 calories
5 g protein
2 g fat
27 g carbohydrate
126 mg sodium
0 mg cholesterol

In medium bowl, pour hot water over raisins; stir in liqueur. Cover and let stand until raisins plump. In 5-quart saucepan or Dutch oven, heat oil. Add onion; sauté about 8 minutes, or until onion begins to brown around the edges. Meanwhile, in small saucepan, bring broth to boil. Add garlic to onion in saucepan. Sauté 2 additional minutes; with fork, stir in curry powder, pepper, pepper flakes, then couscous. Mix well, coating couscous with oil; heat through. Slowly stir in hot broth, being careful not to form lumps. Cover and remove from heat; let stand undisturbed for 5 minutes. Stir in raisins with liquid, mixing well and separating grains of couscous.

*Couscous is now available at most supermarkets.

ESSENCE BRINGS YOU
GREAT COOKING

COUSCOUS SEAFOOD SALAD

Makes 4 servings.

½ cup dry white wine
½ cup water
½ pound bay scallops
12 medium-size shrimp, shelled, cleaned, deveined

DRESSING:
4 tablespoons freshly squeezed lemon juice
1 clove garlic, minced
⅛ teaspoon salt *(optional)*
⅓ cup extra-virgin olive oil

COUSCOUS:
1 tablespoon butter or margarine
2 slices turkey ham or boiled ham, diced
1 small onion, chopped
2 cups chicken broth
¼ teaspoon turmeric
¼ teaspoon ground cardamom
2 cups quick-cooking couscous
1 small red bell pepper, seeded, diced
½ cup cooked tiny green peas

In large saucepan, bring wine and water to simmer. Add scallops; cook until firm, about 2 minutes. Using slotted spoon, remove to medium-size bowl. To remaining simmering liquid, add shrimp; cook until pink and firm, about 3 minutes. Using slotted spoon, remove shrimp to bowl with scallops. In small bowl, combine lemon juice, garlic, and salt (if desired); while beating vigorously with whisk or fork, slowly add oil until blended and thick. Add about 3 tablespoons dressing to seafood mixture, toss to coat; set aside. Meanwhile, to prepare couscous: In medium-size saucepan, melt butter; sauté ham and onion until soft (do not brown). Add chicken broth, turmeric, and cardamom; bring to boil. Stir in couscous; cover pot and remove from heat. Let stand 5 minutes. Transfer couscous to large bowl; fluff with fork. Add red pepper and peas; toss. Add seafood and remaining dressing to couscous mixture. Toss until well mixed. Refrigerate until ready to serve.

ARIS'S KUSH TABULEH

Bulgur wheat salad is a party pleaser! This version by Aris LaTham, a holistic cook who specializes in raw foods, soaks the wheat in carrot juice and as a result is especially tasty and nutritious.

1 cup bulgur
1 cup carrot juice
¼ cup freshly squeezed lemon juice
2 tablespoons tamari or naturally brewed soy sauce
¼ cup Bragg Liquid Aminos*
1 teaspoon ground cumin
1 teaspoon ground coriander
2 teaspoons dried mint leaves
1 teaspoon dried basil
1 cup shredded carrots
1 cup minced fresh parsley
2 scallions, thinly sliced
1 large red bell pepper, seeded, finely diced
1 small cucumber, peeled, finely diced
¼ cup olive oil
Optional garnishes: lettuce leaves, lemon wedges, baby vegetables,
  cherry tomatoes, cucumber slices

Makes 6 servings.

PER SERVING:

207 calories
5 g protein
8 g fat
28 g carbohydrate
364 mg sodium
0 mg cholesterol

In large bowl, combine bulgur with carrot juice, lemon juice, tamari, liquid aminos, cumin, coriander, mint, and basil; refrigerate about 8 hours or until liquid is absorbed. Meanwhile, in medium-size bowl, combine carrots, parsley, scallions, bell pepper, cucumber, and olive oil; mix well. If serving following day or several hours later, store bulgur and vegetable mixtures separately. Drain any excess liquid from bulgur; stir in vegetable mixture, mixing well about 1 hour before serving. For maximum flavor, serve at room temperature. Garnish as desired.

*An all-purpose, nonfermented seasoning made of vegetable protein, which is available in natural-food stores.

ESSENCE BRINGS YOU
GREAT COOKING

BULGUR PILAF

Makes 4 servings.

PER SERVING

146 calories
5 g protein
2 g fat
29 g carbohydrate
140 mg sodium
0 mg cholesterol

½ tablespoon safflower oil or vegetable oil
1 small onion, chopped fine
1 cup uncooked bulgur
2 cups water, vegetable broth, or low-sodium chicken broth
¼ teaspoon salt *(optional)*

In heavy 2-quart saucepan, heat oil. Add onion and sauté about 3 minutes. Stir in bulgur and cook an additional 3 minutes, until onion is translucent. Stir in water and salt (if desired). Bring to boil; reduce heat. Cover and cook for 15 minutes, until liquid is absorbed and the grain tender.

BULGUR HEALTH SALAD

⅔ cup uncooked bulgur

3 cups hot water

1 large ripe tomato, diced

½ cup chopped parsley

1 large scallion, thinly sliced

¼ cup lemon juice

¼ cup vegetable oil

½ teaspoon salt *(optional)*

⅛ teaspoon cayenne pepper

Spinach leaves

1 cucumber or zucchini, scored, sliced crosswise

Tomato wedges

Makes 4 servings.

PER SERVING:

237 calories

4 g protein

14 g fat

26 g carbohydrate

293 mg sodium

0 mg cholesterol

Place bulgur in medium-size bowl; cover with hot water. Let soak for 45 minutes, or until bulgur is light and fluffy; drain in colander or sieve lined with dampened cheesecloth. Wrap cloth around bulgur and gently squeeze to remove remaining water. Mix bulgur in large bowl with tomato, about ⅓ cup parsley, scallion, lemon juice, oil, salt (if desired), and pepper. Mound salad in spinach-lined bowl, on spinach-lined platter, or salad plates. Surround with cucumber slices and tomato wedges. Sprinkle with remaining parsley.

OATMEAL WITH WARM FRUIT COMPOTE

Make this dried fruit medley ahead of time and keep it in the refrigerator to be eaten alone or spooned over hot cereals, waffles, or cottage cheese.

Makes 6 servings.

PER SERVING:

304 calories
7 g protein
3 g fat
67 g carbohydrate
5 mg sodium
0 mg cholesterol

1 12-ounce package dried mixed fruit or any 2-cup combination of dried prunes, apricots, apples, pears, peaches, or figs
3 cups water
¼ cup sugar
1 tablespoon lemon juice
1 3-inch cinnamon stick
1 to 6 servings of cooked oatmeal
Half-and-half or milk, to taste *(optional)*

In 2-quart saucepan, combine fruit, water, sugar, lemon juice, and cinnamon stick. Bring liquid to boil; reduce heat and simmer about 20 minutes. If using apricots, add only during last 10 minutes of cooking to help retain their shape. Serve warm over oatmeal with half-and-half or milk, if desired. Store leftover fruit in refrigerator.

HOMEMADE GRANOLA

Avoid the excessive amounts of sugar and fat in store-bought granola by making your own.

3 tablespoons safflower or other vegetable oil
¼ cup lightly packed brown sugar
2 tablespoons water
⅛ teaspoon ground cinnamon
2 cups rolled oats
1 cup ready-to-eat, no-sugar-added wheat-flakes cereal
½ cup whole unblanched almonds
½ cup raisins, chopped dates, or combination
¼ cup raw or toasted wheat germ
¼ cup sunflower seeds
2 teaspoons sesame seeds

Makes about 4 ½ cups.

PER ½ CUP
SERVING:

249 calories
7 g protein
12 g fat
31 g carbohydrate
46 mg sodium
0 mg cholesterol

Heat oven to 250° F. In small saucepan, combine oil, sugar, water, and cinnamon; heat and stir over low heat until sugar melts. Set aside. In large bowl, combine remaining ingredients. Drizzle with sugar mixture; gently toss to coat dry ingredients. In large, shallow baking pan, spread cereal in thin layer. Bake 30 minutes, stirring frequently to brown cereal evenly. Cool to room temperature. Store in container with tight-fitting lid.

ESSENCE BRINGS YOU
GREAT COOKING

LIGHT MACARONI AND CHEESE

Makes 8 servings.

PER SERVING:

192 calories
10 g protein
4 g fat
27 g carbohydrate
233 mg sodium
8 mg cholesterol

There is debate as to whether pasta originated in Italy or China. But it's a fact that pasta has made itself at home in countries around the world. Baked macaroni and cheese is a quintessential dish in almost all regions of the USA.

1 8-ounce package elbow macaroni
2 tablespoons reduced-calorie, or regular, margarine
1 scallion, thinly sliced
2 tablespoons unbleached all-purpose flour
¼ teaspoon dry mustard
½ teaspoon hot-pepper sauce
½ teaspoon salt *(optional)*
2 cups skim milk
1 cup (4 ounces) shredded fat-reduced natural sharp cheddar cheese
Cooking spray
Paprika

Cook macaroni according to package directions. Heat oven to 350° F. Meanwhile, in medium-size saucepan, over medium heat, melt margarine; sauté scallion until tender, about 5 minutes. Blend flour, mustard, sauce, and salt (if desired); cook, stirring constantly, 1 minute. Gradually stir in milk; cook, stirring, until thickened, about 10 minutes. Remove from heat; add cheese, stirring until melted. Drain macaroni; stir into cheese mixture. Into ½-quart baking dish coated with cooking spray, spoon macaroni mixture; sprinkle with paprika. Bake until set, about 25 minutes.

OLD-FASHIONED BAKED MACARONI

½ pound uncooked elbow macaroni

3 large eggs, at room temperature

½ teaspoon dry mustard

½ teaspoon salt *(optional)*

½ teaspoon ground black pepper or ¼ teaspoon cayenne pepper

3 cups milk

2 cups shredded sharp cheddar cheese

2 tablespoons finely minced onion

2 tablespoons butter or margarine, cut into small pieces

Makes 8 servings.

PER SERVING:

306 calories

14 g protein

15 g fat

27 g carbohydrate

363 mg sodium

122 mg cholesterol

Cook macaroni according to package directions. Meanwhile, heat oven to 350° F. Grease 2-quart baking dish; set aside. In large bowl, combine eggs, mustard, salt (if desired), and pepper; beat until frothy. Gradually blend in milk. Drain macaroni. Into prepared dish, pour half the macaroni; sprinkle evenly with 1 cup cheese and onion. Add remaining macaroni; pour egg mixture over macaroni. Sprinkle with remaining cheese; dot top with butter. Bake 45 minutes.

Use a Big Pot

Use at least a 6-quart pot when cooking pasta. A stockpot or large kettle are ideal. A large pot allows the pasta to move around while cooking in rapidly boiling water—this helps prevent the pieces from sticking together. Adding one tablespoon of oil to the water also helps keep the pasta separate.

ESSENCE BRINGS YOU
GREAT COOKING

NOODLES WITH SPICY PEANUT SAUCE

Makes 4 servings.

PER SERVING:

733 calories
28 g protein
27 g fat
96 g carbohydrate
433 mg sodium
0 mg cholesterol

½ pound uncooked fettuccine, linguine, spaghetti, or Oriental noodles
½ cup creamy peanut butter
1 cup water
2 tablespoons low-sodium soy sauce
2 tablespoons lemon juice
1 tablespoon tahini (sesame paste, *optional*)
1 teaspoon crushed red pepper
½ teaspoon ground or 1 tablespoon grated fresh ginger
⅛ teaspoon garlic powder
1 scallion, sliced
½ cup unsalted peanuts

Cook pasta according to package directions. Meanwhile, in small saucepan, stir together peanut butter and water. Simmer over low heat, stirring constantly until smooth. Stir in soy sauce, lemon juice, tahini (if desired), pepper, ginger, and garlic powder. Bring to boil, stirring occasionally. Drain pasta and transfer to platter or plates; top with peanut sauce. Sprinkle with scallion and nuts.

LINGUINE PRIMAVERA

Newly sprung vegetables are featured in this seasonal classic; prepare with any delectable combination of fresh, tender produce.

1 pound uncooked flavored or plain linguine
2 tablespoons butter, margarine, or olive oil
1 medium-size onion, finely chopped
1 large garlic clove, minced
1 yellow summer squash, cut into thin strips
1 cup fresh sweet peas or frozen green peas, thawed
1 cup small whole mushrooms
1 small red bell pepper, seeded, cut into thin strips
½ pound fresh asparagus, cut into 2-inch pieces
½ pound French-cut green beans (very thin) or yard-long beans, cut into
  2-inch pieces
4 steamed artichoke hearts, cut lengthwise into wedges
½ teaspoon salt *(optional)*
¼ teaspoon ground pepper
¼ cup heavy cream
½ cup freshly grated Parmesan cheese

Makes 8 servings.

PER SERVING:

355 calories
13 g protein
9 g fat
56 g carbohydrate
302 mg sodium
23 mg cholesterol

> PASTA is economical, easy to prepare, and healthful.

Cook linguine according to package directions. Meanwhile, in large skillet, heat butter; add onion, garlic, remaining vegetables, salt (if desired), and pepper. Stir-fry until vegetables are of desired tenderness, 3 to 5 minutes. Drain linguine; in large bowl, toss with cream and Parmesan cheese. Transfer pasta to platter or plates; top or toss with vegetables and serve.

ESSENCE BRINGS YOU
GREAT COOKING

NEW SPAGHETTI AND MEATBALLS

Makes 4 to 6 servings.

PER EACH OF
6 SERVINGS:

588 calories
26 g protein
22 g fat
71 g carbohydrate
875 mg sodium
42 mg cholesterol

1 pound ground turkey
¼ cup dry bread crumbs
½ cup chopped onion
1 large garlic clove, minced
¼ teaspoon salt (optional)

2 tablespoons olive or vegetable oil
4 cups Easy All-Purpose Tomato Sauce (see page 58)
8 ounces uncooked fusilli (corkscrew spaghetti) or pasta shape of
   choice
Optional garnish: sprigs of fresh oregano

In medium-size bowl, combine all meatball ingredients; mix well. Shape mixture into 1-to-2-inch balls. In Dutch oven, heat oil; add meatballs. Sauté, rotating meatballs until evenly browned. Remove meatballs; pour off and discard all but 2 tablespoons of pan drippings. Prepare Easy All-Purpose Tomato Sauce, using drippings from meatballs instead of oil. Add meatballs to tomato sauce during last 10 minutes of cooking. Meanwhile, cook fusilli according to package directions. Drain pasta; transfer to platter or plates. Ladle with meatball sauce. Garnish with fresh oregano.

ESSENCE BRINGS YOU
GREAT COOKING

142

LIGHT LASAGNA

3 cups Easy All-Purpose Tomato Sauce (see page 58)
9 uncooked curly edged lasagna noodles
2 cups low-fat (1-percent) cottage cheese
2 cups shredded part-skim mozzarella cheese
½ cup freshly grated Parmesan cheese
1 egg, lightly beaten
¼ cup chopped fresh parsley

Makes 10 servings.

PER SERVING:

405 calories
26 g protein
12 g fat
46 g carbohydrate
736 mg sodium
53 mg cholesterol

Prepare Easy All-Purpose Tomato Sauce. As sauce simmers, cook noodles according to package directions. Heat oven to 375° F. In medium-size bowl, combine cottage cheese, 1 cup mozzarella, ¼ cup Parmesan, egg, and parsley; stir until well mixed. Drain noodles and spread on flat surface. Lightly grease 13-by-9-by-2-inch baking pan; spread about ⅓ of sauce on bottom. Top with 3 noodles, then layer with half of cheese mixture. Repeat layers ending with noodles. Spread noodles and cheese with remaining sauce. Sprinkle with reserved mozzarella and Parmesan cheeses. Bake until hot and bubbly, about 40 minutes. Let sit 15 minutes before cutting into rectangles to serve.

What The Heck Is Al Dente?

The translation of this Italian term is "to the tooth." This translates into pasta that has a bit of resistance when you bite into it—cooked through, yet pleasantly firm. Cooking times depend not so much on the size of the pasta, but on its thickness. For best results, follow package directions and test a piece or two as the pasta cooks.

SLIM-LINE FETTUCCINE ALFREDO

We've taken out the cream but not the creamy taste.

Makes 6 servings.

PER SERVING:

261 calories
9 g protein
12 g fat
29 g carbohydrate
193 mg sodium
56 mg cholesterol

8 ounces uncooked fettuccine
2 tablespoons butter or margarine
1 cup half-and-half
¼ teaspoon ground white or black pepper
1 cup grated Parmesan cheese
Optional garnish: chopped fresh parsley

Cook fettuccine according to package directions. Meanwhile, in Dutch oven or large skillet, melt butter. Stir in half-and-half and pepper. Over medium heat, simmer, stirring frequently, until mixture thickens slightly, about 5 minutes. Stir in Parmesan; cook, stirring constantly, just until cheese is melted. Drain fettuccine well. Add to sauce; toss to coat. If sauce begins to separate, stir in a little more half-and-half and cook over low heat until smooth. Garnish with parsley.

ESSENCE BRINGS YOU
GREAT COOKING

LINGUINE GEECHEE ROSA

Paul Carter Harrison, playwright, essayist, and inspired cook, boldly flavors his linguine and clam sauce with sun-dried tomatoes and an extra helping of garlic.

1 pound uncooked spinach linguine
2 tablespoons olive oil
8 scallions, chopped
6 garlic cloves, minced
4 6½-ounce cans chopped clams, reserve juice
2 teaspoons dried oregano
Freshly ground black pepper to taste
1 cup sun-dried tomatoes
2 tablespoons lemon juice
¼ cup butter, melted
½ cup grated Parmesan cheese

Makes 8 servings.

PER SERVING:

390 calories
19 g protein
13 g fat
52 g carbohydrate
238 mg sodium
77 mg cholesterol

Cook linguine according to package directions. Meanwhile, in large skillet, heat oil; sauté scallions and half the garlic, about 3 minutes. Add clam juice, oregano, and pepper; simmer about 10 minutes. Stir in tomatoes; simmer 10 additional minutes. Stir in clams and lemon juice; cook until just heated through. Drain linguine; return to pot. Toss with butter, cheese, and remaining garlic. Transfer to platter or plates; spoon with sauce.

WARM PASTA SALAD

Bill Duke, actor and director, is also a vegetarian. This salad is one he likes to make for guests.

Makes 5 servings.

PER SERVING:

350 calories
11 g protein
8 g fat
62 g carbohydrate
262 mg sodium
0 mg cholesterol

- 8 ounces uncooked spinach or artichoke rotelli (or other dried pasta)
- 1 tablespoon olive oil
- 5 scallions, chopped
- 4 or 5 garlic cloves, minced
- 1 cup sliced fresh mushrooms
- 1 head romaine or red-leaf lettuce, leaves separated, well rinsed, dried torn into bite-size pieces
- 6 Italian plum tomatoes, quartered
- 1 cup alfalfa or other sprouts
- 5 ears fresh corn, steamed 2 minutes, kernels removed, or if unavailable, 2 cups no-salt-or-sugar-added canned whole-kernel corn
- 5 pitted ripe olives

SALAD DRESSING:
- 2 tablespoons sodium-reduced soy sauce or 2 tablespoons Bragg Liquid Aminos*
- 1 tablespoon olive oil
- ¼ teaspoon cayenne pepper
- ½ tablespoon maple syrup

Cook pasta according to package directions. Meanwhile, in medium-size skillet, heat oil; sauté scallions, garlic, and mushrooms until tender, about 5 minutes. To prepare salad dressing: In small bowl or jar with tight-fitting lid, combine dressing ingredients; beat or shake vigorously until thickened and blended; set aside. Drain pasta. In large salad bowl, combine with mushroom mixture. Gently toss together remaining salad ingredients. Beat or shake dressing again; drizzle over salad. Toss to coat.

*An all-purpose, nonfermented seasoning made of vegetable protein, which is available in natural-food stores.

SEA AND SHELLS SALAD

4 cups uncooked small shell pasta, elbow macaroni, or other small
   pasta shape
½ cup mayonnaise
½ cup sour cream
3 tablespoons lemon juice
2 tablespoons capers
½ teaspoon salt *(optional)*
¼ teaspoon dry mustard
¼ teaspoon hot pepper sauce
1 cup sliced celery
1 cup diced cucumber
3 cups diced cooked seafood (use any combination of shrimp, scallops,
   lobster, crabmeat, tuna, salmon, and whitefish)
Lettuce leaves

Cook pasta according to package directions. Meanwhile, in large bowl, combine mayonnaise, sour cream, lemon juice, capers, salt (if desired), dry mustard, and pepper sauce; stir until blended. Mix in celery, cucumber, and seafood. Cover and refrigerate about 1 hour to chill. Serve on bed of crisp lettuce leaves.

Makes 4 to 6 servings.

PER EACH OF
6 SERVINGS:

518 calories
24 g protein
21 g fat
56 g carbohydrate
492 mg sodium
130 mg cholesterol

ESSENCE BRINGS YOU
GREAT COOKING

Breads—Quick
and Otherwise

Recipes

BASIC BISCUITS

BUTTERMILK BISCUITS

CINNAMON NUT ROLLS

HERB BISCUITS

SWEET POTATO BISCUITS

CORN BREAD I

CORN BREAD II

CHEESE-JALAPEÑO CORN BREAD

JALAPEÑO CORN STICKS

CHEESE CORN STICKS

SOUTHERN CORN BREAD DRESSING

GIBLET–CORN BREAD DRESSING VARIATION

JALAPEÑO–CORN BREAD DRESSING

DELECTABLE CORN BREAD–OYSTER DRESSING

SPOON BREAD

WHOLE WHEAT DINNER ROLLS

OATMEAL ROLLS

Recipes

HERB CHEESE MONKEY BREAD

CHEESE HERB BREAD

SWEET POTATO BREAD

ONION CHEESE BREAD

WAKE-UP APPLE-WALNUT MUFFINS

HONEY-ORANGE CORN MUFFINS

BANANA-PECAN MUFFINS

ORANGE–PEANUT BUTTER MUFFINS

BLUEBERRY CORN MUFFINS

OATMEAL-RAISIN MUFFINS

BROCCOLI CHEESE MUFFINS

BANANA-BRAN PANCAKES

CINNAMON APPLE PANCAKES

CORNMEAL PANCAKES

ORANGE-VANILLA FRENCH TOAST

NUTTY BANANA TOAST

CINNAMON TOAST

EASY STICKY PECAN TREATS

THERE'S a certain joy in waking up to fragrant biscuits for breakfast or sitting down to hot rolls for dinner. The aroma fills the house and our hearts. So many of our good times involve "breaking bread" with family and friends. Cornbread, corn sticks, hoe cakes, buttermilk biscuits, and spoon bread are all a part of the continuity with our past.

If you love the idea of home baking, but feel you just don't have the time, quick breads are the answer. Breads are divided into two main types—quick and yeast. Quick breads, such as biscuits, are leavened by the addition of baking soda or baking powder. As their name implies, they are quickly made because little or no kneading or rising is required. Yeast breads are a little more involved, but with a bit of planning are quite manageable. While the bread is rising or baking, you're free to do other things.

Made with the good-for-you grains discussed in the Grits and Other Great Grains chapter, the following recipes can serve the beginning cook as well as the serious baker.

YEAST is a living plant that feeds on the sugar in dough and produces the gas that makes dough expand and rise. It also adds a unique aroma and flavor.

FINISHING TOUCHES

Crisp crust: Brush with water before baking.

Shiny crust: Brush with 1 egg beaten with 1 tablespoon water before baking. Sprinkle with sesame seeds, poppy seeds, whole oats, or dried onion flakes, if desired.

Soft crust: Brush loaf with milk or melted butter before or after baking.

When You Need to Knead

Don't be intimidated—this step appears to be more difficult than it actually is. (Once you get the basic motion down, you might, however, be tempted to add rhythm and flair.) Dust hands and work surface (board or pastry cloth) lightly with flour to prevent sticking. Form the dough into a ball; place on floured surface.

1. Using the heels of your hands, push dough down and away from you.

2. Pick up the edge of the dough farthest from you; fold it over the edge closest to you.

3. Give the dough a quarter turn.

4. Continue to push, fold, and turn.

Knead until dough is smooth and elastic, about 8 to 10 minutes. If the dough sticks as you work, sprinkle surface and hands lightly as needed. Kneading can be done in a food processor fitted with the proper blade or in a mixer with a dough hook. This makes it easier, but the "hands on" satisfaction is lost.

ESSENCE BRINGS YOU
GREAT COOKING

153

BISCUITS

In the bread universe, biscuits are a world unto themselves. Angel, baking powder, beaten, buttermilk, cheese, cornmeal, and sweet potato are popular variations of this tender, flaky type of bread. Light-as-a-feather beaten biscuits are so labor-intensive—1,000 strokes—they have all but disappeared from home kitchens. At the other extreme, there's no need to rely on ready-to-bake biscuit dough that pops out of a paper tube when you whack it against the edge of the kitchen counter. You may be surprised to know how easy it is to make golden, tender, flaky biscuits. It takes only about 15 minutes to prepare the dough and less than 15 minutes to bake—such a wonderful return of flavor and nutrients for time spent.

Biscuit Shortcuts

Instead of rolling out the dough with a rolling pin, it may be easier for you to just pat it out to an even thickness with your hands. Another time-saver is to shape the flattened dough into a rectangle, then simply cut it into squares.

BASIC BISCUITS

Makes 12 to 15 biscuits.

PER BISCUIT:

144 calories
3 g protein
7 g fat
17 g carbohydrate
212 mg sodium
3 mg cholesterol

2¼ cups unbleached all-purpose flour
4 teaspoons baking powder
½ teaspoon salt *(optional)*
2 teaspoons butter or margarine
⅓ cup solid vegetable shortening
⅔ cup milk

Heat oven to 400° F. In large mixing bowl, sift together 2 cups flour, baking powder, and salt (if desired). With fingers or pastry blender, work in butter and shortening until mixture is consistency of coarse meal. Add milk; using fork, blend well. Sprinkle remaining flour on smooth surface. Scrape mixture from bowl onto floured surface. Knead dough by rolling and pressing down with hands 5 or 6 times. Using rolling pin coated with flour, roll out dough to ½-inch thickness. Cut out rounds with 1½-inch biscuit cutter or rim of glass. Place on ungreased cookie sheet about 1½ inches apart. Bake 10 to 12 minutes.

BUTTERMILK BISCUITS

This versatile recipe can be used to make flaky, delicate biscuits or spicy sweet rolls.

2 cups unbleached all-purpose flour
2 teaspoons baking powder
¼ teaspoon baking soda
½ teaspoon salt *(optional)*
⅓ cup solid vegetable shortening
¾ cup buttermilk

Makes about 18 biscuits.

PER BISCUIT:

84 calories
2 g protein
4 g fat
10 g carbohydrate
118 mg sodium
.37 mg cholesterol

Heat oven to 450° F. In large bowl, combine flour, baking powder, baking soda, and (if desired) salt; using fork, mix well. Using pastry blender, cut in shortening until mixture resembles coarse crumbs. Add buttermilk; using fork, mix just until mixture forms soft dough and leaves side of bowl (it may be a bit sticky). Turn dough out onto lightly floured surface; knead 6 to 8 times to mix thoroughly. Roll out dough to ½-inch thickness. With floured 2-inch round cutter, cut out biscuits. On ungreased baking sheet, place biscuits about 1 inch apart for crusty biscuits, nearly touching for soft-sided biscuits. Press dough scraps together, reroll, and cut until all dough is used. Bake until golden, about 12 to 15 minutes.

No Buttermilk On Hand?

It's easy to make your own substitute. Simply mix 2¼ teaspoons vinegar and enough whole milk to make ¾ cup. Let the mixture stand several minutes until thickened.

ESSENCE BRINGS YOU
GREAT COOKING

CINNAMON NUT ROLLS

Makes about 12 rolls.

½ cup packed light or dark brown sugar
1 teaspoon ground cinnamon
½ cup coarsely chopped pecans or walnuts
½ cup raisins
Buttermilk Biscuits dough (see previous recipe)
3 tablespoons butter or margarine, softened or melted

Heat oven to 425° F. In medium-size bowl, combine sugar, cinnamon, nuts, and raisins; mix well. Prepare biscuit dough according to preceding recipe through kneading step. Roll out dough into ¼-inch-thick 15-by-9-inch rectangle. Spread with 2 tablespoons butter. Sprinkle evenly with nut mixture; gently pat mixture to adhere to dough. Beginning at wide side of rectangle, carefully roll dough jelly-roll style. Use fingertips to press seam closed. Cut roll crosswise into 1-inch-thick slices. On greased baking sheet or in greased 9-inch round cake pan, arrange rolls about ½ inch apart. Brush tops with remaining butter. Bake until golden, about 15 minutes. Serve warm.

HERB BISCUITS

2 cups sifted, unbleached all-purpose flour
2½ teaspoons baking powder
½ teaspoon salt *(optional)*
2 tablespoons chopped fresh parsley
6 tablespoons cold unsalted butter or margarine, cut into small pieces
⅔ cup milk
1 tablespoon honey or molasses

Makes 10 to 12 biscuits.

PER BISCUIT:

163 calories
3 g protein
7 g fat
20 g carbohydrate
199 mg sodium
21 mg cholesterol

Heat oven to 400° F. Into medium-size mixing bowl, sift together flour, baking powder, and salt (if desired). Add parsley. Using pastry blender or rotary or electric hand mixer, blend butter into dry ingredients until mixture resembles coarse cornmeal. Using fork, add milk and honey. Stir until dough starts to form ball. On lightly floured surface, knead gently about 30 seconds, shaping into ball. Gently pat or roll out dough to ½-inch thickness. Using cookie or biscuit cutter, cut out 2-inch rounds, squares or diamonds; gather scraps, roll out again, and cut out shapes. Place biscuits on ungreased baking sheet or atop casserole. Bake 12 to 15 minutes or until golden brown.

SWEET POTATO BISCUITS

Makes 12 biscuits.

PER BISCUIT:

250 calories
4 g protein
8 g fat
40 g carbohydrate
386 mg sodium
20 mg cholesterol

1½ cups cooked mashed sweet potatoes
½ cup butter or margarine, melted if potatoes are not hot
¼ cup sugar
2 tablespoons milk
3½ cups unbleached all-purpose flour
4½ teaspoons baking powder
1 teaspoon salt *(optional)*

Heat oven to 425° F. In large bowl, combine sweet potatoes, butter, sugar, and milk; mix well. Into potato mixture, sift flour, baking powder, and salt (if desired). Using pastry blender, mix well. Using hands, work mixture into soft dough; chill. Roll or pat dough to ½-inch thickness; cut with 2½-inch biscuit cutter. Arrange on greased baking sheet. Place on top shelf of oven; bake about 15 minutes, until light golden brown. Serve warm.

CORN BREAD I

Southern-style corn bread is made with white cornmeal and little or no sugar, unlike its yellow and sweet northern counterpart. A classic dressing begins with tasty corn bread.

1 cup unbleached all-purpose flour
2 teaspoons baking powder
½ teaspoon salt (*optional*)
1 cup cornmeal
2 large eggs
1 cup milk
¼ cup vegetable oil, or melted butter or margarine

Heat oven to 425° F. Into large bowl, sift flour, baking powder and salt (if desired). Stir in cornmeal; mix well. In medium-size bowl, beat eggs lightly; stir in milk and oil until blended. Pour this over cornmeal mixture; stir only until moistened (do not overmix). Into greased 9-by-9-inch baking pan, pour batter. Bake until wooden pick inserted in center comes out clean, 20 to 25 minutes.

Makes 9 servings corn bread; 6 cups crumbled corn bread for dressing.

PER SERVING:

190 calories
5 g protein
8 g fat
23 g carbohydrate
220 mg sodium
51 mg cholesterol

It is believed that bread baking was the first form of cooking. The Bible makes many references to bread—"the staff of life." Religions from Christianity to Islam to Hinduism use bread in symbolic ways.

ESSENCE BRINGS YOU
GREAT COOKING

CORN BREAD II

Makes 9 servings.

PER SERVING:

199 calories
4 g protein
7 g fat
28 g carbohydrate
368 mg sodium
27 mg cholesterol

1½ cups unbleached all-purpose flour
¾ cup white or yellow cornmeal
1 tablespoon baking powder
2 tablespoons sugar
1 teaspoon salt *(optional)*
1 large egg, beaten slightly
1 cup milk
¼ cup melted shortening

Heat oven to 400° F. In large bowl, sift together flour, cornmeal, baking powder, sugar, and salt (if desired). In medium-size bowl, combine egg, milk, and shortening. Add liquid ingredients to dry ingredients all at once, stirring quickly and vigorously only until mixture is mixed and has lumpy appearance, but no longer. Turn into greased 8-inch or 9-inch square pan. Bake 30 minutes or until done. Cut into 9 squares.

Dry ingredients have a limited shelf life, especially leavening ingredients. Check expiration date on packages before use. Store in tightly sealed containers away from heat and moisture.

CHEESE-JALAPEÑO CORN BREAD

1½ cups cornmeal
1 teaspoon baking soda
½ teaspoon salt *(optional)*
3 large eggs
1 16-ounce can cream-style corn
1 cup buttermilk
½ cup melted vegetable shortening or oil
1 cup shredded cheddar cheese
⅓ to ½ cup jalapeño peppers, seeded, thinly sliced, or finely chopped

Heat oven to 350° F. Grease well-seasoned 10-inch cast-iron skillet or 9-by-11-inch baking pan; set aside. In large bowl, mix cornmeal, baking soda, and salt (if desired). In medium-size bowl, lightly beat eggs; stir in corn, buttermilk, and shortening until well mixed. Pour liquid mixture into dry ingredients; stir well. Pour half the batter into prepared skillet; sprinkle with half the cheese and half the peppers. Add remaining batter; sprinkle evenly with remaining cheese and peppers. Bake 30 to 40 minutes or until golden brown and surface springs back when lightly touched.

Cut into 16 wedges.

PER SLICE:

177 calories
5 g protein
10 g fat
17 g carbohydrate
322 mg sodium
48 mg cholesterol

Cheese Herb Bread (page 174).

ESSENCE BRINGS YOU
GREAT COOKING

JALAPEÑO CORN STICKS

Makes 14 corn sticks.

PER CORN STICK:

110 calories
2 g protein
6 g fat
11 g carbohydrate
124 mg sodium
23 mg cholesterol

Vegetable oil or cooking spray for greasing mold
1 cup sifted unbleached all-purpose flour
1 tablespoon sugar *(optional)*
2 teaspoons baking powder
½ teaspoon salt *(optional)*
½ teaspoon ground cumin
1 cup yellow cornmeal
½ cup solid vegetable shortening
¼ cup jalapeño peppers, roasted, chopped
2 large eggs
1 cup milk

Heat oven to 400° F. Grease two 7-stick corn-stick molds; heat molds about 5 minutes. In large bowl, add flour, sugar, baking powder, salt (if desired), and cumin. Stir in cornmeal until blended. With pastry blender, wire whisk, or a knife held in each hand, cut in shortening until mixture resembles coarse crumbs; stir in peppers and set aside. In small bowl, beat eggs slightly; stir in milk. Add liquid mixture to flour mixture all at once; stir until dry mixture is moistened. Carefully remove heated molds from oven; spoon batter into molds. Bake 20 minutes or until golden brown. Serve warm.

ESSENCE BRINGS YOU
GREAT COOKING

CHEESE CORN STICKS

Vegetable oil or cooking spray for greasing molds
1 tablespoon baking powder
1½ cups yellow cornmeal
½ cup whole wheat flour
2 teaspoons salt *(optional)*
1 large egg
1 cup skim milk
¼ cup vegetable oil
1 small jalapeño pepper, finely chopped
½ cup shredded, low-sodium cheddar cheese

Heat oven to 425° F. Grease two 7-stick corn-stick molds; heat molds about 5 minutes. In medium-size bowl, combine cornmeal, flour, baking powder, and salt (if desired). In small bowl, beat egg lightly; blend in milk and oil. Stir liquid mixture into dry ingredients; stir just until combined. Gently mix in jalapeño pepper and cheese. Remove molds from oven; evenly spoon batter into each section. Bake 15 minutes or until golden brown; remove and serve warm.

Makes 14 corn sticks.

PER CORN STICK:

126 calories
4 g protein
5 g fat
16 g carbohydrate
348 mg sodium
18 mg cholesterol

ESSENCE BRINGS YOU
GREAT COOKING

SOUTHERN CORN BREAD DRESSING

Bake corn bread a day ahead to simplify preparation on day of serving.

Makes about 8 cups;
12 servings.

PER SERVING:

238 calories
6 g protein
14 g fat
23 g carbohydrate
497 mg sodium
52 mg cholesterol

4 slices bread (white, whole wheat, or combination)
½ cup (1 stick) butter or margarine
1 cup chopped onion
2 cups chopped celery (including some leaves)
¼ cup chopped fresh parsley
1 teaspoon rubbed or ground sage, or to taste
1 teaspoon chopped fresh thyme or ½ teaspoon dried thyme
½ teaspoon poultry seasoning
½ teaspoon ground black pepper
½ teaspoon salt *(optional)*
5 cups crumbled Corn Bread (see page 161)
3 large eggs, slightly beaten
1½ to 2 cups Turkey Broth (see page 331)

Heat oven to 350° F. Cut bread into ½-inch cubes. In shallow pan, spread cubes; toast, stirring once, until dried out and edges slightly brown, about 8 minutes. Transfer to large bowl. In large skillet, melt butter; add onions and celery. Over low heat, sauté until tender (but not mushy), about 8 minutes. Remove from heat; stir in parsley, sage, thyme, poultry seasoning, pepper, and salt (if desired). To bowl with bread cubes, add corn bread and vegetable mixture. Stir in eggs and 1½ cups broth. If mixture seems dry, add remaining ½ cup broth. Taste and, if necessary, adjust seasonings. To cook inside turkey: Spoon dressing into body cavity (do not pack); spoon any additional dressing into neck cavity and/or buttered baking dish. To bake dressing separately: Spoon into large greased baking dish; cover loosely. To cook along with turkey, add to oven during last 30 to 45 minutes roasting time.

GIBLET–CORN BREAD DRESSING VARIATION

Cook giblets according to directions in Turkey Broth and Giblets recipe (page 331). Proceed according to Southern Corn Bread Dressing recipe (page 166). Add chopped giblets to corn bread mixture after adding vegetable mixture.

Makes 14 servings.

PER SERVING:

230 calories
9 g protein
12 g fat
20 g carbohydrate
435 mg sodium
110 mg cholesterol

Dressing Down the Fat

Here's how to keep the rich flavor and get rid of some of the fat in dressing. (1) Instead of stuffing the dressing into the turkey, bake the dressing in a separate dish; this keeps fat from the turkey from soaking into the dressing. (2) Use less butter, margarine, or oil to sauté the onion, celery, and other seasonings for the dressing; using cooking spray will cut fat even further. (3) Skim any fat from homemade or purchased broth, or use vegetable broth.

JALAPEÑO–CORN BREAD DRESSING

Makes 12 servings.

PER SERVING:

278 calories
13 g protein
12 g fat
29 g carbohydrate
815 mg sodium
105 mg cholesterol

1 pound mild turkey bulk sausage
1½ cups chopped celery
1 bunch scallions, chopped (including tops)
1 small red bell pepper, seeded, diced
6 cups crumbled Corn Bread (see page 161)
6 slices dried bread, cubed, toasted
⅓ cup jalapeño peppers, seeded, thinly sliced, minced
1 teaspoon poultry seasoning
1 teaspoon salt *(optional)*
2 large eggs, lightly beaten
1½ cups Turkey Broth (see page 331)
Optional garnishes: jalapeño peppers, cilantro sprigs

Heat oven to 350° F. In large unheated skillet, break up sausage. Over low heat, cook turkey until some fat is rendered; stir to break into small pieces. Add celery, scallions, and bell pepper; sauté until sausage is no longer pink and celery is tender, about 8 minutes. Meanwhile, in large bowl, combine corn bread and bread cubes. Add sausage-celery mixture, jalapeño peppers, poultry seasoning, and salt (if desired); toss to mix well. Stir in eggs and broth. Into lightly greased 3-quart baking dish, spoon dressing; partially cover and bake 45 to 50 minutes. Garnish as desired.

Stuffing a Turkey.

DELECTABLE CORN BREAD–OYSTER DRESSING

½ cup butter or margarine

1 cup chopped onion

1 cup chopped celery

2 cups oysters, drained, liquid reserved

¼ cup chopped parsley

4 cups crumbled corn bread

4 cups cubed stale white or French bread

1 teaspoon salt *(optional)*

¼ teaspoon ground black pepper

2 teaspoons poultry seasoning

2 large eggs, beaten

1½ cups chicken broth

Optional garnish: sage sprig

Makes 12 servings.

PER SERVING:

243 calories
8 g protein
14 g fat
20 g carbohydrate
579 mg sodium
104 mg cholesterol

Heat oven to 350° F. In 6-quart Dutch oven over medium heat, melt butter. Sauté onion and celery in hot butter until tender, about 8 minutes. Chop oysters; add to vegetables. Cook about 2 minutes; remove from heat. Stir in remaining ingredients; mix well. If stuffing poultry, lightly spoon dressing into bird cavity. Spoon remaining dressing into greased casserole dish; bake, covered, along with the poultry during the last 45 minutes of baking time.

> **N O T E**
>
> If dressing is made in advance, do not add liquid to other ingredients until just before baking, to prevent the dressing from becoming soggy.

ESSENCE BRINGS YOU
GREAT COOKING

SPOON BREAD

Not actually a bread, this baked cornmeal side dish is served by spooning it onto the plates.

Makes 6 servings.

PER SERVING:

199 calories
6 g protein
9 g fat
21 g carbohydrate
288 mg sodium
127 mg cholesterol

- 1½ cups water
- 1 cup yellow or white cornmeal
- 1 cup milk
- 1 teaspoon sugar
- ½ teaspoon salt *(optional)*
- 3 tablespoons butter or margarine
- 3 large eggs, separated

Heat oven to 375° F. In medium-size heavy saucepan over medium heat, bring water to boil. Using wooden spoon or whisk, stir in cornmeal until blended, lumps are dissolved, and mixture thickens, about 5 minutes. Stir in milk, sugar, salt (if desired), and butter until blended. Remove from heat. In small bowl, beat egg yolks; stir into cornmeal mixture. In deep bowl, beat egg whites until soft peaks form; fold into cornmeal mixture. Into well-greased 1½-quart baking dish, pour mixture. Bake until nicely browned on top and wooden pick inserted in center comes out clean, about 45 minutes. Serve immediately.

WHOLE WHEAT DINNER ROLLS

2 cups water

¾ cup solid shortening

2 tablespoons molasses

3¾ cups unbleached all-purpose flour

3 cups whole wheat flour

½ cup sugar

2 teaspoons salt

2 packages active dry yeast

2 large eggs

Makes 36 rolls.

PER ROLL:

133 calories
3 g protein
9 g fat
20 g carbohydrate
123 mg sodium
12 mg cholesterol

In small saucepan, heat water, shortening, and molasses until shortening melts. In large mixing bowl, at low speed, blend mixture with 2 cups unbleached flour, 1 cup whole wheat flour, sugar, salt, yeast, and eggs. With wooden spoon, stir in remaining flours. Place dough on lightly floured board, knead 5 minutes. Turn dough over and over in greased bowl so that surface of dough is greased. Cover dough with towel; let stand in warm, draft-free place until doubled, about 1 hour. Punch dough down. Using shortening, generously grease 13-by-9-by-2-inch pan and 8-by-8-by-2-inch pan. Heat oven to 375° F. Divide dough into 36 pieces; shape into balls. In prepared pans, arrange balls side by side. Cover and let rise until doubled, about 1 hour. Bake 20 minutes or until golden brown.

ESSENCE BRINGS YOU
GREAT COOKING

OATMEAL ROLLS

Makes about 36 rolls.

PER ROLL:

107 calories
3 g protein
2 g fat
19 g carbohydrate
128 mg sodium
8 mg cholesterol

2 cups scalded milk, heated to just below boiling
1 cup rolled oats
1 package active dry yeast, dissolved in ⅓ cup warm water
½ cup packed brown sugar
3 tablespoons shortening, melted
1 large egg
2 teaspoons salt *(optional)*
5 to 6 cups unbleached all-purpose flour

Into large bowl, pour milk over oats; cool to lukewarm. Add yeast, sugar, shortening, egg, and salt (if desired). Beat in about 3 cups flour, enough to make spongelike texture. Let rise about 1 hour. Add between 2 and 3 cups flour to make soft dough. On lightly floured surface, knead dough until smooth and elastic. Cover and let rise in warm place until doubled in bulk. Roll out to ½-inch thickness. Cut lengthwise and crosswise into about 36 squares; shape into balls. Place 2 inches apart on greased baking sheets. Cover; let rise until doubled, about 30 minutes. Meanwhile, heat oven to 350° F. Bake about 20 minutes, until golden. Serve warm.

How to Shape Dinner Rolls.

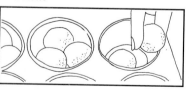

Pan Rolls

Crown Rolls

Bow Knot Rolls

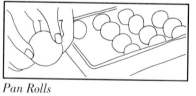

Cloverleaf Rolls

Swirl Rolls

Crescent Rolls

ESSENCE BRINGS YOU
 GREAT COOKING

HERB CHEESE MONKEY BREAD

This savory homemade bread slashes rising time by up to 50 percent with rapid-rise yeast.

3½ to 4½ cups unbleached all-purpose flour
1 package rapid-rise dry yeast
3 tablespoons sugar
⅓ cup grated Parmesan cheese
3 teaspoons Italian herb-seasoning blend
1 teaspoon salt *(optional)*
¼ cup water
¾ cup milk
2 tablespoons margarine or butter
1 large egg, at room temperature
⅓ cup melted butter or margarine

Makes 1 loaf;
16 servings.

PER SERVING:

169 calories
4 g protein
7 g fat
22 g carbohydrate
242 mg sodium
16 mg cholesterol

In large mixing bowl, combine 3½ cups flour, yeast, sugar, cheese, 2 teaspoons seasoning blend, and salt (if desired). In small saucepan, combine water, milk, and 2 tablespoons butter; heat over low heat until hot but not boiling (125° to 130° F). Stir hot liquid mixture into dry ingredients. Stir in egg; beat until smooth. Stir in only enough of remaining 1 cup flour to make a soft dough. On lightly floured surface, knead until smooth and elastic, about 8 to 10 minutes. Cover; let rest 10 minutes. Divide dough into 32 pieces; roll into 1-inch balls. To shape loaf, dip balls into ⅓ cup melted margarine or butter; in greased 10-inch tube pan, arrange balls in layers. Sprinkle with remaining herb seasoning. Cover; let rise in warm, draft-free place until double in size, about 30 minutes. Meanwhile, heat oven to 375° F. Bake 40 minutes or until golden brown. Let cool in pan on rack for 20 minutes. Turn out onto serving plate. Serve warm.

CHEESE HERB BREAD

This savory loaf is classified as a quick bread. There's no waiting for rising, because it's made with baking powder and baking soda instead of yeast.

Makes 1 round loaf;
12 servings.

PER SERVING:

185 calories
6 g protein
8 g fat
21 g carbohydrate
260 mg sodium
58 mg cholesterol

- 1 cup whole wheat flour
- 1 cup unbleached all-purpose flour
- 2 teaspoons baking powder
- ½ teaspoon baking soda
- ½ teaspoon salt *(optional)*
- 4 tablespoons cold butter or margarine, cut into pieces
- 1 tablespoon finely chopped fresh basil or 1 teaspoon dried basil
- 1 tablespoon chopped fresh oregano or 1 teaspoon dried oregano
- 1 tablespoon chopped fresh thyme or 1 teaspoon dried thyme
- 1 cup grated sharp or extra-sharp cheddar cheese
- 2 large eggs
- ¼ cup honey or molasses
- ¾ cup milk

Heat oven to 350° F. In large bowl, combine flours, baking powder, baking soda, and salt (if desired); stir to mix well. Using pastry blender or a table knife held in each hand, cut in butter until mixture resembles coarse crumbs. Stir in herbs and cheese until distributed evenly. In medium-size bowl, using whisk or fork, beat eggs and honey. Stir in milk. Pour liquid ingredients over dry ingredients. Using wooden spoon, stir just enough to moisten dry ingredients. Spoon into greased, waxed-paper-lined 8-inch round pan. Place pan on center oven rack. Bake 45 to 50 minutes. Cool in pan on rack 10 minutes; remove from pan and cool on rack. To serve, cut into wedges or slice crosswise.

SWEET POTATO BREAD

⅓ cup solid vegetable shortening

¼ cup sugar

2 large eggs

½ cup molasses

1 cup sweet potatoes or yams, cooked, peeled, mashed

2 cups unbleached all-purpose flour

¼ teaspoon baking powder

1 teaspoon baking soda

½ teaspoon salt *(optional)*

½ teaspoon powdered cinnamon

½ teaspoon powdered nutmeg

½ teaspoon ground cloves

¼ cup raisins

⅔ cup chopped walnuts

Heat oven to 350° F. In large bowl, combine shortening, sugar, and eggs. Beat until light and fluffy. Stir in molasses and sweet potatoes. Sift dry ingredients and spices. Add to mixture. Add raisins and chopped walnuts. Blend well. Turn into a greased 9-by-5-by-3-inch loaf pan. Bake 1 hour. Turn out of pan and cool completely on baking rack.

Makes 1 loaf; 9 1-inch thick slices.

PER SLICE:

349 calories

7 g protein

14 g fat

50 g carbohydrate

242 mg sodium

47 mg cholesterol

> GIVE US DAY BY DAY OUR DAILY BREAD.
> —Luke 11:3

ESSENCE BRINGS YOU GREAT COOKING

ONION CHEESE BREAD

Makes 8 servings.

PER SERVING:

212 calories
6 g protein
14 g fat
16 g carbohydrate
395 mg sodium
51 mg cholesterol

1 tablespoon solid vegetable shortening
½ cup onion, chopped
1 large egg, beaten
½ cup milk
1½ cups biscuit mix
1 cup cheddar cheese, grated
2 teaspoons poppy seeds
2 tablespoons melted butter

Heat oven to 375° F. In small saucepan, melt shortening; sauté onion until transparent, about 3 minutes. In medium-size bowl, combine egg and milk. Add biscuit mix. Stir just until biscuit mix is moist. Stir in onion, ½ cup cheese, and poppy seeds. Spread dough into well-greased 8-inch round cake pan. Sprinkle remaining cheese on top and drizzle with butter. Bake about 30 minutes.

- Mix ingredients just until all dry particles are moistened; the batter will be sightly lumpy. Overmixing causes a tough texture, unattractive tunnels, and peaked rather than rounded tops.
- Use an ice-cream scoop to fill muffin cups easily.
- Fill any empty muffin cups with water before baking.
- Remove muffins from tins immediately after baking to prevent them from becoming soggy.

WAKE-UP APPLE-WALNUT MUFFINS

Vegetable oil or cooking spray for greasing tin
2 cups unbleached all-purpose flour
¼ cup sugar
1 tablespoon baking powder
½ teaspoon cinnamon
½ teaspoon salt *(optional)*
2 large eggs
¾ cup milk
¼ cup butter or margarine, melted, or vegetable oil
1 small apple, peeled, cored, chopped
½ cup chopped walnuts
1 tablespoon sugar *(optional)*
¼ teaspoon cinnamon *(optional)*

Makes 12 muffins.

PER MUFFIN:

181 calories
5 g protein
8 g fat
23 g carbohydrate
273 mg sodium
48 mg cholesterol

Have ingredients at room temperature. Heat oven to 400° F. Grease 12 2½-inch muffin-tin cups; set aside. Into large bowl, sift flour, sugar, baking powder, cinnamon, and salt (if desired). In small bowl, beat eggs slightly with fork. Stir in milk, butter, apple, and nuts. Add liquid mixture to dry mixture all at once. Stir lightly only until dry ingredients are moistened; let lumps remain. Spoon batter into muffin cups about ⅔ full. (Add water to any empty muffin cups.) For muffins that are extra spicy and sweet, in small bowl or on waxed paper, mix sugar and cinnamon; sprinkle on batter. Bake muffins 20 to 25 minutes until golden and wooden pick inserted in center comes out clean.

ESSENCE BRINGS YOU
GREAT COOKING

HONEY-ORANGE CORN MUFFINS

These "anytime" muffins, by Andrea Jones of Catering with a Caribbean Flair, are great with a hot beverage in the morning, packed in lunch boxes, or served as part of a weekend brunch.

Makes 12 muffins.

PER MUFFIN:

233 calories
3 g protein
14 g fat
24 g carbohydrate
177 mg sodium
18 mg cholesterol

Vegetable oil or cooking spray
1 cup yellow cornmeal
1 cup unbleached all-purpose flour
3 teaspoons baking powder
½ teaspoon salt *(optional)*
1 large egg
¼ cup honey
¾ cup orange juice
¾ cup vegetable oil

Grease and flour 12 2½-inch muffin-tin cups. Heat oven to 400° F. In large bowl, combine cornmeal, flour, baking powder, and salt (if desired); mix well and set aside. In medium-size bowl, beat egg; stir in honey, orange juice, and oil, mixing well. Add liquid mixture all at once to dry ingredients; stir until flour is incorporated; avoid overmixing. Fill muffin cups about ¾ full. Wipe pan clean of spills. Bake 15 to 20 minutes or until edges of muffins are golden and a toothpick comes out clean when inserted in the center. Remove muffins from pan onto wire rack. Serve warm.

NOTE

Muffins are best when served warm right after baking. However, they can be baked in advance, then wrapped in foil and reheated in a 450° F oven for about 5 minutes. To make ahead, combine flour, sugar, baking powder, cinnamon, and salt (if desired) and store tightly covered for several days until ready to use.

BANANA-PECAN MUFFINS

These homemade muffins go from freezer to oven to table in just seven minutes. Pop them in the oven as you get ready for work.

Vegetable oil or cooking spray
1½ cups unbleached all-purpose flour
⅔ cup firmly packed brown sugar
1 teaspoon baking soda
¼ teaspoon salt *(optional)*
2 medium-size ripe bananas
½ cup vegetable oil
2 large eggs
2 teaspoons grated orange peel
½ cup chopped pecans
½ cup pecan halves

Grease and flour 12 2½-inch muffin-tin cups. Heat oven to 375° F. In large bowl, combine flour, sugar, baking soda, and salt (if desired); mix well and set aside. In food processor, puree bananas or mash with fork until smooth. In medium size bowl, combine bananas, oil, eggs, orange peel, and chopped pecans. Add liquid mixture all at once to dry ingredients. Mix just until flour is incorporated; avoid overmixing. Fill muffin cups about ¾ full; top with pecan halves. Wipe pan clean of spills. Bake 15 minutes or until an inserted wooden toothpick comes out clean; do not overbake. Remove muffins from pan onto wire rack. Serve warm.

Makes 12 muffins.

PER MUFFIN:

268 calories
3 g protein
16 g fat
29 g carbohydrate
128 mg sodium
35 mg cholesterol

ESSENCE BRINGS YOU
GREAT COOKING

ORANGE–PEANUT BUTTER MUFFINS

Makes 12 muffins.

PER MUFFIN:

197 calories
4 g protein
9 g fat
27 g carbohydrate
165 mg sodium
18 mg cholesterol

¼ cup peanut oil
⅓ cup honey
⅓ cup chunky-style peanut butter
¼ cup orange marmalade
1 large egg
1 cup orange juice
1½ cups unbleached all-purpose flour
½ teaspoon baking soda
½ teaspoon salt *(optional)*

Heat oven to 400° F. In large mixing bowl, combine first 6 ingredients; beat until smooth. In medium-size bowl, combine remaining ingredients; gently stir into peanut butter mixture. Spoon into 12 2½-inch greased or paper-lined muffin cups; fill to top. Bake about 20 minutes or until wooden pick inserted in center comes out clean. Serve warm or transfer to cooling rack.

ESSENCE BRINGS YOU
GREAT COOKING

BLUEBERRY CORN MUFFINS

Vegetable oil
1¼ cups yellow cornmeal
1 cup unsifted unbleached all-purpose flour
½ cup packed brown sugar
1 teaspoon baking soda
½ teaspoon ground cinnamon *(optional)*
½ teaspoon salt (*(optional)*
1 large egg
1 cup buttermilk
¾ cup vegetable oil
1 cup fresh blueberries or frozen blueberries, thawed

Makes 12 muffins.

PER MUFFIN:

267 calories
4 g protein
15 g fat
31 g carbohydrate
188 mg sodium
18 mg cholesterol

Heat oven to 400° F. With pastry brush, grease 12 2½-inch muffin-tin cups or 36 miniature cups. (Omit greasing if paper or foil baking cups are used.) In large mixing bowl, using fork, mix cornmeal, flour, sugar, baking soda, and (if desired) cinnamon and salt. In small bowl, using a fork, beat egg slightly; then stir in milk and oil. Add egg mixture and blueberries all at once to flour mixture. Using spoon, stir just until dry ingredients are moistened; batter should be lumpy. Spoon batter into muffin cups; wipe pan clean of any spills. Bake muffins 20 to 25 minutes or until they have risen, are golden brown, and wooden pick inserted in center comes out clean and dry. Immediately remove muffins from pan onto wire rack; serve at once, or keep warm by leaving in cups. To prevent soggy bottoms, tilt muffins, allowing steam to escape.

OATMEAL-RAISIN MUFFINS

Sweetened with molasses, these moist gems are rich in minerals and high in fiber.

Makes 12 muffins.

PER MUFFIN:

231 calories
5 g protein
10 g fat
30 g carbohydrate
187 mg sodium
19 mg cholesterol

- Vegetable oil
- 1½ cups rolled oats
- 1 cup unbleached all-purpose flour
- ¼ cup packed brown sugar
- 1 tablespoon baking powder
- ½ teaspoon salt *(optional)*
- ½ cup raisins
- ½ cup chopped nuts
- 1 large egg
- ⅔ cup milk
- ⅓ cup vegetable oil
- ⅓ cup unsulfured molasses

Heat oven to 400° F. With pastry brush, lightly oil 12 2½-inch muffin-tin cups. In large bowl, using fork, mix oats, flour, sugar, baking powder, salt (if desired), raisins, and nuts. In medium bowl, whisk or beat egg with fork, then stir in milk, oil, and molasses until blended. Pour egg mixture all at once into dry ingredients; stir just until dry ingredients are moistened. Spoon batter into prepared muffin cups, filling them about ¾ full. Bake about 18 minutes or until golden-brown and wooden pick inserted in center comes out clean. Serve warm or at room temperature.

ESSENCE BRINGS YOU
GREAT COOKING

BROCCOLI CHEESE MUFFINS

These savory muffins make a great alternative to dinner rolls or bread.

Water
1 ½ cups chopped fresh broccoli
2 cups unbleached all-purpose flour
1½ tablespoons baking powder
1 tablespoon sugar *(optional)*
½ teaspoon salt *(optional)*
½ teaspoon paprika
1 large egg
⅓ cup melted butter or margarine or vegetable oil
½ cup milk
½ cup sour cream
1 cup shredded cheddar cheese
1 small scallion, sliced thin

Makes 6 muffins.

PER MUFFIN:

387 calories
12 g protein
22 g fat
35 g carbohydrate
681 mg sodium
93 mg cholesterol

In large saucepan ¾ full with water, bring water to boil. Add broccoli; blanch 30 seconds; remove with strainer. Rinse with cold water; pat dry with paper towels. Set aside. Heat oven to 400° F. Grease 6 6-ounce glass baking cups or muffin-tin cups; set aside. Into large bowl, sift flour, baking powder, sugar, salt (if desired), and paprika; set aside. In medium-size bowl, beat egg slightly; stir in butter, milk, sour cream, and ¾ cup cheese until well mixed. Stir in scallion and broccoli, mixing well. Add liquid mixture to dry ingredients all at once. Stir only until mixed; batter will be very thick and lumpy. Spoon into prepared baking cups; sprinkle tops with remaining cheese. Place cups on baking sheet; bake 30 to 35 minutes or until wooden pick inserted in center comes out clean.

Pancakes to Flip Over

For tender, golden pancakes, follow these easy tips:

1. Heat griddle to 375° or 400° F; grease evenly to avoid sticking. Avoid over greasing; the fat will be absorbed into the pancakes and produce more of a fried cake.

2. Turn pancakes only once during cooking. They are ready to turn when tops are puffed and full of bubbles that are just beginning to burst.

3. Batter that becomes too thick on standing can be thinned with a little more liquid.

Banana-Bran Pancakes.

BANANA-BRAN PANCAKES

1 cup oat bran
1 cup unbleached all-purpose flour
1 tablespoon sugar
½ teaspoon baking powder
½ teaspoon ground cinnamon
¼ teaspoon baking soda
2 large egg whites
1½ cups buttermilk
1 tablespoon vegetable cooking oil (additional oil needed for greasing griddle)
2 medium-size bananas, cut into ¼-inch-thick slices

In medium-size bowl, mix together dry ingredients. In small bowl, lightly beat egg whites; stir in buttermilk and 1 tablespoon oil. Using whisk or fork, beat just until combined. Add liquid mixture to dry ingredients; stir just until combined. Use large nonstick skillet or griddle, or lightly brush or spray pan with oil; place over medium heat. For each pancake, group 3 to 4 banana slices in skillet. Pour about ¼ cup batter over bananas; cook until top is bubbly and underside golden. Using pancake turner, flip and cook on other side. Transfer as done to heated platter or warm oven; keep warm. Repeat until batter is finished, brushing skillet with oil as needed. Delicious with maple syrup, honey, or all-fruit preserves.

Makes 10 pancakes.

PER PANCAKE:

131 calories
5 g protein
3 g fat
24 g carbohydrate
106 mg sodium
1 mg cholesterol

ESSENCE BRINGS YOU
GREAT COOKING

CINNAMON APPLE PANCAKES

If the idea of making pancakes for breakfast on a weekday morning seems impossible, fix the batter the night before and enjoy this A. M. taste treat.

Makes 4 servings.

PER SERVING:

337 calories
8 g protein
16 g fat
40 g carbohydrate
429 mg sodium
63 mg cholesterol

- 1 ¼ cups all-purpose unbleached flour
- 1 tablespoon sugar
- 1 tablespoon baking powder
- 1 teaspoon cinnamon
- ¼ teaspoon salt *(optional)*
- 1 large egg
- 1 ¼ cups milk (use 1 cup for thicker pancakes)
- 3 ½ tablespoons vegetable oil (additional oil needed for greasing skillet)
- 1 apple (Rome Beauty and McIntosh are good choices), peeled, cored, thinly sliced, coarsely chopped; sprinkle apple with 1 tablespoon lemon juice to prevent browning if preparing in advance

In large bowl, mix flour, sugar, baking powder, cinnamon, and salt (if desired). In small bowl, beat egg; stir in milk and oil. Pour egg mixture into flour mixture and stir only until dry ingredients are moistened. Gently stir in chopped apples. Heat large skillet or griddle over medium-high heat, until an added drop of water sizzles. Brush lightly with oil. Pour batter by about ¼ cupfuls onto skillet, making a few pancakes at a time. Cook until bubbles appear on surface and burst. Turn pancakes and cook about 30 seconds, or until bottom is lightly browned. Serve pancakes hot with maple syrup, if desired.

CORNMEAL PANCAKES

½ cup boiling water
½ cup yellow cornmeal
½ cup unbleached all-purpose flour
1 tablespoon baking powder
1 teaspoon sugar *(optional)*
¼ teaspoon salt *(optional)*
¼ cup milk
3 tablespoons vegetable oil
1 large egg, lightly beaten

In large mixing bowl, pour boiling water over cornmeal; stir until blended. In small bowl, combine flour, baking powder, sugar, and salt (if desired); mix well. In measuring cup, combine milk, oil, and egg; stir until blended. Heat griddle or large cast-iron skillet over medium-high heat, or heat an electric griddle to 350° F. Add flour and liquid mixtures to cornmeal; stir just until dry ingredients are moistened. Coat griddle with cooking spray; reduce heat to medium. For each pancake, pour about ¼ cup batter onto griddle. Cook, turning pancakes only once when tops are bubbly and edges are browned. Repeat procedure until all batter is used.

Makes 12 pancakes; 4 servings.

PER SERVING:

80 calories
2 g protein
4 g fat
9 g carbohydrate
135 mg sodium
18 mg cholesterol

ESSENCE BRINGS YOU
GREAT COOKING

ORANGE-VANILLA FRENCH TOAST

Refrigerate batter-dipped bread overnight for a speedy, nourishing breakfast in the morning.

Makes 4 slices toast.

PER SLICE:

295 calories
10 g protein
16 g fat
30 g carbohydrate
380 mg sodium
110 mg cholesterol

2 large eggs
¾ cup skim milk, half-and-half, or cream
¼ cup orange juice
1 tablespoon sugar or honey
1 teaspoon grated orange rind *(optional)*
1 teaspoon ground cinnamon
½ teaspoon vanilla extract
4 slices wheat bread (cut from unsliced loaf for thicker slices)
4 tablespoons butter or margarine
1 8-ounce container low-fat vanilla yogurt
Optional garnish: orange slices, watercress sprigs

In large shallow bowl or pie plate, using fork, beat eggs lightly. Stir in milk, orange juice, sugar, orange rind (if desired), ½ teaspoon cinnamon, and vanilla. Dip both sides of each slice of bread into batter. In large skillet, melt half of butter. Add 2 slices bread and fry over medium heat until lightly browned; turn each and brown other side. Remove to warm platter or keep warm in 200° F oven. Add remaining butter to skillet; panfry remaining bread slices. Spoon yogurt over toast; sprinkle with remaining cinnamon. Serve warm; garnish with orange slices and watercress.

NUTTY BANANA TOAST

No time to cook? Try this quick and nourishing toast surprise.

1 slice raisin, 7-grain, or other whole grain bread, toasted
2 tablespoons peanut, cashew, sunflower, or other nut butter
1 small banana, sliced
1 tablespoon honey

Spread toast with nut butter. Top with banana slices. Drizzle or spread with honey.

Makes 1 serving.

PER SERVING:

401 calories
11 g protein
17 g fat
57 g carbohydrate
249 mg sodium
0 mg cholesterol

CINNAMON TOAST

This is a grown-up version of a childhood favorite.

Makes 1 serving.

1 slice French or whole grain bread
1 teaspoon butter or margarine
5 or 6 pecan halves *(optional)*
1 teaspoon brown sugar or honey
⅛ teaspoon ground cinnamon

Heat broiler or toaster oven. Meanwhile, lightly spread 1 side of bread with butter. Dot bread with pecans, if you like. In small bowl, mix sugar and cinnamon; sprinkle over butter and nuts. Place under broiler until sugar melts, about 1 minute (watch closely to avoid burning).

EASY STICKY PECAN TREATS

½ cup chopped pecans
¼ cup butter or margarine, melted
¼ cup packed brown sugar
¼ cup light or dark corn syrup
½ teaspoon ground cinnamon
5 plain English muffins, split, lightly toasted

In small bowl, mix pecans, butter, sugar, corn syrup, and cinnamon. Spread nut mixture over each muffin half. Arrange on broiler-proof pan or rack. Broil 6 inches from heat, 2 to 3 minutes or until bubbly. Serve warm.

Makes 10 buns.

PER BUN:

205 calories
3 g protein
9 g fat
27 g carbohydrate
267 mg sodium
0 mg cholesterol

CHAPTER FIVE

Eggs and Cheese

Recipes

PERFECT FRIED EGGS

PERFECT POACHED EGGS

HUEVOS RANCHEROS

CREAMY SCRAMBLED EGGS IN BAKED TOMATO CUPS

CREAMY SCRAMBLED EGGS

EGG-CEPTIONAL TOMATO CUPS

TURKEY HASH WITH BAKED EGGS

HASH-BAKED EGGS

SPANISH POTATO OMELET WITH SPANISH SAUCE

CHEESY VEGETABLE FRITTATA

COTTAGE CHEESE–SAUSAGE SCRAMBLE

CHEESE AND VEGETABLE QUICHE

GARDEN QUICHE

COLLARD GREEN QUICHE

SPINACH-NUT QUICHE

SPINACH-MUSHROOM QUICHE

CABBAGE AND CHEESE PIE

Recipes

SWEET PEPPER AND CRABMEAT QUICHE

TOMATO CHEESE QUICHE

LOBSTER DEVILED EGGS

CHEESE SAUCE

CHEESY EGG AND MUSHROOM BAKE

ZUCCHINI AND CHEDDAR CHEESE SOUP

CHEESE-STUFFED ZUCCHINI

CHEESE SOUP

BAKED CHEESE-STUFFED MUSHROOMS

ALMOND-CARAMEL BRIE

CREAMY BLUE-CHEESE DIP

NOODLE AND CHEESE CASSEROLE

EASY THREE-CHEESE LASAGNA

SHRIMP EGG FOO YUNG

EASY ITALIAN-STYLE MANICOTTI

HOT CRAB AND CHEESE SANDWICHES

RASPBERRY YOGURT SHAKE

SUNRISE HEALTH SHAKE

Recipes in this chapter do not include nutritional analysis for sodium content
when salt is listed as an optional ingredient.

EGGS

IT'S eggs that raise angel-food cakes to their heights, but we seem to love them most when deviled. Eggs have extraordinary capabilities—they puff soufflés, bind meat loaf and dressing, clarify stock, emulsify oil into mayonnaise, glaze breads and rolls, and thicken ice cream and custard!

The image of eggs as nature's almost perfect food was cracked in recent years by studies that linked foods with high levels of cholesterol to increased risk of heart disease. It now makes sense to limit the number of egg yolks (this is where the 5 grams of fat and 213 milligrams of cholesterol in a large egg are located) to four per week. This obviously does not mean that eggs should be altogether avoided. Eggs have a great deal of nutritional value and can play an important role in a well-balanced eating plan. They contain high-quality protein, and all of the essential amino acids are present in patterns that are readily utilized by the body. Eggs also contain phosphorus, iron, iodine, riboflavin, and vitamins A, B_{12}, D, and E. You get all of the above for just 75 calories per large egg.

While the yolk is rich in cholesterol, protein predominates in the white. An easy way to reduce cholesterol is to use a 2 or 3 to 1 ratio of whites to yolks when cooking.

BREAKFAST

In the days of the old South, breakfast was served at the crack of dawn. As a major repast, the meal was substantial and stuck to the ribs. Tables were laden with scrambled and fried eggs, country ham and red-eye gravy, slab bacon, hash-browned potatoes, fried apples, grits, flapjacks, and biscuits.

Today, the workday still stretches from sunup to sundown, but instead of the hard labor of farming, most work is sedentary. Obviously, the breakfast of old is obsolete. Yet breakfast is still considered the most important meal of the day. It jump-starts your day with a boost of energy and contributes to overall productivity. Breakfast also provides a precious moment to pause with your loved ones before everyone rushes off in different directions.

A little organization the night before can put a healthful, satisfying morning meal on the table in minutes, or even seconds. Fifteen seconds is all it takes to blend a power breakfast shake!

GETTING GOOD GRADES

The grade of an egg refers to its quality at the time the egg is packed. Standard consumer grades are AA, A, and B. Double A is the top grade and when broken onto a plate will stand tall. The yolk is firm and the white is thick and covers a small area. As the egg ages, the grade drops and the egg flattens accordingly.

Buy eggs that are refrigerated. Check the appearance of each egg; do not buy any that are cracked or soiled. Keep eggs in the containers they are purchased in; their porous shell will be less likely to absorb refrigerator odors. Do not transfer eggs to the cute cutouts on your refrigerator door. Eggs can be stored in the refrigerator about four weeks.

BROWN VERSUS WHITE

There is no known nutritional or taste difference in eggs with white shells and those with brown shells. The color of the shell is characteristic of the laying hen's breed. Yet many consumers choose to pay a higher price for brown eggs.

MISNOMER

Though often called "hard-boiled eggs," when properly cooked, these eggs are not boiled, but placed in cold water and simmered gently for 10 to 15 minutes. The more apt name is "hard-cooked eggs."

To prevent that greenish ring from forming around the yolk of a hard-cooked egg, cook over low heat, then immediately plunge the cooked eggs into cold water.

To remove a piece of eggshell that has fallen into an egg mixture, use another piece of eggshell as a scoop.

DOES SIZE COUNT?
Egg size is based upon the net weight per dozen.
Jumbo—30 ounces
Extra large—27 ounces
Large—24 ounces
Medium—21 ounces
Small—18 ounces
Peewee—15 ounces

Large is the standard egg size used in this and most cookbooks. Sizes are interchangeable except in recipes for cakes, custards, and other foods with delicately balanced ingredients. As a general guide, substitute 2 jumbo or 4 small for 3 large eggs.

PERFECT FRIED EGGS

Makes 2 servings.

PER SERVING:

126 calories
6 g protein
11 g fat
.69 g carbohydrate
64 mg sodium
228 mg cholesterol

1 tablespoon unsalted butter or margarine
2 large eggs
⅛ teaspoon salt *(optional)*
⅛ teaspoon ground black, white, or cayenne pepper

   In skillet or griddle, over medium heat, melt butter. Meanwhile, break an egg into saucer or small shallow bowl, being careful not to break yolk. Slip egg from saucer into skillet; repeat with second egg. Reduce heat to low. For sunny-side-up eggs, cook 3 to 4 minutes, basting with butter in skillet, or cook until whites are firm and opaque and yolks are of desired consistency. For over-easy eggs, as soon as whites are firm turn eggs with wide spatula; cook just until yolks are of desired consistency. Transfer eggs from skillet to plates or platter; sprinkle with salt (if desired) and pepper.

ESSENCE BRINGS YOU
GREAT COOKING

PERFECT POACHED EGGS

This no-fat-added method of cooking eggs is a healthful choice. Poached eggs are especially tasty eaten atop whole wheat toast. Breaking each egg into a saucer, and slipping it into the water, helps the egg hold its shape.

Water or vegetable bouillon
Large eggs

To medium-size nonstick saucepan or deep skillet, add 2 inches water (some believe that adding a tablespoon of vinegar will prevent egg white from spreading while cooking). Over medium-high heat, bring to boil. Reduce heat to keep water at constant simmer. One at a time, break eggs into saucer; slide egg into water. Simmer, occasionally spooning egg with water from saucepan, until cooked to desired firmness, about 3 to 5 minutes. Using slotted spatula or spoon, transfer eggs to paper towels. Drain and, if desired, trim edges.

PER EGG:

75 calories
6 g protein
5 g fat
.61 g carbohydrate
64 mg sodium
212 mg cholesterol

ESSENCE BRINGS YOU
GREAT COOKING

HUEVOS RANCHEROS

This Mexican dish features eggs in a hot and spicy tomato sauce atop flavorful corn tortillas.

Makes 2 servings.

PER SERVING:

FRIED

473 calories
16 g protein
35 g fat
25 g carbohydrate
643 mg sodium
472 mg cholesterol

POACHED

371 calories
16 g protein
24 g fat
25 g carbohydrate
643 mg sodium
439 mg cholesterol

1 tablespoon olive or vegetable oil
1 small onion, finely chopped (about ¼ cup)
1 garlic clove, minced
1 14-ounce can peeled tomatoes, chopped
2 canned whole green chilies, chopped
1 teaspoon dried oregano
¼ teaspoon salt *(optional)*
⅛ teaspoon ground cumin
4 Perfect Fried Eggs or Perfect Poached Eggs (see page 198 and page 199)
1 tablespoon butter or margarine
2 corn tortillas

   In 10-inch skillet, heat oil; sauté onion and garlic several minutes until onion is transparent. Stir in tomatoes, chilies, oregano, salt (if desired), and cumin; simmer about 12 minutes. Meanwhile, prepare Perfect Fried or Poached Eggs. Using wide spatula, transfer soft-cooked eggs to simmering sauce. In small skillet, melt butter. One at a time, cook each tortilla about 30 seconds. Place tortilla in each of 2 shallow individual serving dishes. Gently remove eggs, with large spoon, from sauce; place atop tortillas. Spoon with additional sauce. Serve immediately.

CREAMY SCRAMBLED EGGS IN BAKED TOMATO CUPS

12 firm, ripe, medium-size tomatoes
1 teaspoon salt *(optional)*
Creamy Scrambled Eggs (see following recipe)
Optional garnish: Belgian endive leaves

Heat oven to 350° F. Using sharp knife, slice tops carefully from tomatoes; scoop out and discard seeds and pulp, leaving ½-inch-thick shell. Sprinkle tomato hollows with salt (if desired); place cut-sides-down on rack to drain, about 15 minutes. Into large baking pan, place rack with inverted tomatoes; bake until tender yet firm, about 8 minutes. Meanwhile, prepare Creamy Scrambled Eggs. Spoon generous amount of eggs into tomato cups. Arrange on platter; garnish with leaves of Belgian endive. Serve right away.

Makes 12 servings.

PER SERVING:

194 calories
11 g protein
14 g fat
7 g carbohydrate
239 mg sodium
304 mg cholesterol

ESSENCE BRINGS YOU
GREAT COOKING

CREAMY SCRAMBLED EGGS

When making breakfast or brunch for a bunch, you can build a menu around these easy eggs.

Makes 12 servings.

PER SERVING:

173 calories
10 g protein
14 g fat
2 g carbohydrate
230 mg sodium
304 mg cholesterol

- 16 large eggs
- ½ cup water or milk
- ½ teaspoon salt *(optional)*
- ⅛ teaspoon cayenne pepper
- ¼ cup butter or margarine
- 1 8-ounce package low-fat cream cheese, cut into ½-inch cubes
- 2 tablespoons chopped fresh chives or parsley

In large bowl, beat eggs, water, salt (if desired), and pepper just until combined. In large, 12-inch skillet, over medium heat, melt 2 tablespoons butter; tilt skillet to coat. Pour in half the egg mixture; cook over low heat. As eggs begin to set, with spatula gently stir from bottom to allow uncooked egg to flow to bottom of pan. Sprinkle half the cream-cheese cubes and 1 tablespoon chives on top of eggs. Gently stir and lift cooked portion occasionally. (To avoid dry, crumbly eggs, do not stir continuously.) Cook until eggs are no longer runny and cheese has melted. Transfer to warm serving platter; keep warm. Cook remaining egg mixture in same manner. Sprinkle cooked eggs with remaining chives.

EGG-CEPTIONAL
TOMATO CUPS

2 tablespoons mayonnaise

1 teaspoon prepared mustard

3 hard-cooked large eggs, coarsely chopped

¼ cup thinly sliced celery

2 tablespoons minced green bell pepper

1 tablespoon minced onion

Dash of cayenne pepper or ground white pepper

2 medium-size ripe tomatoes

Lettuce leaves *(optional)*

Makes 2 servings.

PER SERVING:

249 calories

11 g protein

20 g fat

8 g carbohydrate

228 mg sodium

327 mg cholesterol

In medium-size bowl, blend mayonnaise and mustard. Stir in eggs, celery, bell pepper, onion, and pepper until mixed. Cover and refrigerate until chilled. Cut each tomato into 8 wedges without cutting through to bottom; open to form cup. Place each tomato on plate lined with lettuce. Spoon egg mixture into tomato centers. (If making only 1 stuffed tomato, remaining egg salad can be refrigerated for 1 day and used as sandwich filling or to stuff celery or other vegetables.)

ESSENCE BRINGS YOU
GREAT COOKING

TURKEY HASH WITH BAKED EGGS

Makes 4 servings.

PER SERVING:

402 calories
31 g protein
18 g fat
28 g carbohydrate
228 mg sodium
294 mg cholesterol

2 cups diced or chopped cooked turkey
1 pound small red-skinned potatoes, cooked, cubed
1 small green or red bell pepper, or combination, seeded, chopped
1 small onion, diced
1 tablespoon unbleached all-purpose flour
¾ teaspoon salt (optional)
2 teaspoons chopped fresh sage or ½ teaspoon ground sage
¼ teaspoon ground black pepper
3 tablespoons butter or margarine
½ cup milk or chicken broth
4 large eggs
½ teaspoon paprika
Optional garnishes: cherry tomatoes, fresh sage leaves

In large bowl, combine turkey, potatoes, bell pepper, onion, flour, salt (if desired), sage, and black pepper; mix well. In large ovenproof skillet, melt butter. Add turkey mixture; stir until well mixed and flour is blended. Cook, stirring occasionally, until ingredients are lightly browned, about 8 minutes. Slowly stir in broth until blended. Simmer about 5 minutes or until bubbly. Heat oven to 350° F. Using back of spoon, make 4 round indentations in hash, or transfer mixture to 4 individual-serving baking dishes and make indentation in each. Break an egg into saucer, then slide egg into indentation; repeat for each. Sprinkle eggs with paprika. Place skillet or baking dishes in oven; bake until eggs are set and of desired consistency, about 15 minutes. Garnish with tomatoes and sage leaves.

It was a southern tradition to serve foods left from the previous day's dinner for the following morning's breakfast. Fried chicken, fish, or even pork chops often rounded out the first meal of the day. Leftovers are also a practical approach for today's cooks. Add chopped, already-cooked foods to scrambled eggs, omelets, and frittatas. Or place atop whole wheat bread, sprinkle with low-fat cheese, then toast or broil.

HASH-BAKED EGGS

Hash and eggs is not for breakfast only. When creatively prepared and served with a salad or vegetable, it becomes a fine dinnertime meal.

2 tablespoons butter or margarine
2 12-ounce cans corned beef hash
4 large eggs
¼ cup milk
¼ teaspoon ground black pepper

Heat oven to 375° F. Lightly butter four 5- or 6-ounce custard cups or other ovenproof dishes. Line each cup with ¼ of hash; break an egg into each. Pour 1 tablespoon milk over each egg; sprinkle with pepper and dot with butter. Bake about 12 minutes or until eggs are set. Serve with spinach salad.

Makes 4 servings.

PER SERVING:

443 calories
22 g protein
30 g fat
20 g carbohydrate
1,048 mg sodium
286 mg cholesterol

ESSENCE BRINGS YOU
GREAT COOKING

SPANISH POTATO OMELET

Makes 2 servings.

PER SERVING:

428 calories
15 g protein
29 g fat
25 g carbohydrate
909 mg sodium
425 mg cholesterol

Spanish Sauce (see following recipe)
1 tablespoon olive oil or butter
4 large eggs
¼ cup water
¼ teaspoon salt *(optional)*
Dash freshly ground black pepper
1 medium-size cooked potato, sliced
Optional garnishes: pimiento-stuffed olives, flat-leaf parsley

Prepare Spanish Sauce; set aside. In 10-inch omelet pan or skillet, heat oil over medium-high heat; tilt pan to coat. Meanwhile, in medium-size bowl beat 2 eggs, 2 tablespoons water, ⅛ teaspoon salt (if desired), and pepper; pour mixture into skillet. With spatula, push cooked portion of eggs toward center of pan; tilt pan so that uncooked eggs will run onto pan surface. While egg surface is still moist and creamy, arrange half of potato slices over half of omelet. Spoon with one quarter of Spanish Sauce; fold omelet in half over sauce. Remove from pan to platter; spoon with one quarter of remaining sauce. Keep warm. Prepare second omelet the same way with remaining ingredients. Garnish omelets with olives and parsley.

Spanish Sauce

Makes 1 cup.

PER CUP:

264 calories
4 g protein
18 g fat
21 g carbohydrate
1,560 mg sodium
0 mg cholesterol

1 tablespoon olive oil
½ cup chopped onion
½ cup chopped green bell pepper
½ cup sodium-reduced tomato sauce
2 tablespoons sliced pimiento-stuffed Spanish olives
1 tablespoon chopped parsley
¼ teaspoon salt *(optional)*
Dash freshly ground black pepper
1 tablespoon dry sherry

In medium-size skillet, heat oil; sauté onion and green pepper, about 5 minutes. Stir in remaining ingredients; simmer uncovered, about 10 minutes.

ESSENCE BRINGS YOU
GREAT COOKING

CHEESY VEGETABLE FRITTATA

This unfolded omelet makes a great brunch or dinner meal.

2 tablespoons unsalted butter or margarine

1 cup sliced mushrooms

1 small garlic clove, minced

1 small zucchini, cut in ¼-inch-thick slices

8 large eggs

½ cup milk

1 teaspoon dried oregano

½ teaspoon cayenne pepper

1 dash hot pepper sauce

1 cup cubed low-sodium cheese

1 medium-size tomato, diced

2 tablespoons chopped parsley

Makes 6 servings.

PER SERVING:

253 calories

16 g protein

19 g fat

5 g carbohydrate

246 mg sodium

321 mg cholesterol

Heat oven to 350° F. In 10-inch ovenproof skillet, melt butter; sauté mushrooms, garlic, and zucchini. Meanwhile, in mixing bowl, beat eggs, milk, oregano, pepper, and pepper sauce. Pour egg mixture over vegetables in skillet. Cover and cook, without stirring, until edges are set, about 1 to 2 minutes. Gently lift cooked portion with spatula to allow uncooked portion to flow to bottom. When eggs are lightly browned on bottom, sprinkle top with cheese, tomato, and parsley. Bake about 5 minutes, or until cheese is melted and eggs cooked through. Cut into wedges and serve immediately.

COTTAGE CHEESE— SAUSAGE SCRAMBLE

This hearty dish is a good choice for a brunch buffet.
Serve with a tossed salad, fresh fruit cup, and bread basket.

Makes 12 servings.

PER SERVING:

228 calories
17 g protein
16 g fat
3 g carbohydrate
496 mg sodium
341 mg cholesterol

2 cups thinly sliced smoked kielbasa sausage
18 large eggs
½ cup milk
1 pint cream-style cottage cheese
¼ cup chopped chives
1 teaspoon salt *(optional)*
½ teaspoon cayenne pepper
½ teaspoon black pepper

In large, unheated skillet, place sausage. Over low heat, cook until sausage renders some fat. Increase heat to medium and cook until heated through. In medium-size mixing bowl, using whisk, beat eggs and remaining ingredients lightly. Stir egg mixture into skillet until combined with meat. As mixture begins to set, stir occasionally from bottom. Cook until eggs are thickened throughout but still moist.

CHEESE AND VEGETABLE QUICHE

Though this recipe makes just one single-serving quiche, consider

doubling it and freezing the other quiche for a future quick heat-and-eat meal.

⅓ frozen piecrust

¼ cup shredded fat-reduced cheddar, Jarlsberg or other
    semi-hard cheese

1 large egg

1 egg white

⅛ teaspoon salt (*optional;* omit if cheese and vegetables have
    added salt)

Dash of ground white pepper

Dash of cayenne pepper

Dash of ground nutmeg

1 cup cooked vegetables (chopped spinach, bell peppers, broccoli,
    potatoes, string beans, mushrooms)

1 small scallion, thinly sliced

Makes 1 serving.

PER SERVING:

541 calories

26 g protein

30 g fat

41 g carbohydrate

788 mg sodium

251 mg cholesterol

Heat oven to 425° F. Fold ends of pastry toward center to make more round; roll into thin 8-inch circle. Fit into 5½-inch individual pie pan or baking dish; tuck edges under and crimp. Using fork, prick bottom and sides of pastry. Prebake crust, about 5 minutes, until firm and just beginning to color; remove from oven, cool slightly. Sprinkle cheese evenly over piecrust. In medium-size bowl, mix together remaining ingredients. Carefully pour egg mixture into pie pan. Bake, uncovered, 10 minutes at 425° F; reduce heat to 325° F. Bake until knife inserted near center comes out clean, about 20 additional minutes. Cool on wire rack, about 10 minutes. Delicious served with a crisp green salad.

See page 210 for Quiche Notes.

ESSENCE BRINGS YOU
GREAT COOKING

Quiche Notes

1. Partially or fully bake the crust before filling to prevent it from becoming soggy.
2. Brushing the bottom and sides of the baked crust with egg yolk or butter before filling also helps prevent sogginess.
3. Watch carefully for doneness; do not overbake. If center is still somewhat moist when removed from the oven, as it sits, it will continue to bake from retained heat.
4. Overbaking can cause a quiche to curdle and turn watery.
5. Let the quiche sit for several minutes to firm up before slicing.
6. Quiche is delicious warm and at room temperature.

GARDEN QUICHE

Use leftover vegetables to save money and a frozen deep-dish pie shell to save time.

Makes 6 servings.

PER SERVING:

476 calories
16 g protein
31 g fat
34 g carbohydrate
476 mg sodium
206 mg cholesterol

Pastry for 9-inch piecrust
½ tablespoon margarine
5 large eggs
1 13-ounce can evaporated milk
2 tablespoons minced onion
1 tablespoon chopped parsley or 1 teaspoon dried parsley, basil, oregano, or other herb
¼ teaspoon salt *(optional)*
½ teaspoon ground white or cayenne pepper
1 10-ounce package frozen mixed vegetables or 2 cups leftover vegetables, drained
½ cup shredded processed American cheese

Heat oven to 375° F for metal pan or 350° F for glass. Roll out dough; transfer to 9- or 10-inch quiche dish or pie pan. Ease dough into bottom and sides; tuck edges under and crimp. Using fork, prick bottom and sides. Partially bake until crust is just beginning to color, about 12 minutes. Let cool slightly. In large bowl, combine eggs, milk, onion, parsley, salt (if desired), and pepper; beat lightly until mixed. Stir in vegetables and cheese. Pour into prepared pie shell. Bake until puffed slightly and knife inserted near center comes out clean, about 35 to 45 minutes. Remove from oven; let stand about 10 minutes before cutting into wedges.

COLLARD GREEN QUICHE

Pastry for 9-inch piecrust
4 large eggs
1 cup half-and-half
½ teaspoon salt *(optional)*
½ teaspoon ground black or cayenne pepper
½ teaspoon dried oregano
½ cup chopped onion
¼ cup chopped green pepper
⅓ cup fresh or canned mushrooms, chopped
3 cups chopped cooked fresh or frozen collard greens, drained, squeezed dry
1¼ cups grated mild cheddar cheese
¾ cup shredded mozzarella cheese

Makes 6 servings.

PER SERVING:

521 calories
19 g protein
37 g fat
30 g carbohydrate
484 mg sodium
192 mg cholesterol

Heat oven to 375° F for metal pan or 350° F for glass. Roll out dough; transfer to 9- or 10-inch quiche dish or pie pan. Ease dough onto bottom and sides; tuck edges under and crimp. Using fork, prick bottom and sides. Partially bake until crust is just beginning to color, about 12 minutes. Let cool slightly. In large bowl, beat eggs and half-and-half lightly. Add salt (if desired), pepper, oregano, onion, green pepper, mushrooms, and collard greens; set aside. In small bowl, mix cheeses together. Sprinkle half of cheese mixture on piecrust. Pour egg mixture on top of cheese. Sprinkle remaining cheese on top. Bake until knife inserted halfway between center and outside edge comes out clean, about 45 to 60 minutes. Let sit 10 minutes before cutting into wedges.

NOTE

To save time, cook collard greens in 1 cup water in a pressure cooker for 15 minutes.

ESSENCE BRINGS YOU
GREAT COOKING

211

SPINACH-NUT QUICHE

Makes 6 servings.

PER SERVING:

518 calories
19 g protein
38 g fat
28 g carbohydrate
354 mg sodium
180 mg cholesterol

Pastry for 9-inch piecrust
1 pound fresh spinach, thoroughly rinsed, thick stems removed
4 large eggs
1 cup half-and-half
1 cup milk
½ teaspoon salt *(optional)*
¼ teaspoon ground nutmeg
⅛ teaspoon cayenne pepper
¼ pound Swiss cheese, shredded (about 1 cup)
½ cup pignoli nuts, lightly roasted
Optional garnishes: tomato slices, tomato rose, small spinach leaf

Heat oven to 375° F for metal pan or 350° F for glass. Roll out dough; transfer to 9- or 10-inch quiche dish or pie pan. Ease dough onto bottom and sides; tuck edges under and crimp. Using fork, prick bottom and sides. Partially bake until crust is just beginning to color, about 12 minutes. Let cool slightly. Meanwhile, place spinach in steamer basket and steam over boiling water until wilted, about 5 minutes. Remove spinach, pat dry with paper towels, then chop coarsely. In large bowl, using wire whisk, beat eggs, half-and-half, milk, salt (if desired), nutmeg, and pepper. Stir in cheese, spinach, and nuts. Place prepared baking dish on baking sheet; pour mixture into piecrust. Place baking sheet on rack in lower-middle section of oven. Bake 25 to 30 minutes, or until knife inserted near center comes out clean. Let stand 10 minutes before serving. Garnish with tomato rose and spinach leaf.

SPINACH-MUSHROOM QUICHE

Pastry for 9-inch piecrust

2 tablespoons butter

6 cups fresh mushrooms, cleaned, thinly sliced

4 cups chopped fresh spinach, stems removed

¾ cup thinly sliced scallions with tops

½ cup diced green pepper

1 16-ounce can stewed tomatoes

¼ cup water

2 cups grated Monterey Jack cheese

2 cups grated cheddar cheese

8 large eggs

½ pint half-and-half

1 tablespoon sesame seeds

1 teaspoon paprika

Makes 12 servings.

PER SERVING:

393 calories
17 g protein
29 g fat
17 g carbohydrate
493 mg sodium
194 mg cholesterol

Heat oven to 375° F for metal pan or 350° F for glass. Roll out dough; transfer to 9- or 10-inch quiche dish or pie pan. Ease dough into bottom and sides; tuck edges under and crimp. Using fork, prick bottom and sides. Partially bake until crust is just beginning to color, about 12 minutes. In 12-inch skillet, melt butter; add mushrooms, spinach, scallions, green pepper, tomatoes, and water. Cook uncovered over medium-low heat until liquid is absorbed, about 15 minutes. Place ½ cup of each cheese in food processor or blender. Add eggs and half-and-half. Cover and blend until smooth, about 1 minute. Spoon half of vegetable mixture onto crust; spread evenly. Pour half of egg mixture over vegetables. Sprinkle on half of remaining cheeses. Spoon on remaining vegetables, then egg mixture. Sprinkle on remaining cheeses. Sprinkle on sesame seeds and paprika. Bake 60 minutes or until knife inserted near center comes out clean.

ESSENCE BRINGS YOU
GREAT COOKING

CABBAGE AND CHEESE PIE

Makes 5 servings.

PER SERVING:

222 calories
12 g protein
12 g fat
16 g carbohydrate
237 mg sodium
78 mg cholesterol

1 pound potatoes (about 2 medium-size), peeled, quartered
Water
½ medium-size green cabbage, cored, shredded (about 3 cups)
½ small red or green bell pepper, seeded, cut into thin strips
1½ cups shredded sharp cheddar cheese
1 large egg, beaten
½ teaspoon salt *(optional)*
¼ teaspoon cayenne pepper
4 scallions, chopped

To large saucepan, add potatoes and water to cover; over high heat, bring to boil. Reduce heat to low; cover and simmer about 18 minutes, or until tender; drain well. Meanwhile, to large saucepan with 1 inch water, add cabbage and bell pepper; over high heat, bring to boil. Reduce heat; cover and simmer about 8 minutes, drain well. Heat oven to 350° F. Using fork or potato masher, mash potatoes coarsely in saucepan. Stir in 1 cup cheese, the egg, salt (if desired), cayenne, scallions, and drained cabbage; mix well. Into greased 9-inch pie pan or quiche dish, spread vegetable filling; sprinkle with remaining cheese. Bake 15 minutes, or until heated through and top is bubbly. Let pie sit about 8 minutes before cutting into wedges.

SWEET PEPPER AND CRABMEAT QUICHE

2 medium-size red bell peppers
2 tablespoons butter or margarine
1 small onion, sliced thin
1 9-inch unbaked piecrust
1 cup shredded Swiss cheese
1 cup coarsely flaked crabmeat
4 large eggs
1½ cups half-and-half
3 tablespoons combined chopped fresh parsley and dill
½ teaspoon salt *(optional)*
⅛ teaspoon cayenne pepper

Makes 12 small servings.

PER SERVING:

260 calories
10 g protein
19 g fat
13 g carbohydrate
206 mg sodium
109 mg cholesterol

Heat oven to 350° F. Remove seeds and membranes from peppers; cut lengthwise into ½-inch strips. In 10-inch skillet, over medium heat, melt butter. Add bell peppers and onion; sauté about 4 minutes, until onions are golden and peppers are tender. Remove from heat. Sprinkle pie pastry with cheese; using slotted spoon, place peppers and onions (reserve pan juices) on top of cheese. Sprinkle with crabmeat. In large bowl, combine pan juices from cooked peppers and onions, eggs, half-and-half, herbs, salt (if desired), and cayenne. Using fork or whisk, beat until well mixed. Place pie pan on baking sheet; pour egg mixture into pastry shell. Place quiche on baking sheet in oven. Bake about 45 minutes, until golden or when knife inserted in center comes out clean. Let stand 10 minutes before serving.

TOMATO-CHEESE QUICHE

Makes 6 servings.

PER SERVING:

434 calories
15 g protein
30 g fat
27 g carbohydrate
432 mg sodium
171 mg cholesterol

4 firm ripe tomatoes
½ teaspoon salt *(optional)*
1 cup grated sharp cheddar cheese
1 unbaked piecrust
4 large eggs
1½ cups milk
⅛ teaspoon cayenne pepper
2 teaspoons minced onion
2 tablespoons grated Parmesan cheese

Heat oven to 350° F. Peel and core tomatoes. Sprinkle with salt. Let stand for 15 minutes; drain. Sprinkle cheddar on bottom of piecrust. Cut tomatoes into wedges; place over cheese. Beat eggs with milk; add pepper and minced onions to mixture. Stir to blend. Pour mixture over filling. Sprinkle Parmesan cheese on top of pie. Bake until wooden pick inserted near center comes out clean, about 60 minutes.

LOBSTER DEVILED EGGS

Crabmeat, tuna, or other seafood can replace the lobster in this version of stuffed eggs.

6 hard-cooked large eggs
3 to 4 tablespoons mayonnaise
1 teaspoon Dijon mustard, or to taste
¼ cup finely chopped lobster
¼ teaspoon salt *(optional)*
¼ teaspoon cayenne or white pepper
Optional garnishes: chopped or slivered ripe olives, pimiento, capers, chopped scallions, watercress leaves

Shell eggs. So eggs will sit flat, cut slices from each end or opposite sides; chop trimmings and reserve. Remove yolks gently; place in small bowl with trimmings. Using fork, mash yolks. Add mayonnaise, mustard, lobster, salt (if desired), and pepper; stir until well mixed but not mushy. Using spoon or piping bag, fill hollow of egg white with yolk mixture. Add garnish of choice.

Makes 12 stuffed halves.

PER STUFFED HALF:

71 calories
4 g protein
6 g fat
.48 g carbohydrate
78 mg sodium
111 mg cholesterol

ESSENCE BRINGS YOU
GREAT COOKING

Cheese

Cheese is intense. This concentrated form of milk ranks with meat and fish in its quality of protein. Natural cheese is made by the centuries-old process of separating milk solids (curd) from the liquid (whey). Rennet (an enzyme that coagulates milk) and bacteria trigger the process. This same basic procedure produces hundreds of different tastes and textures of cheeses.

When cooking with cheese, generally use low heat and cook for a short time. Excessive heat and overcooking will make cheese stringy or rubbery and cause it to separate. When making a sauce, add cheese near the end of cooking and continue stirring over low heat just long enough to melt the cheese and blend it with other ingredients.

CHEESE SAUCE

Makes about 1½ cups sauce (12 2-tablespoon servings).

PER SERVING:

70 calories
4 g protein
5 g fat
2 g carbohydrate
53 mg sodium
16 mg cholesterol

1 tablespoon butter or margarine
1 tablespoon unbleached all-purpose flour
¼ teaspoon salt *(optional)*
Dash of ground pepper or paprika
½ cup milk
¾ cup shredded cheese (cheddar, Gruyère, Monterey Jack, or American-style cheese)

In medium-size saucepan over low heat, melt butter. Stir in flour, salt (if desired), and pepper until blended. Add milk; simmer, stirring constantly, until thick and smooth. Add cheese; stir just until melted.

CHEESY EGG AND MUSHROOM BAKE

2 tablespoons butter or margarine
1 large scallion, chopped
1½ cups sliced fresh mushrooms
2 tablespoons unbleached all-purpose flour
1½ cups milk
½ teaspoon salt (optional)
⅛ teaspoon cayenne pepper
6 hard-cooked large eggs, quartered lengthwise
½ cup shredded cheddar cheese

Makes 4 servings.

PER SERVING:

303 calories
17 g protein
22 g fat
10 g carbohydrate
286 mg sodium
362 mg cholesterol

Heat oven to 375° F. In medium-size saucepan over medium-high heat, heat butter. Add scallions and mushrooms; sauté about 5 minutes until tender. Blend in flour; cook, stirring constantly, about 1 minute. Slowly stir in milk, salt (if desired), and pepper. Bring to boil, stirring constantly. Lower heat; simmer 1 to 2 minutes. In 1½-quart baking dish arrange eggs; pour sauce over eggs. Sprinkle with cheese. Bake about 12 minutes; place under broiler several minutes until cheese is lightly browned. Serve with a crisp tossed salad.

ZUCCHINI AND CHEDDAR CHEESE SOUP

Makes 3 servings.

PER SERVING:

202 calories
4 g protein
12 g fat
12 g carbohydrate
832 mg sodium
11 mg cholesterol

1 tablespoon butter or margarine
1 cup sliced zucchini
1 small garlic clove, minced
¼ teaspoon crushed thyme leaves
1 11-ounce can condensed cheddar-cheese soup
1 soup can water
½ cup canned tomatoes drained, chopped

   Melt butter in saucepan. Add zucchini, garlic, and thyme; cook until tender, about 5 minutes. Add soup; gradually stir in water and tomatoes. Heat thoroughly, 5 to 8 minutes, stirring occasionally.

ESSENCE BRINGS YOU
GREAT COOKING

CHEESE-STUFFED ZUCCHINI

This tasty cheese spread can be used to stuff the vegetables of your choice, or as a dip. Mushroom caps, cherry tomatoes, bell peppers, and endive are good picks. This assortment makes an eye-catching and healthful party tray.

1 cup low-fat cottage cheese
1 3-ounce package calorie-reduced cream cheese, softened
¼ cup finely chopped chives
1 tablespoon chopped fresh dill
1 teaspoon celery seed
1 teaspoon lemon juice
3 medium-size zucchini
Optional garnishes: chives, dill

In medium-size bowl, blend cheeses. Stir in chives, dill, celery seed, and lemon juice; mix well. Cover and chill at least 1 hour. Rinse zucchini thoroughly; blot dry with paper towels. Slice crosswise into 1-inch-thick rounds. Using small spoon or melon baller, scoop out about half of pulp; fill hollows with herb-cheese spread; top with garnish.

Makes approximately 30 canapés.

PER CANAPÉ:

14 calories
1 g protein
.60 g fat
.94 g carbohydrate
47 mg sodium
2 mg cholesterol

ESSENCE BRINGS YOU
GREAT COOKING

CHEESE SOUP

Makes 4 servings.

PER SERVING:

253 calories
10 g protein
20 g fat
8 g carbohydrate
486 mg sodium
63 mg cholesterol

3 tablespoons butter or margarine
2 tablespoons finely chopped onion
1 tablespoon unbleached all-purpose flour
1 cup beef broth
2 cups milk
¾ cup grated cheddar cheese
1 teaspoon paprika

In 4-quart saucepan, melt butter; add onions. Cook over medium heat 3 minutes, stirring constantly. Stir in flour until smooth. Cook 2 additional minutes. Add beef broth. Slowly add milk, stirring constantly. Heat just to boiling; reduce heat. Add cheese and paprika, stirring until cheese melts and soup is very hot.

BAKED CHEESE-STUFFED MUSHROOMS

4 large mushrooms, thoroughly cleaned
1 tablespoon butter or margarine
¼ cup crumbled blue, shredded mozzarella, cheddar, or other cheese
¼ cup seasoned dry bread crumbs
⅛ teaspoon ground black pepper
1 tablespoon vegetable oil
Optional garnishes: watercress, parsley sprigs

Heat oven to 425° F. Remove stems from mushrooms; set caps aside and chop stems. In medium-size skillet over medium heat, melt butter. Sauté mushroom stems, stirring frequently, until tender and all liquid has evaporated, about 8 minutes. Remove skillet from heat; stir in cheese, bread crumbs, and pepper. Brush outside of mushroom caps with oil. Fill mushroom hollows with cheese mixture; arrange on baking sheet. Bake until cooked through, about 10 minutes. Arrange on bed of watercress or garnish with parsley.

Makes 2 servings.

PER SERVING:

242 calories
7 g protein
18 g fat
14 g carbohydrate
694 mg sodium
28 mg cholesterol

ESSENCE BRINGS YOU
GREAT COOKING

ALMOND-CARAMEL BRIE

Charles Stamps, a Brooklyn-based caterer, presents dishes that have an understated elegance. This round of baked brie is impressive yet easy to make.

Makes 20 appetizers.

PER APPETIZER:

171 calories
10 g protein
14 g fat
2 g carbohydrate
286 mg sodium
45 mg cholesterol

1 2-pound wheel brie cheese
¼ cup confectioners' sugar
½ cup sliced almonds
Optional garnishes: apple wedges, seedless grapes, other ripe fresh fruit

Heat broiler to 500° F. On broiler-proof dish, place brie. Sprinkle top with sugar. Arrange almonds around edge in pattern. Broil just until sugar caramelizes, about 1 to 2 minutes. Garnish with apple and grapes.

CREAMY BLUE CHEESE DIP

4 ounces blue cheese
8 ounces cream cheese
½ cup grated Parmesan cheese
½ cup sour cream
½ cup mayonnaise
Dash of hot pepper sauce

   In medium-size bowl, beat blue cheese and cream cheese until blended. Stir in remaining ingredients; mix well. Refrigerate several hours, or until well chilled.

Makes 2½ cups.

PER TABLESPOON:

60 calories
2 g protein
6 g fat
.43 g carbohydrate
92 mg sodium
12 mg cholesterol

ESSENCE BRINGS YOU
GREAT COOKING

NOODLE AND CHEESE CASSEROLE

Cottage cheese keeps calories low and adds creaminess.

Makes 4 servings.

PER SERVING:

410 calories
20 g protein
16 g fat
47g carbohydrate
378 mg sodium
142 mg cholesterol

1 8-ounce package medium-wide noodles
1¼ cups plain low-fat yogurt
1 cup small-curd cottage cheese
3 tablespoons butter or margarine, melted
½ teaspoon salt *(optional)*
⅛ teaspoon ground black or white pepper
1 large egg, beaten

Heat oven to 350° F. Cook noodles according to package directions until slightly underdone. Drain and rinse under cold water. In medium-size mixing bowl, combine noodles and other ingredients; stir well to blend. Pour into well-greased 1½-quart casserole. Bake for 30 minutes.

EASY THREE-CHEESE LASAGNA

A baked pasta dish, like this one from 16-year-old Xandi Wesley of Montclair, New Jersey, is always welcome at a potluck.

Water
12 lasagna noodles
1 tablespoon olive oil
4 large eggs
1 16-ounce carton (2 cups) ricotta cheese
10 ounces (2½ cups) shredded mozzarella cheese
½ cup freshly grated Parmesan cheese
¼ cup chopped fresh parsley
1 teaspoon ground black pepper
1 28-ounce jar chunky-style spaghetti sauce

Makes 8 to 12 servings.

PER EACH OF 10 SERVINGS:

407 calories
21 g protein
19 g fat
39 g carbohydrate
675 mg sodium
125 mg cholesterol

In large pot of boiling water, cook noodles with olive oil according to package directions until cooked through but firm. Heat oven to 350° F. Meanwhile, in medium-size bowl, beat eggs lightly; stir in ricotta, 2 cups mozzarella, ¼ cup Parmesan, half the parsley, and pepper until well mixed. Lightly grease 11-by-9-by-2-inch baking dish; spoon and spread about ¾ cup sauce over bottom of dish. Arrange (slightly overlapping) 4 noodles lengthwise in pan; spread noodles with about ½ the cheese mixture. Spread with about ¾ cup sauce. Repeat layering with 4 noodles, remaining cheese mixture, and ¾ cup sauce. Top with remaining noodles and sauce; sprinkle with mozzarella, Parmesan, and parsley. Bake, uncovered, until hot and bubbly, about 50 minutes. Let stand at least 10 minutes before slicing. Cut into 8, 10, or 12 squares; serve from dish.

SHRIMP EGG FOO YUNG

Makes 4 servings.

6 large eggs
1 green onion, sliced thin diagonally
¼ teaspoon salt *(optional)*
⅛ teaspoon cayenne pepper
2 cups bean sprouts, well drained
1 5-ounce can shrimp or ¾ cup cooked shrimp, chopped
2 tablespoons vegetable oil
Egg Foo Yung Sauce (see following recipe)
Rice, shredded lettuce, or chow mein noodles

In large bowl, beat eggs. Add onion, salt (if desired), pepper, bean sprouts, and shrimp; mix well. In large skillet over medium heat, heat oil. Into skillet, drop egg mixture by spoonfuls, forming patties. Cook until underside is golden, about 2 minutes. Turn with wide spatula; brown other side. Add additional oil to skillet to cook remaining mixture if necessary. Serve with Egg Foo Yung Sauce over rice, shredded lettuce, or chow mein noodles. Also delicious with green peas and spiced tea.

Egg Foo Yung Sauce

Makes 4 servings.

1 tablespoon cornstarch
2 teaspoons sugar
2 tablespoons soy sauce
1 cup chicken or vegetable broth

In small saucepan, combine cornstarch and sugar. Stir in soy sauce and broth until blended. Over medium heat, cook, stirring constantly until mixture thickens and boils.

ESSENCE BRINGS YOU
GREAT COOKING

EASY ITALIAN-STYLE MANICOTTI

This cheese-and-spinach-stuffed pasta dish is made quickly using prepared spaghetti sauce; select a quality brand for near-homemade flavor.

8 ounces uncooked manicotti
2 large eggs, beaten
2 tablespoons finely chopped onion
½ cup grated Parmesan cheese
2 cups creamed cottage cheese
1 10-ounce package frozen chopped spinach, thawed, squeezed to drain
1 cup shredded mozzarella cheese
½ teaspoon ground nutmeg
2 cups no-salt-added spaghetti sauce or Easy All-Purpose Tomato Sauce (see page 58)

Makes 7 servings.

PER SERVING:

350 calories
21 g protein
14 g fat
35 g carbohydrate
476 mg sodium
87 mg cholesterol

Cook manicotti according to package directions. Meanwhile, heat oven to 350° F. Grease 13-by-9-inch (3-quart) baking dish. In large bowl, combine eggs, onion, ¼ cup Parmesan, cottage cheese, spinach, mozzarella, and nutmeg; mix well. Drain manicotti; rinse with cold water. Fill each with cheese mixture; arrange side by side in baking dish. Pour spaghetti sauce over manicotti; sprinkle with remaining Parmesan. Bake until hot and bubbly, about 35 to 45 minutes.

ESSENCE BRINGS YOU
GREAT COOKING

HOT CRAB AND CHEESE SANDWICHES

Makes 4 servings.

PER SERVING:

471 calories
24 g protein
28 g fat
31 g carbohydrate
743 mg sodium
110 mg cholesterol

4 English muffins, split
2 tablespoons butter or margarine
8 ounces crabmeat, well drained, chopped
2 teaspoons lemon juice
¼ cup mayonnaise
2 tablespoons minced onion
1 teaspoon prepared horseradish
2 medium-size tomatoes, sliced
8 slices cheddar or Swiss cheese

Spread cut sides of English muffin halves with butter; toast lightly. In medium-size bowl, combine crabmeat, lemon juice, mayonnaise, onion, and horseradish; mix well. Spread crab mixture over muffin halves; broil just until heated through, about 1 to 2 minutes. Top each muffin half with tomato and cheese slices. Broil several minutes, until heated through and cheese melts. Serve with warm or chilled asparagus spears.

Yogurt

Though widely consumed in other parts of the world for centuries, yogurt is relatively new to the United States. At first thought of as a "health food," yogurt is now widely available in an array of flavors and with added ingredients that can detract from its wholesomeness. In the plain, stripped-down form, yogurt is ordinary milk to which a culture, *lactobacillus bulgaricus*, has been added. This friendly bacteria multiplies quickly to create yogurt. In our systems, this same bacteria goes to work on harmful bacteria in the intestinal tract, helping to keep the tract healthy. Yogurt, because of its easy digestibility, is a good source of calcium and other nutrients found in milk for those who are lactose-sensitive. Use yogurt as a healthful substitute for sour cream and high-fat dairy products when making baked goods, salad dressings, and casseroles.

RASPBERRY YOGURT SHAKE

Makes 4 servings.

PER SERVING:

130 calories
6 g protein
1 g fat
26 g carbohydrate
72 mg sodium
5 mg cholesterol

1 10-ounce package sweetened frozen raspberries
1 8-ounce container plain, vanilla, or fruit-flavored low-fat yogurt
1 cup skim milk, chilled

In blender or food processor, combine all ingredients; process until thick and creamy. For thicker shakes, place mixture in freezer until almost frozen; blend again before serving.

SUNRISE HEALTH SHAKE

You can consider this nutrient-rich drink a meal in a glass.

¾ cup orange juice or apricot nectar

¼ cup low- or nonfat yogurt

½ banana, sliced

1 tablespoon wheat germ (nontoasted is considered more nutritious)

1 tablespoon honey *(optional)*

In blender or food processor, combine all ingredients (for thicker shake, add 2 crushed ice cubes); blend at high speed until creamy, about 30 seconds.

Makes 1 serving.

PER SERVING:

199 calories

7 g protein

2 g fat

41 g carbohydrate

42 mg sodium

3 mg cholesterol

ESSENCE BRINGS YOU
GREAT COOKING

CHAPTER SIX

Seafood—Fish and Shellfish

Island Codfish and Peppers (page 263).

Recipes

OVEN-FRIED CATFISH I

OVEN-FRIED CATFISH II

CRUNCHY BAKED FISH FILLET

GOLDEN PANFRIED PORGIES

BAKED STUFFED RED SNAPPER

BAKED CATFISH ALMONDINE

CATFISH WITH SWEET PEPPERS

CATFISH FINGERS

STEAMED GINGER SALMON WITH WINTER VEGETABLES

POACHED SALMON WITH CUCUMBER SAUCE

POACHED RED SNAPPER WITH ORANGE-CHIVE SAUCE

TERIYAKI SALMON

BAKED COD

FILLET OF SOLE DIANE

FLOUNDER FLORENTINE

ESCOVITCH FISH

ISLAND CODFISH AND PEPPERS

SALT-FISH FRITTERS

CREOLE FISH AND RICE BAKE

GRILLED TILEFISH WITH BLACK BEAN SALSA

WINE-MARINATED FISH STEAKS

GRILLED HALIBUT STEAKS WITH CILANTRO-LIME BUTTER

Recipes

GRILLED STUFFED BROOK TROUT

CRISPY HERB-GRILLED SEA BASS

STIR-FRY GINGER SHRIMP AND VEGETABLES

SHRIMP CREOLE

SHRIMP JAMBALAYA

SEA SCALLOP STIR-FRY

SOFT-SHELL CRAB SANDWICHES WITH HERB MAYONNAISE

MARYLAND CRAB CAKES WITH SPICY MUSTARD SAUCE

FRENCH-FRIED OYSTERS WITH SWEET AND SOUR SAUCE

SEAFOOD GUMBO

CATFISH GUMBO

FISHERMAN'S STEW

CALDO DE PEIXE (FISH SOUP)

OYSTER BISQUE

ST. LUCIAN FISH BROTH

LOBSTER SALAD

QUICK SALMON HASH

TEMPTING TUNA PIE

PASTA-TUNA SALAD

TUNA PATÉ

ZESTY CRAB DIP

ONLY one-fourth of the earth's surface is covered by land. The rest is water! Oceans, seas, and networks of rivers, streams, lakes, bays, and bayous provide a vast diversity of finned and shelled creatures for our sustenance. America is blessed with a natural bounty. The coastal states—from New England, down along the sea islands and low country of South Carolina and Georgia, around the Florida peninsula, and up the West Coast to Alaska—all have deep-rooted seafood traditions. Fish is celebrated in song, at seafood festivals, and at mealtime throughout the day.

As word spreads inland about the natural goodness of seafood and how easy it is to prepare, more and more people are becoming hooked.

Fish and shellfish can add healthfulness and variety to your eating style. Fish provides one of the most concentrated sources of high-quality protein. One 3½-ounce serving supplies about half the total protein required daily by your body. A good source of vitamins and minerals as well, fish supplies thiamine, riboflavin, pantothenic acid, niacin, phosphorous, potassium, iron, iodine, zinc, and selium. If you are counting calories, an average 3½-ounce serving of fish has fewer than 100. Learning to cook seafood in ways that enhance its natural flavor and keep its calories low can net you great taste and good nutrition.

OMEGA-3 FATTY ACIDS

Scientists pondered why the Inuits of Alaska and other groups of people who eat large amounts of fish that are high in fat and cholesterol have low rates of heart disease. Research revealed the protective factor to be a class of polyunsaturated fats called omega-3 fatty acids. All fish contain omega-3 fatty acids, but those from the colder waters—salmon, bluefin tuna, mackerel, bluefish, herring, halibut, sardines, and sablefish—have the highest amounts.

These oils can not only lower blood cholesterol and triglyceride levels but also help prevent the sort of blood clots that are involved in heart attacks and strokes. To take advantage of the health benefits of omega-3, it is recommended that you eat fish at least twice a week, in servings of up to 5 ounces each.

> "Dreaming about fish means someone is pregnant."
>
> —Folk Saying

HOW TO BUY FISH

Start by shopping at a busy fish market or a supermarket with a top-notch fish department. A brisk business indicates a high turnover of stock—thus fresher fish. It is best to go with the flow—that is, ask the merchant which fish came in that day and choose from among them. If your heart was set on flounder but the snapper looks fresher—go with the snapper. The fresher the fish, the better tasting the dish. Fish in the same category of lean or fat are interchangeable in most recipes. See fish categories listed under "Cooking Guide for Fish."

FISH TERMINOLOGY

- WHOLE OR "IN THE ROUND" FISH—the fish as it comes from the water; nothing has been altered. Only for the experienced or those with the stomach to handle gutting.

- DRAWN FISH—a whole fish that's been gutted—viscera removed. The fins and scales are usually removed as well.

- DRESSED OR PAN DRESSED—gutted and scaled (if necessary); fins removed and head and tail possibly removed.

- FILLETS—sides of the fish removed from the backbone in lengthwise cuts. Boneless, may have skin on one side.

- STEAKS—cross-section slices of large dressed fish; may have a section of the backbone remaining.

GETTING FRESH

- WHOLE FISH—*Eyes* are bright, clear, and bulging slightly; *gills* are red or bright pink; *scales* are shiny, bright, and tightly attached to skin, or

HOW MUCH TO BUY

FOR EACH SERVING:
Whole, Drawn—¾ to 1 pound
Dressed—½ pound
Fillets or steaks—4 to 6 ounces
Mussels—½ pound (with shells)
Scallops—¼ to ⅓ pound
Shrimp—⅓ to ½ pound with shells
Brook trout—one
Lobster—1 ¼-pound each with shell

skin is shiny; *flesh* is firm and springs back when pressed; *smell* is mild with little or no fishy odor. Stale fish have cloudy, sunken eyes, faded gills, spongy flesh, and smell very fishy.

- FILLET OR STEAKS—Freshly cut edges without browning; firm texture; fresh, mild odor.
- FROZEN—Packages should be tightly sealed and solidly frozen. Contents that are discolored, are tinged with brown, or have ice crystals indicate the fish was thawed and refrozen.
- SCALLOPS— Pinkish, white, or pale yellow in color; firm to the touch, give off clear liquid.
- SHRIMP—Shrimp in the shell should be firm and glistening and have a fragrant saltwater smell.
- CLAMS, MUSSELS, AND LOBSTERS are sold live.

STORAGE

Unwrap the fish and dip it into a bowl of ice water with freshly squeezed lemon juice; blot dry. Loosely wrap in plastic wrap or waxed paper; store in coldest part of the refrigerator. To freeze, wrap tightly in freezer wrap or foil. Properly wrapped lean fish keeps for up to six months at 0° F or lower. Frozen fish with a high fat content will keep no longer than three months without loss of flavor and texture.

AN OUNCE OF PREVENTION

As a safeguard against spoilage when purchasing fresh fish, make the supermarket or fish store your last stop before going home. At the supermarket, pick up the fish last. In your kitchen, to prevent the spread of bacteria after handling raw fish, wash your hands and all items that came in contact with the fish before it was cooked—cutting board, countertop, knife, plate, etc.—with hot soapy water, then rinse thoroughly.

AN ORIGINAL FAST FOOD

Fish is easy to prepare and is ready in minutes. Unlike meat, fish is naturally tender. When cooked too long, fish becomes dry and falls apart. The 10-Minute Rule is an easy guide to perfectly cooked fish. Measure the fish at its thickest part, then allow 10 minutes cooking time per inch of thickness. This rule applies to poaching, baking, broiling, grilling, and panfrying. When done, the flesh will be opaque (translucent when raw) and will flake when you test it by inserting the tip of a blunt knife.

Shellfish cooks even quicker. Shrimp take just 3 to 5 minutes (depending on size) to boil or steam in the shell. When cooked, shrimp turn pink and opaque. Sea scallops are ready in just 3 to 4 minutes, and bay scallops (smaller) take just 30 to 60 seconds. Scallops are done when they turn milky white, opaque, and firm.

When grilling fish, avoid chemically processed charcoal briquettes and chemical starters. They can give cooked foods an unpleasant taste.

COOKING GUIDE FOR FISH

LEAN

The fish in this group have a fat content of 5 percent or less. They are mild in flavor with tender, flaky white or pale flesh that lends itself to varied cooking methods. Because lean fish tends to dry out during cooking, use methods that preserve or add moisture, such as sautéing or steaming. When baking, add broth or other liquid; smother in a blanket of vegetables; or wrap in parchment paper or foil.
- Cod, flounder, grouper, mahimahi, monkfish, ocean perch, pike, red snapper, skate, sea trout, sole, striped bass, tilefish, turbot, or yellowtail snapper.

MODERATELY FATTY

Highly versatile, this category of fish lends itself to almost all popular methods of cooking. Bake, broil, grill, panfry, or poach.
- Brook trout, buffalo fish, carp, porgy, rockfish, or swordfish.

FATTY

These rich-fleshed fish are high in certain polyunsaturated oils. Because their natural oils are self-basting, they respond well to broiling, grilling, and baking. These fish are also a good choice for sautéing, stir-frying, and poaching.
• Bluefish, lake trout, mackerel, pompano, salmon, or whitefish.

DRIED, SALTED, AND SMOKED FISH

Long a part of the human diet, fish is as perishable as it is important. After a short period of time without proper handling, fish begins to deteriorate. Aeons ago, it was discovered that when fish are removed from the water, and water is then removed from the fish, they will keep. Thus, sun drying became a popular method of preservation. This method worked well with some fish, others with higher fat content required salting in addition to drying. Smoking fish over wood was another technique used. Today, modern methods of freezing and canning make these old standards unnecessary, yet because of their unique taste, dried, salted, and smoked fish are still popular. This is especially true throughout the Caribbean, where salted codfish, also known as bacalao, is the national dish of many islands. Bacalao can be purchased in most West Indian and Latin American markets.

To remove the excess salt from salted fish:
• In a large bowl with enough water to cover, soak the fish 8 hours or overnight, changing the water at least twice.
• Drain soaking water and rinse well before cooking.
• Discard cooking water and, if desired, rinse fish after cooking.

THE FISH FRY

The fish fry is a hallowed tradition throughout the southern and midwestern United States. It was at an outdoor fish fry in Delhi, Louisiana,

"Fishes, fishes in the brook
Papa catch 'em with a hook,
Mama fry 'em in the pan.
Baby eat 'em like a man."
—*The Book of Negro Folklore*

"It seemed like a connected community. Everyone had a link to everyone else. Folks really cared about one another. There were chitlin' switches and giant fish fries."
—*Ray Charles*

commemorating the Esther Toombs School Reunion, that I experienced this unique social event and gastronomical treat at its fullest. On that occasion, catfish was king, but other local variations might feature amberjack, perch, small-mouth bass, mullet, grouper, walleye, or crabbies. The process is basically the same everywhere: Fish are coated lightly with cornmeal or batter, fried in oil, and served up golden and crispy on the outside and sweet and succulent on the inside. This seafood feast is usually rounded out with hush puppies, coleslaw, and fresh corn on the cob.

But what about all that grease if you're trying to cut back on fat? Using proper frying techniques can keep the fat in check.

When fish is fried at the correct temperature of 350° to 375° F, the heat causes protein in the fish's surface to form a seal that keeps it from absorbing excess oil and protects its natural flavor. Besides . . . you don't get to attend a real fish fry everyday. So when you do, enjoy it and adjust your fat and calorie intake for the rest of the meal and the day!

CATFISH

To the agriculture of the Old South, bolls of cotton were what farm-raised catfish have become to aquaculture of the New South. Mississippi leads the way in producing this breed that has been termed "the fish of the future." Through modern technology, this formerly shunned bottom-feeding scavenger has surfaced with a delicate, sweet taste that makes it a popular choice with everyday home cooks as well as trendy chefs.

LEFTOVERS

Leftover fish can save you time and money. Use leftovers to make or add to seafood salads, such as tuna, shrimp, or crabmeat salad. Use salads to make sandwiches, or to stuff tomatoes or avocados. Leftover fish can also be used to make delicious fish cakes or croquettes.

FISH FRY RULES:

1. Limit the amount of oil in the skillet or kettle to a level deep enough to rise only halfway up the fish's sides.

2. Maintain a constant oil temperature between 350° and 375° F. Use a fat or candy thermometer for accuracy.

3. As fish is cooking, use long-handled tongs or a frying strainer for turning. Transfer the fish to several layers of paper towels for draining excess surface fat. Drain both sides, changing the paper as needed.

BUYING CANNED FISH

First, consider the intended use. For salmon: If appearance is important, purchase the more expensive chinook and sockeye varieties, which break easily into chunks. For loaves and patties where appearance is not as important, use less expensive chum and pink varieties. For tuna: When appearance is important, buy fancy or solid-pack. Chunk-style tuna is good for casseroles and sandwich fillings. If cost is a key factor, the smaller the pieces, the lower the price. If calories are important, select water-packed instead of oil-packed. No-salt-added or reduced-salt varieties are available if sodium is a concern.

BUYING SHRIMP

Shrimp are the most popular shellfish in the United States. Most shrimp are frozen and thawed for sale; they are rarely sold fresh. Shrimp are usually sold headless as the head is more perishable. The designated size is based on the number of shrimp in a pound (names can differ).
• Colossal—under 10 per pound
• Jumbo—10 to 15 per pound
• Large—15 to 20 per pound
• Medium—24 to 30 per pound
• Small—40 to 60 per pound
• Tiny—up to 100 or more per pound

PEELING AND DEVEINING SHRIMP

Though it looks unappetizing and is occasionally gritty, the dark vein on a shrimp's back is safe to eat. For aesthetics' sake, remove it if you wish.
• Just above the tail, hold the shrimp firmly between your thumb and first two fingers.
• Using your other hand, pull off the body.
• Strip away the rest of the shell by peeling from the underside. It should come off in one or two sections.

SHELLFISH

When it comes to shellfish, crustaceans—crab, lobster, and shrimp—are the most prized. Luxuries from the sea, crustaceans make a meal more of a special occasion.

- The tail can be removed or left intact for appearance and added flavor.
- To devein, lay the shrimp on its side; using a sharp paring knife, make a shallow slit along the back from the head almost to the tail. This will expose the vein, which can be lifted out with the tip of the knife. Scrape away any residual dirt. Rinse with cold water.

GUMBO

Gumbo is our most famed seafood dish. Spawned in New Orleans, gumbo is literally a melting pot of cultures. The early French settlers of the area brought their love of fish stew—bouillabaisse. Lacking the fish they knew in France, they used the crabs and shrimp found in local waters. The following wave of Spanish settlers added tomatoes and rice to the pot. Choctaw Indians, the original inhabitants of the area, added a sprinkling of filé powder—ground sassafras leaves. Africans then stirred in their culinary know-how and their *kin-gumbo* (okra)—thus the name of the dish.

Gumbo is improvisational—no two cooks make it exactly the same way, nor does any cook make it the same way twice. There are seafood gumbos, chicken gumbos, ham and sausage gumbos, and even a special gumbo for Lent, *z' herbes*, made with seven different greens. The one common factor, however, is that real gumbo begins with a roux. Roux comes from the French term *roux beurre*, meaning brownish butter. A roux is a mixture of flour or cornstarch and butter or other fat cooked until it develops the desired color and intensity to flavor, thicken, and meld the dish in which it is used. In New Orleans, roux is equated with things mystical.

> ## TO REMOVE THE SMELL OF FISH FROM YOUR HOUSE
>
> Slice an orange in half and stud each half on the rind side with whole cloves. Boil the orange in water until the fish odor is gone.

ESSENCE BRINGS YOU GREAT COOKING

OVEN-FRIED CATFISH I

Makes 4 servings.

PER SERVING:

169 calories
24 g protein
5 g fat
5 g carbohydrate
437 mg sodium
66 mg cholesterol

4 4-ounce farm-raised catfish fillets or other lean, firm fish such as fresh
   cod, tile, sea bass, or whiting, skinned
½ cup cornflake crumbs
½ teaspoon paprika
½ teaspoon salt *(optional)*
¼ teaspoon ground black or white pepper
½ cup buttermilk, skim, or evaporated milk or 2 beaten egg whites
Vegetable cooking spray
Optional garnishes: lemon wedges, capers, dill sprigs

Heat oven to 350° F . Rinse fillets with cold water; blot dry with paper towels. In food-storage bag or shallow dish, combine crumbs, paprika, salt (if desired), and pepper; mix thoroughly. Into shallow dish, pour buttermilk or egg whites. Dip each fillet into liquid, coating well; dredge in crumb mixture until completely coated. In baking dish coated with cooking spray, arrange fillets in single layer. Bake, uncovered, until fish flakes when tested with knife, about 8 to 10 minutes. Using wide spatula, transfer to platter or plates; garnish as desired.

OVEN-FRIED CATFISH II

This method of baking fish yields the popular fried taste and look with less trouble and fewer calories.

1 pound catfish fillets (or cod, scrod, flounder, or other fish suitable for frying)
1 teaspoon salt *(optional)*
½ teaspoon freshly ground black pepper
2 tablespoons vegetable oil
½ cup cornflake crumbs
Optional garnish: watercress sprigs

Heat oven to 500° F . Rinse fillets with cold water, dry thoroughly with paper towels. Season with salt (if desired) and pepper. Place oil in shallow dish. Dip fillets in oil, then coat thoroughly with crumbs. On lightly greased baking pan, arrange fish. Bake 10 minutes or until cooked through, without turning. Transfer to platter or plates; garnish with watercress sprigs. Delicious served with tartar sauce, coleslaw, lemon wedges, and baked shoestring potatoes.

Makes 4 servings.

PER SERVING:

208 calories
21 g protein
12 fat
3 g carbohydrate
644 mg sodium
65 mg cholesterol

ESSENCE BRINGS YOU
GREAT COOKING

CRUNCHY BAKED FISH FILLET

Makes 4 servings.

PER SERVING:

326 calories
24 g protein
7 g fat
20 g carbohydrate
826 mg sodium
137 mg cholesterol

1 pound fish fillets
1 egg
¼ teaspoon salt *(optional)*
2 cups cornbread stuffing mix, finely crushed
¼ cup butter or margarine, melted

Heat oven to 350° F . Cut fillets into serving-size pieces. In shallow dish, beat egg with salt (if desired). Dip each fish fillet in egg mixture, then roll in stuffing mix, coating well. Place on foil-lined baking sheet; drizzle with butter. Bake 20 to 25 minutes until crispy, golden, and fish is cooked through. Delicious served with oven-baked potatoes cut in halves or quarters, green beans, and tartar sauce.

GOLDEN PANFRIED PORGIES

4 small porgies (about 3 pounds)
½ cup cornmeal
½ cup all-purpose or whole-wheat flour
1 teaspoon salt *(optional)*
¼ teaspoon black pepper or ⅛ teaspoon cayenne pepper
¼ cup evaporated milk
⅓ cup vegetable oil
2 tablespoons unsalted butter or margarine
Optional garnishes: lemon wedges, watercress

Makes 4 servings.

PER SERVING:

284 calories
24 g protein
8 g fat
26 g carbohydrate
612 mg sodium
58 mg cholesterol

Dress fish by scaling and removing entrails and fins; head and tail can be left intact, if desired. Rinse fish in cold running water to remove all blood and viscera; dry well. In large shallow dish, combine cornmeal, flour, salt (if desired), and pepper. Into another shallow dish or bowl, pour milk. Dip fish first into milk, then into cornmeal mixture, coating completely; place on waxed paper or wire rack for several minutes to set coating. In heavy 10-or 12-inch skillet—preferably cast-iron—heat oil and butter until sizzling but not smoking. Add fish, allowing enough space between them for even cooking. (Cook in two batches if necessary.) Fry fish about 5 minutes until golden on first side. Turn carefully and cook until golden on other side. An inch-thick fish will cook in about 10 minutes; avoid overcooking. Drain on paper towels. Arrange fish on serving platter; garnish with lemon wedges and watercress.

BAKED STUFFED RED SNAPPER

Makes 6 servings.

PER SERVING:

382 calories
41 g protein
16 g fat
19 g carbohydrate
802 mg sodium
78 mg cholesterol

5-to-6-pound whole red snapper, cleaned and dressed
1 teaspoon salt *(optional)*
¼ teaspoon ground black pepper
1 teaspoon celery seed
1 teaspoon chopped thyme leaves
2 medium garlic cloves, minced
Juice of 2 limes
Optional garnishes: lime wedges, watercress

STUFFING:
3 tablespoons butter or margarine
2 yellow onions, sliced
1 small green bell pepper, seeded, chopped
1 garlic clove, chopped
3 cups fresh bread crumbs
12 green olives, chopped
½ cup chopped peanuts

Rinse fish thoroughly in cold running water to remove all blood and viscera; blot dry with paper towels. In small bowl, combine ½ teaspoon salt (if desired), ⅛ teaspoon pepper, celery seed, thyme, garlic, and lime juice; mix well. Rub fish well with mixture, inside and out. Place in large rectangular baking dish. Cover and refrigerate 2 hours. To make stuffing, in medium saucepan, melt 2 tablespoons of butter over low heat; when hot add onions, bell pepper, and garlic. Sauté vegetables several minutes until tender. Remove saucepan from heat; stir in bread crumbs, olives, peanuts, and remaining salt (if desired), and pepper. Heat oven to 400° F . Remove fish from refrigerator; fill with stuffing mixture. Dot fish with remaining butter; bake 40 minutes or until fish flakes when tested with knife. Remove from oven; transfer to serving platter. Garnish with lime and watercress.

ESSENCE BRINGS YOU
GREAT COOKING

BAKED CATFISH
ALMONDINE

4 catfish fillets, about 4 ounces each (cod, tile, or other white-fleshed,
  lean fish can be used)
½ teaspoon crushed, dried oregano
½ teaspoon salt *(optional)*
¼ teaspoon ground black pepper
¼ cup lemon juice
1½ tablespoons margarine
¼ cup sliced almonds
Optional garnishes: lemon wedges, watercress

Rinse fish quickly under cold running water; blot dry with paper towels. Season with oregano, salt (if desired), and pepper. In shallow baking pan, pour lemon juice over fillets. Cover pan; marinate fillets in refrigerator 30 minutes. Preheat oven to 475° F . Dot fish with 1 tablespoon margarine. Bake 10 to 12 minutes per inch thickness of fish or until flesh is white, opaque, and flakes when tested with knife. Meanwhile, in small skillet, melt remaining margarine; add almonds and sauté until lightly browned, about 5 minutes. Spoon cooking juices from baking pan and almonds over each portion. Garnish with lemon wedges and watercress.

Makes 4 servings.

PER SERVING:

217 calories
22 g protein
13 g fat
3 g carbohydrate
389 mg sodium
65 mg cholesterol

ESSENCE BRINGS YOU
GREAT COOKING

CATFISH WITH SWEET PEPPERS

Makes 4 servings.

PER SERVING:

362 calories
25 g protein
22 g fat
15 g carbohydrate
462 mg sodium
144 mg cholesterol

3 small sweet bell peppers (use different colors for added visual appeal)

3 tablespoons butter or margarine

¼ cup milk

1 large egg

½ cup all-purpose, unbleached flour

½ teaspoon salt *(optional)*

¼ teaspoon cayenne pepper

4 farm-raised catfish fillets

2 tablespoons vegetable oil

2 tablespoons fresh lemon juice

1 teaspoon Worcestershire sauce

Optional garnish: chives

Remove seeds from peppers; cut into thin strips. In large skillet, heat 1 tablespoon butter; add peppers and sauté about 5 minutes or just until tender. Remove to platter and keep warm. In shallow bowl, combine milk and egg; beat lightly. In large shallow dish, combine flour, salt (if desired), and pepper. Dip fillets in milk mixture, then in flour mixture. In same skillet, heat 1 tablespoon butter and oil. Add fish and cook about 5 minutes on each side or until cooked through and golden. Meanwhile, in small saucepan, combine remaining butter, lemon juice, and Worcestershire sauce; heat through. Transfer fish to platter with peppers. Spoon fillets with sauce; garnish with chives.

ESSENCE BRINGS YOU
GREAT COOKING

CATFISH FINGERS

½ cup yellow cornmeal
1 teaspoon chili powder
½ teaspoon salt *(optional)*
½ teaspoon dried oregano
1 egg
⅓ cup milk
1 cup vegetable oil
4 catfish fillets, cut diagonally into 1½-inch-
  thick strips
Optional garnish: cilantro or parsley sprigs

In medium-size bowl, combine cornmeal, chili powder, salt (if desired), and oregano. In another bowl, lightly beat together egg and milk. Dip fish in egg mixture, then dredge in cornmeal mixture. In large deep skillet or electric fryer, heat oil to 350° F .* Fry fish, in several batches if necessary, until cooked through and golden, about 5 minutes. Transfer cooked pieces to absorbent paper to drain. Garnish with cilantro or parsley sprigs. Delicious served hot with herb mayonnaise, honey mustard sauce, salsa, or tartar sauce.

Makes 8 servings.

PER SERVING:

224 calories
12 g protein
16 g fat
8 g carbohydrate
225 mg sodium
65 mg cholesterol

*Cooking at correct temperature is important. Fish will be greasy and soggy if the fat is not hot enough. Too-high temperatures may break down the fat, rendering it unsuitable for cooking.

ESSENCE BRINGS YOU
GREAT COOKING

STEAMED GINGER SALMON WITH WINTER VEGETABLES

A bamboo steamer basket that fits into a wok is an ideal way to steam fish and vegetables; however, a foldout metal steamer that fits inside a large saucepan or Dutch oven also works well.

Makes 2 servings.

PER SERVING:

315 calories
27 g protein
17 g fat
15 g carbohydrate
101 mg sodium
71 mg cholesterol

Water
1 tablespoon mild olive oil
2 medium-size carrots, sliced or julienned
½ small green cabbage, cored, shredded
2 scallions, cut diagonally into several pieces
1 tablespoon fresh grated ginger or 1 teaspoon ground ginger
1 tablespoon minced parsley
1 small garlic clove, minced
2 4-ounce salmon fillets (catfish, grouper, fresh cod, monkfish, red
   snapper, and whitefish are also good choices)
1 tablespoon butter, melted *(optional)*

If using bamboo steamer basket, add 1 inch water to wok or large skillet; or if using foldout or other steamer, add water up to 1 inch beneath steamer. Over high heat, bring water to boil. Place length of cheesecloth over bottom of bamboo steamer, leaving ends hanging over edge (to make removing plate easier). Using half the oil, grease large heatproof plate (one that will fit in or on steaming utensil). On plate, arrange carrots, cabbage, and scallions; place plate on cheesecloth in bamboo steamer. Cover steamer and place in wok or skillet; reduce heat to medium. Steam vegetables about 5 minutes. Meanwhile, in small bowl, mix together ginger, parsley, and garlic. Using remaining oil, lightly grease fish fillets; spread with ginger mixture. Arrange fillets over vegetables in steamer. Cover and steam until fish is opaque all the way through, about 10 minutes. When salmon is cooked, using cheesecloth or pot holders, lift plate from basket. Drizzle fish and vegetables with small amount of olive oil or melted butter (if desired).

POACHED SALMON WITH CUCUMBER SAUCE

4 salmon fillets or steaks (about 4 to 6 ounces each)
Water
3 tablespoons wine vinegar
2 tablespoons salt *(optional)*
Optional garnishes: lettuce leaves, paprika, dill sprigs

In large skillet or poaching pan, arrange fillets. Add water to cover fish by ½ inch, wine vinegar, and salt (if desired). Cover pan; set over medium-high heat. When water begins to steam, reduce heat to low. Poach fish 8 to 10 minutes per inch of thickness. To serve warm, lift rack from poacher, draining liquid back into poacher, or use wide spatula to remove fish to warm platter. To serve cold, set uncovered skillet in 1 to 2 inches cold water; when poaching liquid has cooled, cover and refrigerate up to 24 hours. Arrange chilled salmon on platter lined with lettuce. Sprinkle with paprika; garnish with dill. Serve with cucumber sauce (see following recipe).

Makes 4 servings.

PER SERVING:

191 calories
24 g protein
10 g fat
.14 g carbohydrate
853 mg sodium
71 mg cholesterol

ESSENCE BRINGS YOU
GREAT COOKING

Cucumber Sauce

Makes about 1½ cups.

PER SERVING:

94 calories
2 g protein
7 g fat
6 g carbohydrate
159 mg sodium
24 mg cholesterol

1 large cucumber, peeled, halved
1 teaspoon vinegar
1 teaspoon sugar
¼ teaspoon salt *(optional)*
1 cup light sour cream
1 tablespoon chopped fresh dill or 1 teaspoon dried dill

Scoop out and discard seeds from cucumber. Into medium-size bowl, shred cucumber on large holes of manual grater. Toss with vinegar, sugar, and salt (if desired). Fold in sour cream and dill. Cover and refrigerate several hours before serving.

POACHED RED SNAPPER WITH ORANGE-CHIVE SAUCE

2 cups orange juice

2 cups dry white wine

1 cup water

1 bunch chives, coarsely chopped

1 stalk celery, sliced

½ teaspoon salt *(optional)*

1 teaspoon white peppercorns or ¼ teaspoon ground white pepper

1 3-pound whole red snapper, dressed (fillets or steak can also be used)

Optional garnishes: citrus-fruit slices (orange, lemon, and/or lime) and seaweed

Makes 10 servings.

PER SERVING:

61 calories

12 g protein

.8 g fat

0 g carbohydrate

27 mg sodium

22 mg cholesterol

In 17-inch fish poacher or covered roasting pan, combine juice, wine, water, half the chives, celery, salt (if desired), and peppercorns. Place over 2 burners; bring to boil. Meanwhile, rinse snapper under cold running water. Place fish on poaching rack or wrap it in cheesecloth for easy removal. Reduce heat almost to simmer. Lower fish into poaching liquid; top with remaining chives, citrus slices, and seaweed (if desired). Cover and begin timing. Poach fish approximately 10 minutes per inch at thickest point. Regulate heat so broth remains continuously just below simmer (boiling liquid can break up or toughen fish). Fish is cooked when it appears white and flakes when tested. Remove rack with fish; transfer snapper to serving platter. If desired, make sauce from poaching liquid by straining it through layers of cheesecloth, then rapidly boiling until reduced to desired thickness; ladle sauce over poached fish. Garnish with fruit and seaweed.

ESSENCE BRINGS YOU
GREAT COOKING

TERIYAKI SALMON

This flavorful recipe, prepared with no added fat, is from the popular Canyon Ranch Spa in Lenox, Massachusetts.

Makes 6 servings.

PER SERVING:

323 calories
27 g protein
10 g fat
31 g carbohydrate
776 mg sodium
71 mg cholesterol

1½ pounds salmon steaks
½ cup sodium-reduced soy sauce
2 tablespoons rice or cider vinegar
1 large garlic clove, minced
1 tablespoon ground ginger
1½ cups frozen unsweetened apple juice concentrate, thawed
   (undiluted)
½ cup finely chopped scallions
Optional garnish: whole scallions, trimmed

Divide salmon into six 4-ounce portions. In medium-size bowl or blender, combine soy sauce, vinegar, garlic, ginger, and apple juice; whip or process marinade until blended. Stir in chopped scallions; set aside. In 9-by-13-by-2-inch glass baking dish, arrange salmon; pour marinade over fish. Cover and marinate in refrigerator 10 to 24 hours, occasionally turning salmon to distribute marinade evenly. Heat oven to 350° F . Bake salmon in marinade 10 minutes per inch of thickness or until fish flakes when tested with knife. Transfer fish to platter or plates; spoon with marinade. Garnish with scallions. Delicious served with pasta.

BAKED COD

Vegetable cooking spray
4 fresh cod steaks (about 3 ounces each)
2 tablespoons lemon juice
2 teaspoons melted margarine
1 tablespoon chopped parsley
Paprika

Heat oven to 450° F . Spray large shallow baking pan with cooking spray. Arrange steaks in pan. In small mixing bowl, combine lemon juice, margarine, and parsley; mix well. Drizzle mixture over fish. Sprinkle with paprika. Bake 8 to 10 minutes or until fish flakes easily when tested. Using wide spatula, transfer fish to platter or plates.

Makes 4 servings.

PER SERVING:

89 calories
15 g protein
2 g fat
.75 g carbohydrate
68 mg sodium
37 mg cholesterol

ESSENCE BRINGS YOU
GREAT COOKING

FILLET OF SOLE DIANE

Makes 4 servings.

PER SERVING:

198 calories
21 g protein
10 g fat
4 g carbohydrate
404 mg sodium
76 mg cholesterol

3 tablespoons butter or margarine
2 cups sliced fresh mushrooms
¼ cup fresh chopped onion
¼ cup fresh chopped parsley
1 teaspoon dried chives
1 fish or chicken bouillon cube
⅛ teaspoon cayenne pepper
2 tablespoons white wine
1 tablespoon Worcestershire sauce
1 pound fresh fillet of sole

In large skillet, heat butter or margarine. Add mushrooms and onion; sauté until tender, about 10 minutes. Stirring constantly, add parsley, chives, bouillon cube, pepper, wine, and Worcestershire sauce; mix well. Arrange fish fillets on top of mushroom mixture. Cover and cook 8 to 10 minutes; remove from heat. With wide spatula, place fillets on large platter. Spoon mushroom mixture on top. Delicious served with steamed broccoli.

FLOUNDER FLORENTINE

3 tablespoons butter or margarine
1 10-ounce bag fresh spinach, rinsed
1 pound flounder fillets
¼ teaspoon salt *(optional)*
2 tablespoons lemon juice
Optional garnish: lemon wedges

Makes 4 servings.

PER SERVING:

184 calories
21 g protein
10 g fat
3 g carbohydrate
358 mg sodium
76 mg cholesterol

In large skillet over medium heat, melt 1 tablespoon butter. Add spinach; stir and cook several minutes until spinach wilts or reaches desired tenderness. Remove to serving platter and cover to keep warm. Sprinkle flounder with salt (if desired). In same skillet, melt 1 tablespoon butter. Add flounder; cook about 3 minutes on each side or until fish flakes when tested with tip of knife. Using wide spatula, carefully remove fish from skillet and place atop spinach. Add lemon juice and remaining butter to pan. Make thin sauce by stirring and scraping pan to loosen any particles. Spoon lemon-butter mixture over fish and spinach. Garnish with lemon wedges. Delicious with fresh sliced tomatoes.

ESCOVITCH FISH

This Jamaican-style marinated fish can be served warm as a main dish or chilled as an appetizer.

Makes 6 main-dish servings.

PER SERVING:

258 calories
24 g protein
13 g fat
10 g carbohydrate
259 mg sodium
42 mg cholesterol

2 tablespoons olive oil
1 medium-size onion, thinly sliced
2 medium-size carrots, scraped and thinly sliced or julienned
1 small bell pepper, seeded, cut into strips
⅓ cup vinegar, preferably cane or malt
2 tablespoons fresh lemon juice or lime juice
1 bay leaf
½ teaspoon salt *(optional)*
¼ teaspoon cayenne pepper
⅛ teaspoon ground mace
1½ pounds kingfish, snapper or other whitefish steaks or fillets, cut crosswise into halves
¼ cup all-purpose flour
½ teaspoon ground black pepper
½ cup vegetable oil
Optional garnishes: olives, chopped pimiento

In medium-size skillet, heat olive oil; sauté onion, carrots, and bell pepper until onion is transparent, about 5 minutes. Stir in vinegar, lemon juice, bay leaf, salt (if desired), pepper, and mace. Simmer 10 minutes. Meanwhile, briefly rinse fillets; blot dry with paper towels. Dredge in mixture of flour and black pepper. In large skillet, heat vegetable oil until hot. Add fish, fry until golden brown, about 4 minutes on each side. Remove fish to platter; spoon with hot vegetable marinade. Serve right away or marinate overnight. Garnish with olives or pimiento.

WINE-MARINATED FISH STEAKS

For a healthful cookout for a crowd, these flavor-steeped steaks are a good choice. The recipe can be reduced to feed fewer folks.

1 cup light olive oil
½ cup dry white wine or freshly squeezed lemon juice
½ teaspoon ground black or white pepper
¼ teaspoon salt *(optional)*
2 bay leaves
1 scallion, thinly sliced
2 garlic cloves, minced *(optional)*
1 tablespoon fresh chopped or 1 teaspoon dried thyme, parsley, dill, or herb of choice
4 pounds (1-inch-thick) fish steaks (firm fish such as codfish, halibut, or swordfish)

Makes 16 servings.

PER SERVING:

219 calories
20 g protein
14 g fat
.26 g carbohydrate
95 mg sodium
49 mg cholesterol

In large plastic food-storage bag, combine all ingredients except fish; rotate bag to mix marinade. Place bag in large bowl or pan; add fish to bag. Close bag; rotate fish several times to completely coat; marinate 1 hour in refrigerator. Meanwhile, prepare grill; arrange coals around edge of fire bed instead of center, to allow fish to cook by indirect heat. Arrange fish steaks on greased grid, or place steaks in greased grilling basket, then place on grid; reserve leftover marinade. Grill, brushing occasionally with marinade, until fish flakes when tested with tip of knife, about 5 minutes on each side.

ESSENCE BRINGS YOU
GREAT COOKING

GRILLED HALIBUT STEAKS WITH CILANTRO-LIME BUTTER

Makes 8 servings.

PER SERVING:

154 calories
24 g protein
6 g fat
.10 g carbohydrate
328 mg sodium
36 mg cholesterol

8 1-inch-thick halibut steaks (about 4 ounces each)
1 teaspoon salt *(optional)*
½ teaspoon ground white pepper
3 tablespoons vegetable oil
Cilantro-Lime Butter (see following recipe)
Optional garnish: cilantro

Prepare grill according to manufacturer's directions; place grid about 5 inches from coals. Light coals; then quickly rinse fish with cold running water; blot dry with paper towels. Sprinkle with salt (if desired) and pepper. Brush fish with about 2 tablespoons oil; brush grid with remaining oil. Grill fish about 4 minutes on each side, turning with wide spatula. Cook just until fish is opaque and flaky when tested with a fork; do not allow to dry out. For easier handling and to help keep steaks intact, place them in hinged wire basket for grilling. Transfer steaks to platter or serving plates. Top each with piece of Cilantro-Lime Butter; garnish with cilantro. Serve right away.

Cilantro-Lime Butter

½ cup (stick) butter or margarine, slightly softened
⅓ cup chopped cilantro
1 tablespoon freshly squeezed lime juice

In medium-size bowl, combine ingredients using rubber spatula or wooden spoon; mix well. On large sheet of waxed paper, shape butter mixture into log of desired thickness. Wrap log with waxed paper. Refrigerate until butter is firm, about 1 hour. To serve, slice crosswise into ½-inch-thick pieces or about equivalent of 1 tablespoon.

Makes ¾ cup, or 12 tablespoons.

PER TABLESPOON:

68 calories
.12 g protein
8 g fat
.24 g carbohydrate
78 mg sodium
20 mg cholesterol

ESSENCE BRINGS YOU
GREAT COOKING

GRILLED STUFFED
BROOK TROUT

Makes 4 servings.

PER SERVING:

380 calories
25 g protein
26 g fat
10 g carbohydrate
527 mg sodium
96 mg cholesterol

4 small whole dressed brook trout
½ teaspoon salt *(optional)*
1 tablespoon lemon juice
4 tablespoons butter or margarine
½ cup chopped onion
½ cup diced celery
½ cup chopped mushrooms
1¼ cups fresh bread crumbs or packaged stuffing mix
½ teaspoon poultry seasoning
¼ teaspoon ground black pepper
2 tablespoons vegetable oil
Optional garnishes: bell peppers, celery leaves, mushrooms

Prepare grill for cooking. Rinse trout with cold running water; blot dry. Season inside and out with salt (if desired) and lemon juice. While coals warm, heat butter in large skillet; add onion, celery, and mushrooms. Sauté until soft, about 5 minutes. Remove from heat; stir in bread crumbs and seasonings. Lightly brush fish and grilling basket with oil; add fish and garnishes; close and secure basket. If grilling basket is unavailable, wrap fish in foil, pierce in several places to allow smoke to penetrate. When coals are covered with gray ash, grill fish about 8 to 9 minutes per inch of thickness, turning once. Garnish with bell peppers.

ESSENCE BRINGS YOU
GREAT COOKING

CRISPY HERB-GRILLED SEA BASS

2 2½-pound sea bass, dressed, heads and tails intact
1 teaspoon salt *(optional)*
½ teaspoon coarsely ground black pepper
½ cup chopped mixed fresh herbs (thyme, parsley, and chives are
   good choices)
⅓ cup corn oil
1½ cups dry, plain bread crumbs
½ teaspoon paprika
Optional garnishes: sprigs of fresh herbs, lemon slices

Makes 10 servings.

PER SERVING:

233 calories
23 g protein
10 g fat
11 g carbohydrate
402 mg sodium
47 mg cholesterol

Rinse fish thoroughly in cold running water to remove all blood and viscera; blot dry with paper towels. Rub inside of fish with salt (if desired), pepper, and half of chopped herbs. Rub outside of fish with 2 tablespoons oil; press bread crumbs and remaining herbs evenly onto fish to coat. If needed, moisten fish with small amount of remaining oil to help bread crumbs stick; sprinkle with paprika. Place fish in oiled grill basket, or place directly on grill 5 inches over medium direct heat. Drizzle each side of fish with oil during cooking. Cook fish about 10 minutes on each side, or until it flakes easily when tested with knife and crumbs are crisp and golden. Garnish with herb sprigs and lemon slices.

Oven method: Heat oven to 350° F . Place prepared fish on greased baking sheet. Drizzle each side of fish with oil. Cook fish about 15 minutes, or until it flakes easily when tested with fork and crumbs are crisp and golden.

ESSENCE BRINGS YOU
GREAT COOKING

STIR-FRY GINGER SHRIMP AND VEGETABLES

For more pronounced flavor, marinate shrimp for about 30 minutes. Stir-frying is quick cooking, so make sure you have all the ingredients ready before you begin.

Makes 1 serving.

PER SERVING:

373 calories
30 g protein
16 g fat
29 g carbohydrate
776 mg sodium
175 mg cholesterol

¼ pound (about 7 to 8 medium-size) raw shrimp, shelled, deveined
1 tablespoon finely minced fresh gingerroot or 1 teaspoon ground ginger
1 garlic clove, finely minced
1 tablespoon peanut, vegetable, or sesame oil
1 carrot, cut into julienne strips
½ small red bell pepper, seeded, cut into julienne strips
2 cups coarsely chopped bok choy, well rinsed
½ cup bean sprouts, well rinsed, drained
¼ cup low-sodium chicken or vegetable broth, or water
1 teaspoon cornstarch
1 tablespoon sodium-reduced soy sauce
1 tablespoon water

In medium-size bowl, combine shrimp, ginger, and garlic; set aside. In wok or large skillet over medium-high heat, heat ½ oil until it ripples. Add shrimp mixture; cook, quickly stirring and tossing, until shrimp turn pink and opaque, about 3 to 4 minutes. Remove from wok; cover to keep warm. Add remaining oil to wok; when hot, add carrots. Stir-fry about 1 minute. Add bell pepper; stir-fry 1 minute. Add bok choy; stir-fry 1 minute. Stir in sprouts and broth; cover and steam 1 minute. Meanwhile, in small bowl, mix cornstarch with soy sauce and water; stir into vegetable mixture until sauce thickens. Add shrimp; cook just until heated through. Delicious served over rice, or cellophane, chow mein, or Japanese noodles.

SHRIMP CREOLE

Serve over rice or in the center of a Rice Ring for parties. See directions for making Rice Ring on page 118.

2 tablespoons olive oil
1 large onion, chopped
½ cup thinly sliced celery
1 garlic clove, minced or pressed
1½ cups water
1 can (6 ounces) tomato paste
1 bay leaf
1 teaspoon salt *(optional)*
1 teaspoon sugar
½ teaspoon cayenne pepper
1½ pounds large shrimp, peeled, deveined
1 tablespoon lemon juice
Optional garnishes: chopped parsley, lemon slices

Makes 6 to 8 servings.

PER EACH OF 6
SERVINGS:

205 calories
25 g protein
7 g fat
11 g carbohydrate
552 mg sodium
173 mg cholesterol

In large skillet, heat oil; add onion, celery and garlic. Sauté until tender, about 5 minutes. Stir in water, tomato paste, bay leaf, salt (if desired), sugar, and pepper. Simmer uncovered, about 10 minutes. Stir in shrimp and lemon juice; continue to simmer until shrimp are pink and opaque, about 4 minutes. Sprinkle with parsley; garnish with lemon slices.

ESSENCE BRINGS YOU
GREAT COOKING

SHRIMP JAMBALAYA

Makes 6 servings.

PER SERVING:

541 calories
45 g protein
18 g fat
48 g carbohydrate
100 mg sodium
265 mg cholesterol

1 tablespoon vegetable oil
1 tablespoon butter or margarine
½ pound smoked sausage, sliced
1 large onion, chopped
1 large green bell pepper, seeded, chopped
2 garlic cloves, finely chopped
2 large tomatoes, finely chopped, juice reserved, or 1 16-ounce
   can tomatoes
2 bay leaves
1 tablespoon chopped fresh thyme or 1 teaspoon dried thyme
1 tablespoon chopped fresh basil or 1 teaspoon dried basil
⅛ teaspoon salt *(optional)*
½ teaspoon chili powder
⅛ teaspoon cayenne pepper
⅛ teaspoon allspice
2½ cups chicken broth or water
1½ cups long grain or brown rice
2 pounds shrimp, peeled, deveined
3 tablespoons chopped parsley
Optional garnishes: cooked shrimp, fresh basil leaves

In 5-quart saucepot or Dutch oven, heat oil and butter. Sauté sausage until edges are browned. Add onion, green pepper, and garlic; sauté about 5 minutes until tender. Stir in tomatoes (with juice), bay leaves, thyme, basil, salt (if desired), chili powder, pepper, and allspice; mix well. Stir in broth; bring mixture to boil. Stir in rice and fresh shrimp; return to boil. Reduce heat; cover and simmer about 25 minutes or until rice is tender. Stir in parsley during last 5 minutes of cooking time. Remove bay leaves. Garnish with cooked shrimp and basil leaves, if desired.

SEA SCALLOP STIR-FRY

The Oriental art of quick stir-frying helps maintain the nutrients in these low-cal ingredients.

1 tablespoon cornstarch
2 tablespoons sodium-reduced soy sauce
¼ cup chicken broth
2 tablespoons lemon juice or dry sherry
2 tablespoons safflower or vegetable oil
1 pound sea scallops
2 scallions, cut into thick slices
1 small onion, chopped
1 large garlic clove, minced
1 tablespoon gingerroot, minced
2 medium-size carrots, scraped, cut into ½-inch-thick sticks
2 cups fresh snow peas, ends trimmed
1 8-ounce can pineapple chunks, drained

Makes 4 servings.

PER SERVING:

252 calories
23 g protein
8 g fat
22 g carbohydrate
512 mg sodium
37 mg cholesterol

In small bowl, dissolve cornstarch in soy sauce; blend in chicken stock and lemon juice. Set aside. In wok or large skillet, heat oil; add scallops, scallions, onion, garlic, and ginger. Stir-fry, lifting and tossing about 3 minutes until scallops are opaque. Remove from wok. Stir-fry carrots and snow peas about 2 minutes; add pineapple and stir-fry 1 additional minute. Add scallops and cornstarch mixture; cook and stir until thickened, about 1 minute. Delicious served with rice.

SOFT-SHELL CRAB SANDWICHES WITH HERB MAYONNAISE

Fresh soft-shell crabs, a seasonal delicacy, are available from about Memorial Day to Labor Day.

Makes 2 servings.

PER SERVING:

691 calories
38 g protein
41 g fat
43 g carbohydrate
1,330 mg sodium
169 mg cholesterol

¼ cup mayonnaise

2 tablespoons finely minced mixed herbs such as dill, parsley, and watercress

½ teaspoon finely grated lemon peel

⅛ teaspoon hot pepper sauce

4 small soft-shell crabs, cleaned

¼ cup unbleached all-purpose flour

¼ teaspoon salt (*optional*)

¼ teaspoon freshly ground black pepper

3 tablespoons butter or margarine

2 tablespoons peanut oil

2 to 4 lettuce leaves

2 round sandwich or hard rolls, halved

In small bowl or mini food processor, blend mayonnaise, herbs, lemon peel, and hot-pepper sauce; chill until time to serve. Quickly rinse crabs under cold running water; blot dry with paper towels. Using fork, pierce crabs in several places to allow steam to escape during cooking. In plastic or paper food-storage bag, combine flour, salt (if desired), and pepper; shake to mix. Add crabs; shake to coat well. Remove and shake off excess flour. In large skillet over medium-high heat, heat butter and oil until foam subsides. Sauté crabs, turning with tongs, about 3 to 4 minutes on each side or until cooked through and golden brown. Place lettuce leaves on bottom half of rolls; top with crabs. Spoon herb mayonnaise onto crabs or cut side of rolls; cover with top of rolls.

MARYLAND CRAB CAKES WITH SPICY MUSTARD SAUCE

1 egg white
1 tablespoon fresh lemon juice
1 teaspoon dry mustard
¼ teaspoon salt *(optional)*
¼ teaspoon hot pepper sauce, or to taste
⅛ teaspoon cayenne pepper
½ cup mayonnaise
½ cup finely crushed cracker crumbs or dry bread crumbs
1 scallion, sliced
¼ cup finely chopped parsley
½ teaspoon dried thyme
1 pound fresh cooked lump crabmeat, picked through to remove
  all cartilage
2 tablespoons vegetable oil
2 tablespoons butter or margarine
Optional garnish: lemon slices

Makes 8 crab cakes.

PER CRAB CAKE:

291 calories
13 g protein
25 g fat
5 g carbohydrate
546 mg sodium
77 mg cholesterol

   In large mixing bowl, lightly beat egg white. Stir in lemon juice, dry mustard, salt (if desired), hot-pepper sauce, and cayenne pepper; mix well. Using whisk, blend in mayonnaise. Add half of crumbs, scallion, parsley, and thyme; mix well. Using fork, gently stir in crabmeat, being careful not to break into smaller pieces. Using hands, shape crab mixture into eight 2½-inch-thick balls; flatten slightly. On large piece of waxed paper or in large shallow dish, sprinkle remaining crumbs. Place crab cakes, one at a time, into crumbs to coat; turn to coat other side. Gently pat to help crumbs stick. On baking sheet lined with waxed paper, arrange coated cakes. Refrigerate crab cakes at least 1 hour or up to 12 hours. In large (12-inch) skillet, heat oil and margarine over medium heat until hot, not allowing margarine to brown. In two batches, transfer crab cakes to skillet using wide spatula and cook until nicely browned, about 3 minutes on each side. Garnish with lemon slices. Serve with Spicy Mustard Sauce (see following recipe).

Spicy Mustard Sauce

Makes ½ cup;
8 tablespoons.

¼ cup mayonnaise
3 tablespoons Dijon mustard
1 tablespoon milk
¼ teaspoon hot-pepper sauce

In small mixing bowl, combine all ingredients. Mix with whisk or spoon until blended. Cover and refrigerate until serving time.

FRENCH-FRIED OYSTERS WITH SWEET AND SOUR SAUCE

36 large oysters, shucked
1¼ cups finely ground yellow cornmeal
1 teaspoon salt *(optional)*
½ teaspoon ground black pepper
¾ cup milk or cream
1 cup vegetable oil
Sweet and Sour Sauce (see following recipe)
2 medium-size lemons, cut into wedges
Optional garnishes: paprika, flat-leaf parsley sprigs

Makes 6 servings.

PER SERVING:

314 calories
11 g protein
17 g fat
28 g carbohydrate
461 mg sodium
47 mg cholesterol

Drain shucked oysters; blot dry with paper towels. In medium-size bowl, combine cornmeal, salt (if desired), and pepper; mix well. In shallow bowl, combine oysters and milk. On large sheet of waxed paper, sprinkle half of cornmeal mixture; place oysters on top of meal. Sprinkle oysters with remaining meal; turn in meal to completely coat. In large skillet, over medium-high heat, heat oil. Add about 12 to 18 oysters, being careful not to crowd. Panfry, turning once, until golden brown, about 5 minutes. As cooked, using slotted spoon, transfer oysters to absorbent paper to drain. Repeat until all oysters are cooked. Transfer to serving platter or plates. Serve with Sweet and Sour Sauce and lemon wedges; sprinkle with paprika and garnish with parsley.

Sweet and Sour Sauce

Makes 6 servings.

PER SERVING:

79 calories
.09 g protein
0 g fat
21 g carbohydrate
115 mg sodium
0 mg cholesterol

½ cup packed light brown sugar
½ cup water
⅓ cup red-wine vinegar
2 tablespoons catsup
1 teaspoon soy sauce
1 garlic clove, crushed
½ tablespoon cornstarch
2 tablespoons cold water

In small saucepan, combine sugar, water, vinegar, catsup, soy sauce, and garlic. Over medium-high heat, stirring occasionally, bring sauce to boil. In small bowl, blend cornstarch and 2 tablespoons water; stir into sauce. Cook and stir until thickened, about 10 seconds.

ESSENCE BRINGS YOU
GREAT COOKING

SEAFOOD GUMBO

2 tablespoons cooking oil
2 tablespoons all-purpose flour
2 garlic cloves, chopped
1½ cups chopped onions
1 cup diced celery
1 medium-size green pepper, seeded, diced
1 2-pound can whole Italian tomatoes with juice, chopped
4 cups water
2 pounds small raw shrimp, shelled and deveined
2 6½-ounce cans crabmeat
½ pint fresh oysters
2 teaspoons hot-pepper sauce
1 tablespoon Worcestershire sauce
½ cup minced fresh parsley
½ cup sliced green onion
2 teaspoons gumbo filé
1 teaspoons salt (*optional*)
1 teaspoon ground black pepper
8 cups hot cooked rice

Makes 12 servings.

PER SERVING:

361 calories
27 g protein
5 g fat
49 g carbohydrate
688 mg sodium
157 mg cholesterol

In Dutch oven, over low heat, heat oil. Stir in flour until blended. Make roux by cooking slowly and stirring until a rich brown. Add chopped garlic, onion, celery, green pepper, and tomatoes with juice. Cook 10 minutes, stirring occasionally. Add water, shrimp, crabmeat, oysters with juice, hot sauce, and Worcestershire sauce. Cover and cook 5 minutes; remove from heat. Add parsley, green onion, filé, salt (if desired), and pepper. Stir to blend. Serve hot over cooked rice.

ESSENCE BRINGS YOU
GREAT COOKING

CATFISH GUMBO

Makes 6 servings.

PER SERVING:

283 calories
21 g protein
10 g fat
27 g carbohydrate
226 mg sodium
54 mg cholesterol

3 tablespoons margarine
3 tablespoons all-purpose flour
2 medium-size onions, chopped
1 medium-size green bell pepper, seeded, chopped
2 garlic cloves, minced
1 pound fresh okra, tops removed, sliced
¼ cup chopped parsley
1 bay leaf
1 teaspoon dried thyme
½ teaspoon ground black pepper
¼ teaspoon cayenne pepper
3 tomatoes seeded, chopped, or 1 28-ounce can whole tomatoes, chopped
1 8-ounce bottle clam juice
1 to 2 cups water
1¼ pounds catfish fillets, cut into 1½- to 2-inch pieces
1 cup warm cooked rice

In heavy Dutch oven over low heat, melt margarine; stir in flour until blended. Make roux by cooking slowly and stirring until a rich brown. Add onions, bell pepper, and garlic; cook until vegetables are limp, about 5 minutes. Add okra; cook until it loses stringy consistency, about 3 minutes. Stir in parsley, bay leaf, thyme, and peppers; simmer about 5 minutes. Stir in tomatoes, clam juice, and water; simmer about 40 minutes. Add fish; simmer 10 additional minutes. Add spoonful of rice to each bowl; ladle gumbo over rice. Delicious served with French bread.

FISHERMAN'S STEW

2 tablespoons olive oil

2 garlic cloves, minced

1 large onion, finely chopped

2 8-ounce bottles clam juice

4 cups puréed tomatoes

1 dozen raw mussels (fresh mussel shells should be tightly closed or close when tapped)

2 small zucchini, cut into ½-inch slices

2 ears corn, cut into 2-inch pieces

½ teaspoon salt (*optional*)

¼ teaspoon ground black pepper

¼ teaspoon hot-pepper sauce

1 tablespoon chopped fresh chives or 1 teaspoon dried chives

1 tablespoon chopped fresh basil or 1 teaspoon dried basil

1 large bay leaf

1 pound fish fillets, cut into 1-inch cubes

½ pound sea scallops, halved

½ pound medium shrimp, shelled (tails on), deveined

2 tablespoons chopped fresh parsley

Makes 8 servings.

PER SERVING:

228 calories
25 g protein
5 g fat
23 g carbohydrate
442 mg sodium
83 mg cholesterol

In 6-quart stockpot or Dutch oven, heat oil; add garlic and onion. Sauté until tender, about 5 minutes. Stir in clam juice and tomatoes; gently simmer 15 minutes. Meanwhile, scrub mussels; scrape off any loose barnacles; cut off beards. In large saucepan, with about 1 inch water, steam mussels until they open, about 4 to 5 minutes; discard any unopened shells. Set aside. To stockpot, add zucchini, corn, salt (if desired), pepper, pepper sauce, and herbs, except parsley; simmer about 8 minutes. Add fish, scallops, shrimp, and parsley; simmer until all fish is cooked, about 3 to 5 additional minutes. Discard bay leaf. Add mussels. Transfer to tureen or individual bowls.

ESSENCE BRINGS YOU
GREAT COOKING

CALDO DE PEIXE
(Fish Soup)

This chunky main-course soup is from Cape Verde.

Makes 8 servings.

PER SERVING:

290 calories
22 g protein
9 g fat
32 g carbohydrate
356 mg sodium
53 mg cholesterol

1¾ teaspoons salt (*optional*)
1½ cups water
2 to 3 green (unripe) bananas, sliced
1 yellow onion, sliced
4 tablespoons olive oil
2 large garlic cloves, minced
1 bay leaf
1 chili pepper, crushed, or ½ teaspoon cayenne pepper
1 bunch parsley, finely chopped
2 large tomatoes, chopped
4 cups hot water
¼ cup tapioca flour or quick-cooking tapioca
¼ cup dry bread crumbs
½ head small green cabbage, chopped
4 to 6 sweet potatoes, peeled, cut into 1-inch cubes
2 pounds fish fillets, cut into large pieces

In medium-size bowl, dissolve 1 teaspoon salt (if desired) in water; add bananas and soak for 10 to 15 minutes to draw out tart taste. Meanwhile, in large heavy saucepan or Dutch oven, brown onion in oil over medium heat. Add garlic, bay leaf, pepper, parsley, and tomatoes; sauté for several minutes, stirring frequently. Stir in hot water to make broth. In small bowl, combine tapioca and some of hot broth; stir to form thin smooth paste. Bring broth almost to boil; add paste and bread crumbs. Stir vigorously to blend; reduce heat to simmer. Drain bananas well; add to pot along with cabbage, potatoes, and remaining salt. Top vegetable mixture with fish; add additional hot water to cover. Simmer 20 to 30 minutes or until vegetables and fish are cooked through.

OYSTER BISQUE

1 large onion, chopped
2 celery stalks, chopped
2 medium-size potatoes, peeled, chopped into small pieces
3 tablespoons butter
2 cups milk
1 cup half and half
2 8-ounce bottles clam juice
1 fresh bay leaf, minced
1 teaspoon salt *(optional)*
½ teaspoon ground mace
¼ teaspoon white pepper
¼ teaspoon hot-pepper sauce
2 cups (1 pint) fresh oysters with liquor
Optional garnishes: fresh bay leaves, chives

Makes 10 first-course servings.

PER SERVING:

161 calories
7 g protein
9 g fat
13 g carbohydrate
450 mg sodium
52 mg cholesterol

In heavy-bottomed 2-quart saucepan, combine onion, celery, potatoes, and butter. Cook over low heat until vegetables are tender but not brown, about 10 minutes. Stirring constantly to blend, add milk, half and half, and clam juice. Add bay leaf, salt (if desired), mace, white pepper, and hot-pepper sauce. Over low heat, simmer mixture about 10 minutes. Do not let mixture come to boil (excessive heat will cause it to curdle). In batches, purée mixture in blender or food processor, or press mixture through sieve. In small saucepan, cook oysters in their liquor over medium heat until edges curl, about 4 minutes. Pour oysters into purée. Ladle bisque into warm tureen; garnish with bay leaves or chives.

ST. LUCIAN FISH BROTH

Snapper and vegetables are simply and deliciously combined in a
St. Lucian classic. This version by Marcel Inglis, sous chef at Couples
resort in St. Lucia, captured first prize at the island's 1990 hotel and
restaurant culinary competition.

Makes 4 servings.

PER SERVING:

264 calories
28 g protein
14 g fat
7 g carbohydrate
868 mg sodium
74 mg cholesterol

¼ cup butter or margarine
1 medium-size onion, chopped
1 small carrot, thinly sliced or cut into thin strips
1 rib celery, chopped
1 small bell pepper, seeded, chopped, or cut into thin strips
2 garlic cloves, minced
2 pints fish stock, bouillon, or clam juice diluted with water
4 red-snapper fillets (about 1 pound)
1 teaspoon salt *(optional)*; omit if fish stock is salted
½ teaspoon ground black pepper

In kettle or Dutch oven, heat butter. Add vegetables and garlic; sauté until onion is translucent, about 10 minutes. Add fish stock; bring to boil. Reduce heat; simmer 5 minutes. Add snapper; return broth to boil. Reduce heat; simmer 10 additional minutes. Season with salt (if desired) and pepper.

LOBSTER SALAD

Island seafood salads are colorful and lively—much like St. Croix. Local restauranteur Sarah Harvey's versatile recipe is superb with lobster, but the same amount of almost any other seafood can be substituted, with tasty results.

3 tablespoons mayonnaise
1 tablespoon bottled creamy French dressing
½ teaspoon sugar *(optional)*
¼ teaspoon dried crushed oregano
⅛ teaspoon ground black pepper
⅛ teaspoon garlic powder
1 pound cooked lobster meat or other seafood
½ small onion, finely chopped
1 stalk celery, finely chopped
1 small green sweet pepper, seeded, finely chopped
8 leaves leaf-lettuce or other salad greens
1 large tomato, cut into 8 wedges
1 small red onion, peeled, cut crosswise into rings
8 pitted black olives
1 lemon, cut into wedges

In large bowl, combine mayonnaise, dressing, sugar, oregano, black pepper, and garlic powder; stir until blended. Add lobster, chopped onion, celery, and green pepper. Gently stir to combine and coat lobster. Refrigerate at least 30 minutes to chill and allow flavors to blend. On platter or dinner plates, arrange lettuce. Top with lobster salad; add tomato, red onion, olives, and lemon. Delicious served with crackers.

Makes 4 servings.

PER SERVING:

252 calories
25 g protein
2 g fat
11 g carbohydrate
600 mg sodium
88 mg cholesterol

ESSENCE BRINGS YOU
GREAT COOKING

QUICK SALMON HASH

Cook extra potatoes at dinnertime and save them for this hearty hash
—an ideal sunrise meal for the family.

Makes 4 servings.

1 tablespoon vegetable oil
1 small onion, chopped
1 small green bell pepper, seeded, chopped
2 medium-size cooked potatoes, diced
1 7½-ounce can salmon, drained
1 tablespoon lemon juice
¾ cup chicken or vegetable broth
1 tablespoon chopped fresh dill or 1 teaspoon dried dill
½ teaspoon salt *(optional)*
Freshly ground black pepper to taste

In medium-size nonstick skillet, heat oil; sauté onion and green pepper until limp, about 3 minutes. Stir in remaining ingredients. Reduce heat to low; cover and simmer until heated through, about 7 minutes.

TEMPTING TUNA PIE

2 6-ounce cans solid- or chunk-style tuna (use water-packed for fewer calories and sodium-reduced for less salt)
2 cups frozen mixed vegetables, thawed
1 11-ounce can condensed cream-of-mushroom soup (cream-of-chicken and cream-of-celery are also good choices)
⅓ cup skim or evaporated milk
1 tablespoon grated onion
1 tablespoon chopped fresh thyme or 1 teaspoon dried thyme
1 9-inch unbaked piecrust
1 egg white, beaten with 1 tablespoon water
1 tablespoon sesame seeds

Heat oven to 400° F . In 8-inch baking dish or pie pan, combine tuna, vegetables, soup, milk, onion, and thyme; mix well. Place piecrust atop tuna mixture. Turn pastry edge under rim of dish; flute or crimp edge. Cut slits or decorative pattern in piecrust (to form vents for escaping steam). Brush piecrust with egg-white mixture; sprinkle with sesame seeds. Bake 25 to 30 minutes or until filling is bubbly and piecrust is golden brown. To serve, slice or spoon (pie should be soft-set).

Makes 6 servings.

PER SERVING:

342 calories
22 g protein
16 g fat
27 g carbohydrate
878 mg sodium
25 mg cholesterol

ESSENCE BRINGS YOU
GREAT COOKING

PASTA-TUNA SALAD

Feeding a crowd? This easy-to-make salad goes over in a big way.

You can add your own creative touches to this basic recipe.

Makes 12 to 18 servings.

PER EACH OF 12 SERVINGS:

318 calories
25 g protein
32 g fat
108 g carbohydrate
828 mg sodium
24 mg cholesterol

3 pounds medium-size pasta shells
2 10-ounce packages frozen green peas
4 6-ounce cans water-packed tuna, drained
2 cups sliced scallions
2 teaspoons salt (*optional*)
2 teaspoons ground black pepper
¼ teaspoon cayenne pepper
¾ cup sweet-pickle relish
¾ cup pimiento, chopped
2 to 3 cups mayonnaise
Optional garnish: 12 hard-cooked eggs, halved

   Cook pasta and peas according to package directions. Rinse both well under cold running water; drain. Place pasta, peas, and flaked tuna in large mixing bowl. Add scallions, salt (if desired), pepper, cayenne pepper, relish, and pimiento; toss ingredients well with two forks. Add mayonnaise, 1 cup at a time, stirring after each addition. Depending on consistency and taste desired, add more mayonnaise if necessary. Chill several hours or overnight. Garnish with egg halves.

TUNA PATÉ

This appetizer by Seleeda Bell Grantum of Richmond, Virginia, is guaranteed to get your gathering off to a great start!

2 6½-ounce cans water-packed light tuna, drained, flaked
3 hard-cooked eggs, cooled, chopped
1 medium-size onion chopped
3 tablespoons sweet relish
3 tablespoons low-cholesterol mayonnaise
1 teaspoon prepared mustard
1 teaspoon seasoning salt *(optional)*
1 teaspoon paprika
1 teaspoon dried thyme
1 teaspoon dried tarragon
½ teaspoon garlic powder
½ teaspoon hot-pepper sauce
½ cup dry bread crumbs
¼ cup chopped fresh parsley
Optional garnishes: watercress sprigs, lettuce leaves, ripe olives, cherry tomatoes

Makes 20 appetizer servings.

PER SERVING:

62 calories
7 g protein
2 g fat
4 g carbohydrate
227 mg sodium
35 mg cholesterol

In food processor, combine all ingredients except ½ parsley and garnishes; process until blended and smooth. Spoon, packing gently into lightly greased or sprayed 6-by-3-inch loaf pan or 3-cup mold; cover with plastic wrap. Chill at least one hour or until time to serve. Invert onto serving platter; unmold. Sprinkle with remaining chopped parsley; garnish as desired. Delicious spread on crackers or raw vegetables.

ZESTY CRAB DIP

Makes about 2 ½ cups.

8 ounces cooked crabmeat, well drained, all cartilage removed
¼ cup plain yogurt
⅓ cup calorie-reduced mayonnaise
2 tablespoons fresh lemon juice
2 tablespoons minced onion
2 tablespoons chopped pimiento
½ teaspoon hot-pepper sauce
Optional garnishes: cooked crab legs, lemon slices, parsley sprigs

In large bowl, combine all ingredients except garnishes. Refrigerate at least 1 hour to chill and allow flavors to blend; garnish.

CHAPTER SEVEN

Poultry

Recipes

OLD-FASHIONED ROAST CHICKEN

ROAST CAPON WITH ROSEMARY

ROAST CHICKEN WITH GARDEN VEGETABLES

WINE-AND-HERB BAKED CHICKEN

SAGE-BAKED CHICKEN BREASTS

GARLIC-LEMON CHICKEN

AUTHENTIC JAMAICAN JERK CHICKEN

JERK RUB

ARROZ CON POLLO

CHICKEN SATÉ WITH PEANUT SAUCE

MAPLE-BAKED CHICKEN

ZESTY BROILED GARLIC CHICKEN

CHICKEN MARSALA

CHICKEN SUCCOTASH

AUSTIN LESLIE'S PERFECT CRISPY FRIED CHICKEN

HERB OVEN-FRIED CHICKEN

COUNTRY SMOTHERED CHICKEN

CHICKEN AND DUMPLINGS

LEAH'S CHICKEN CREOLE

LATTICE-TOP CHICKEN POT PIE

WEST INDIAN CHICKEN CURRY WITH YELLOW RICE

GROUNDNUT STEW

GINGER CHICKEN AND CASHEW STIR-FRY

Recipes

HAWAIIAN CHICKEN STIR-FRY

CHICKEN WING DRUMETTES A L'ORANGE

GRILLED CHICKEN FAJITAS

OVEN-BARBECUED CHICKEN WINGS

CHICKEN STOCK

BARBECUED CORNISH HENS

CHUTNEY-GLAZED CORNISH HEN

ROAST TURKEY

TURKEY BROTH AND GIBLETS

GRANDMA'S OLD-FASHIONED GIBLET GRAVY

TURKEY POT ROAST

SPICY ORANGE-GLAZED TURKEY DRUMSTICKS

SAVORY TURKEY STEW

TURKEY ROLL WITH CONFETTI VEGETABLE STUFFING

FRUITED TURKEY KABOBS

TURKEY A LA KING

NEW ENGLAND TURKEY CHOWDER

TURKEY HASH

TURKEY-CITRUS SALAD

TURKEY SALAD

TURKEY MEATLOAF

TURKEY MEATBALLS AND SPAGHETTI WITH BASIC
HOMEMADE TOMATO SAUCE

TURKEY WITH PUMPKIN TORTELLINI

ESSENCE BRINGS YOU
GREAT COOKING

WHICH came first—the chicken or the egg? The Bible gives the nod to the chicken. "And the evening and the morning were the fourth day. And God said, 'Let the waters bring forth abundantly the moving creature that hath life, and fowl that may fly above the earth in the open firmament of heaven.'"

Chicken also comes first for many who are choosing to eat a lean, well-balanced diet. Poultry has fewer saturated fats than other meats; it is also lower in calories and cholesterol. To reduce the fat from chicken even further, leave the skin on while cooking (to keep the meat from drying out), then remove the fat-laden skin before eating.

Also tops in taste appeal, chicken was finger-lickin' good long before the Colonel got into the act. Down home, chicken was a special treat reserved for Sunday dinner and when company was coming over. This classic of the old South quickly became a national institution. Almost everyone loves chicken. Part of the appeal is that cooking it is not complicated. Bake, barbecue, braise, broil, fry, "oven" fry, stir-fry, butterfly, stuff, or ground—chicken is agreeable to almost any preparation or seasoning.

PICKING THE BEST BIRD

Free-range chickens have the best flavor and fewest additives. These birds are raised as chickens were in the past—they strut around, peck, and do what chickens do. Mass-produced chickens are tightly caged and never touch the ground or see the sun. The mass producer's gain in volume is the chicken eater's loss in flavor. Free range chickens can cost considerably more. Always buy the best chicken you can afford. Also consider kosher chickens and fresh-killed chickens from butcher shops or your local Asian markets.

When selecting packaged chicken, avoid packages with bruised or shriveled chicken and certainly those with an "off" odor. Packages with an accumulation of liquid have been sitting for a while. Check the "sell by" date stamped on the pack; do not purchase after that date.

Select chicken according to your intended use.

STORING CHICKEN

Store fresh chicken in the coldest part of the refrigerator for up to 2 days. There is no need to rewrap it if the packaging is in good condition. Freeze chicken if it is to be stored for more than two days and up to six months. To freeze, unwrap the chicken and rinse it with cold running water; blot it dry with paper towels. Rewrap the chicken carefully in freezer wrap or aluminum foil.

Plan to use frozen ground chicken within three months.

THAWING

Place frozen chicken in the refrigerator section to thaw; allow about 16 hours for a whole chicken and about 8 hours for parts. Never defrost chicken in the kitchen sink or on the counter; bacteria multiply rapidly at room temperature. For quicker thawing, immerse chicken that is wrapped airtight in a bowl of cold water, changing the water several times.

WHEN IS CHICKEN DONE?

It is vital that chicken is cooked thoroughly to kill any harmful bacteria. Here's how to test for doneness and safety: If cooking chicken parts or pieces, place a piece on a white plate (to see the juice's color easily), cut the thickest part with the tip of a sharp knife. If the juices run clear and not pink, the chicken is done. If pink, cook longer and test again. When cooking a whole chicken, a meat thermometer placed in the thickest meat between the breast and thigh (be sure tip does not touch bone) should read 180° F . Or, with your hand protected by paper towels, the drumstick will move easily in the socket when lifted.

GUARD AGAINST SALMONELLA

Wash your hands before and after handling raw chicken. Using hot soapy water, scrub all items that came in contact with the raw chicken—cutting board (made of nonporous material), knife, countertop, sink, etc. Marinate chicken in the refrigerator, not at room temperature. Eat chicken right after cooking. Wrap and refrigerate leftovers within two hours of cooking.

WASTE NOT; WANT NOT

Use all parts of a whole chicken. Backs, necks, and wing tips make excellent stock for soups and for cooking vegetables, beans, or grains. Rinse, dry, wrap, and collect these parts in the freezer until you have enough. The heart, liver, and gizzard can be used to make giblet gravy or dirty rice.

> Dark and light meat are as different as night and day. Dark meat has less protein and about twice the fat of light meat.

ESSENCE BRINGS YOU
GREAT COOKING

OLD-FASHIONED ROAST CHICKEN

Very easy to prepare, this glistening, golden-brown chicken is a thing of beauty.

Makes 4 to 5 servings.

PER EACH OF 4
SERVINGS:

383 calories
40 g protein
23 g fat
trace carbohydrate
680 mg sodium
140 mg cholesterol

1 3-pound roasting chicken
1 tablespoon butter or margarine, softened
1 teaspoon salt *(optional)*
½ teaspoon ground black pepper

Remove giblets and neck from inside chicken. (If desired, simmer heart, gizzard, and neck in 1 cup water until tender, then chop meat and use in gravy or dressing, or freeze for future use.) Heat oven to 325° F. Remove any visible fat from cavity and folds of chicken. Rinse bird under cold running water; drain and blot dry with paper towel. In small bowl, blend butter with seasonings; rub over skin. Fold neck skin over opening; with chicken breast side up, lift wings up toward neck, then fold under back of bird to balance it. Using kitchen string, tie drumsticks and tail together. Insert meat thermometer into thickness between breast and thigh. On rack in open roasting pan, place chicken breast side up. Roast, uncovered, basting occasionally with pan drippings, until thermometer registers 180° to 185° F or until drumstick moves easily when tested by hand, about 1½ to 2 hours. Let bird sit about 10 minutes before carving or quartering; discard string.

ROAST CAPON WITH ROSEMARY

6-pound capon or roasting chicken
2 teaspoons salt *(optional)*
3 sprigs rosemary
1 tablespoon soft butter or margarine
Optional garnish: rosemary sprig

Heat oven to 425° F. Remove any visible fat from cavity and fold of capon. Rinse bird with cold running water; drain well. Sprinkle inside capon with 1 teaspoon salt (if desired). Tuck rosemary into cavity. Fold neck skin over cavity and fasten to back with skewer. With bird breast side up, lift wings up toward neck, then fold under back of bird so they stay flat. With string, tie legs and tail of bird together. Rub skin with butter, sprinkle with remaining salt (if desired). Set bird on rack in roasting pan. Roast for 15 minutes to brown skin. Reduce temperature to 325° F and roast, basting frequently with pan drippings, for 1 hour and 30 minutes or until drumstick is tender when pressed and moves easily in socket. Lift bird to warm platter; remove skewer and strings. Garnish with rosemary or as desired. Let stand 10 to 15 minutes before carving.

Makes 10 servings.

PER SERVING:

253 calories
31 g protein
13 g fat
0 g carbohydrate
58 mg sodium
94 mg cholesterol

ESSENCE BRINGS YOU
GREAT COOKING

ROAST CHICKEN WITH GARDEN VEGETABLES

Makes 6 servings.

PER SERVING:

459 calories
36 g protein
19 g fat
30 g carbohydrate
499 mg sodium
106 mg cholesterol

1 3-pound roasting chicken
1 tablespoon fresh parsley or 1 teaspoon dried parsley
1 tablespoon fresh thyme or 1 teaspoon dried thyme
1 teaspoon ground sage
1 teaspoon salt *(optional)*
½ teaspoon ground black pepper
2 ribs celery, cut into large pieces
5 sprigs fresh parsley
1 tablespoon vegetable oil
3 white potatoes, peeled, halved
Water
3 large carrots, scraped, cut into chunks
2 cups brussels sprouts, stems trimmed
2 cups baby pattypan squash
¾ cup dry white wine

Remove giblets and neck from inside bird; rinse in cold water, wrap and refrigerate or freeze for later use. Remove any visible fat from cavity and folds of chicken. Rinse bird with cold running water; drain well and blot dry with paper towels. Mix chopped parsley, thyme, sage, salt (if desired), and pepper; rub mixture inside body cavity and over outside. If time permits, cover and refrigerate 12 hours or overnight. Heat oven to 325° F. Fill body cavity with celery and sprigs of parsley. Lift wings up toward neck, then fold them under back of bird to lock in place and balance. Tie drumsticks and tail together with string. Brush bird with oil. Place chicken, breast side up, on rack in open roasting pan or casserole dish. Place cooking thermometer in breast. Roast, uncovered, 1 hour; baste occasionally with pan drippings. Meanwhile, in 3-quart saucepan over high heat, bring potatoes and water to cover to boil. Reduce heat to medium-low, cover and simmer 10 minutes; drain well. Using bulb baster or long-handled spoon, remove all visible fat from roasting pan. Arrange potatoes, carrots, sprouts, and squash around chicken; pour wine over vegetables and bird. Roast, basting occasionally, 40 to 60 additional minutes or until chicken is done, vegetables are tender, and potatoes are browned. Poultry is done when thermometer inserted before cooking reads 180° to 185° F. To test manually, protect your hand with paper towel, then gently move chicken leg up and down; it will move freely when bird is done. Transfer chicken and vegetables to platter. Skim all visible fat from drippings; spoon remaining juices over chicken and vegetables.

Roast Chicken with Garden Vegetables.

WINE-AND-HERB BAKED CHICKEN

1 cup dry white wine
2 tablespoons chopped fresh parsley
1 tablespoon chopped fresh tarragon
½ teaspoon coarsely ground black pepper
½ teaspoon paprika
1 2½ pound broiler-fryer chicken, quartered

Heat oven to 375° F. In 13-by-9-inch baking dish, combine wine and seasonings. Add chicken, turning pieces in wine mixture to coat well. Arrange chicken pieces skin side down. Bake 25 to 30 minutes, basting occasionally. Turn pieces skin side up; bake, basting occasionally, 25 to 30 additional minutes or until browned and tender. Remove chicken and arrange on serving platter. Pour pan juices into small bowl; skim fat from top. Spoon remaining sauce over chicken.

Makes 4 servings.

PER SERVING:

329 calories
33 g protein
16 g fat
1 g carbohydrate
98 mg sodium
106 mg cholesterol

ESSENCE BRINGS YOU
GREAT COOKING

SAGE-BAKED CHICKEN BREASTS

Placing herbs under the skin infuses poultry with extra flavor. This dish is a delicious and pretty choice for a dinner party.

Makes 4 servings.

4 chicken breast halves, skin intact, bones optional, visible fat removed
½ teaspoon salt *(optional)*
½ teaspoon ground black pepper
4 or more fresh sage leaves
1 tablespoon melted butter, margarine, or vegetable oil
¼ cup chicken broth
¼ cup dry white wine
Optional garnish: fresh sage leaves, bay leaves, or herb of choice

Heat oven to 425° F. Rinse chicken with cold running water; blot dry with paper towels. Rub chicken with salt (if desired) and pepper. With fingers, separate (but do not completely detach) chicken skin from flesh to form pocket. Ease sage leaves under skin; press gently to smooth skin back into place. If desired, insert wooden picks through skin and into flesh to keep skin stretched and help prevent it from shrinking while cooking. In shallow flameproof casserole, arrange chicken skin side up; brush with butter. Bake, basting occasionally with pan drippings, until fork-tender, about 40 minutes. Transfer chicken to hot platter and keep warm. To pan drippings, add chicken broth and white wine; stir until blended. Bring to boil; cook until reduced by half. Skim any fat from top. Spoon sauce over chicken. Garnish with sage leaves or other fresh herbs.

GARLIC-LEMON CHICKEN

4 chicken breast halves, boned, skinned, visible fat removed
2 tablespoons unbleached all-purpose flour
¼ teaspoon cayenne pepper or ground black pepper
2 tablespoons olive oil
6 garlic cloves, peeled, left whole
¾ pound medium-size mushrooms, trimmed, quartered or halved
¼ cup fresh lemon juice
¾ cup low-salt chicken broth
1 bay leaf
1 teaspoon chopped fresh thyme leaves or ½ teaspoon dried thyme
Optional garnishes: lemon slices, thyme sprigs, watercress, spinach
  leaves

Makes 4 servings.

PER SERVING:

301 calories
32 g protein
15 g fat
10 g carbohydrate
86 mg sodium
83 mg cholesterol

Rinse chicken with cold running water; blot dry with paper towels. On waxed paper, mix flour and pepper; dredge chicken until coated. In large heavy skillet, heat oil. Cook breasts until nicely browned on one side, about 3 minutes; turn to other side. Add garlic cloves to skillet; sprinkle mushrooms over chicken. Continue cooking, moving mushrooms and chicken so they cook evenly, about 3 minutes. Add lemon juice, broth, bay leaf, and thyme. Cover and cook over low heat until cooked through, about 10 additional minutes. Transfer chicken pieces to warm serving platter or plates. Increase heat to medium-high; cook sauce, stirring occasionally, until reduced by half. Discard garlic and bay leaf; skim any fat from top. Spoon sauce and mushrooms over chicken. Garnish as desired.

ESSENCE BRINGS YOU
GREAT COOKING

AUTHENTIC JAMAICAN JERK CHICKEN

This recipe is excerpted from <u>Jerk: Barbecue from Jamaica</u> by Helen Willinsky (The Crossing Press, Freedom, California).

Makes 8 servings.

PER SERVING:

443 calories
49 g protein
24 g fat
3 g carbohydrate
109 mg sodium
159 mg cholesterol

2 chickens (about 3½ pounds each), cut into serving-size pieces
1 cup Jerk Rub (see following recipe or use ready-made)

Rub chicken pieces with Jerk Rub. In large glass baking dish, arrange chicken; cover and marinate in refrigerator at least 4 hours. For authentic flavor, build fire in grill with combination of coals and pimiento wood (apple wood or hickory wood or plain coals can be used). Lightly grease grid. When hot coals turn white, arrange chicken pieces skin side down on grid. Turn chicken about every 10 minutes, basting with marinade left in dish. Over slow fire, grill approximately 1½ to 2 hours. Or grill about 40 minutes over hotter fire. Chicken is done when flesh feels firm and juices run clear when meat is cut with tip of sharp knife.

Jerk Rub

Paste rubs are the authentic jerk-flavoring method. This is a medium-hot paste; make it hotter by adding more hot peppers or hot-pepper sauce. For less spice, remove the seeds and membranes from the peppers before grinding. Scotch bonnet or habañero peppers are preferred, but you can substitute the milder jalapeño or serrano peppers.

1 onion, finely chopped
½ cup finely chopped scallions
2 teaspoons chopped fresh thyme leaves
1 teaspoon salt *(optional)*
1 teaspoon ground allspice
½ teaspoon ground cinnamon
¼ teaspoon ground nutmeg
1 teaspoon ground black pepper
4 to 6 small Scotch bonnet or habañero peppers, finely chopped

In blender or food processor, combine all ingredients; using pulse speed, mix ingredients until blended. Cover and refrigerate until time to use. Rub seasoning onto poultry, fish, or meat before cooking.

Makes 1 cup.

PER ½ CUP:

57 calories
.2 g protein
.5 g fat
13 g carbohydrate
1,073 mg sodium
0 mg cholesterol

ESSENCE BRINGS YOU
GREAT COOKING

ARROZ CON POLLO

Though simple and inexpensive, this one-pot meal from the Spanish Caribbean islands has an air of festivity.

Makes 6 servings.

PER SERVING:

636 calories
37 g protein
23 g fat
66 g carbohydrate
776 mg sodium
88 mg cholesterol

- 3 tablespoons vegetable oil
- 1 3-pound broiler-fryer chicken, cut into serving pieces
- 1 large onion, chopped
- 2 garlic cloves, minced
- 1 small green bell pepper, seeded, chopped
- 1 16-ounce can tomatoes in juice, cut up
- 1 teaspoon dried thyme
- ½ teaspoon salt *(optional)*
- ½ teaspoon freshly ground black pepper
- 1 bay leaf
- 2 cups chicken broth or water
- 2 cups uncooked long-grain rice
- 1 tablespoon achiote oil or 1 teaspoon achiote paste or turmeric
- 1 10-ounce package green peas, thawed

Remove any visible fat from chicken. Rinse chicken with cold running water; blot dry with paper towels. In large, deep skillet or Dutch oven, heat oil. Cooking a few pieces at a time, evenly brown chicken on all sides; remove and set aside. Discard all but 2 tablespoons fat from skillet. Add onion, garlic, and bell pepper; sauté until onion is translucent, about 7 minutes. Stir in tomatoes with their juice, thyme, salt (if desired), black pepper, bay leaf, and browned chicken. Bring liquid to boil; reduce heat. Cover and simmer 20 minutes. Stir in broth, rice, and achiote; cover and simmer until rice is tender, about 20 minutes. Sprinkle peas over top; cook, uncovered, about 5 additional minutes. Serve hot.

CHICKEN SATÉ WITH PEANUT SAUCE

2 chicken breast halves, boned, skinned, visible fat removed

MARINADE:
2 tablespoons low-sodium soy sauce or tamari
1 tablespoon brown sugar
1 tablespoon fresh lime juice
1 tablespoon vegetable oil
1 small garlic clove, minced
1 teaspoon ground ginger
½ teaspoon ground cumin seed
½ teaspoon crushed red pepper flakes

PEANUT SAUCE:
¼ cup hot water
¼ cup smooth peanut butter
1 tablespoon fresh lime juice
1 teaspoon brown sugar

Makes 2 servings.

PER SERVING:

429 calories
36 g protein
24 g fat
19 g carbohydrate
764 mg sodium
66 mg cholesterol

Cut chicken into 1-inch-wide strips. In medium-size glass bowl, combine marinade ingredients. Add chicken; toss to coat well. Cover and marinate in refrigerator, stirring occasionally, at least 2 hours. Prepare grill or broiler. Meanwhile, prepare peanut sauce: In medium-size bowl, using whisk, blend hot water and peanut butter. Stir in lime juice and brown sugar until blended. Thread chicken on 8-inch wooden skewers that have been soaked in water (to prevent burning), saving leftover marinade. Grill or broil, about 5 inches from heat source, 10 to 12 minutes, turning frequently and basting with leftover marinade. Serve chicken saté with peanut sauce for dipping.

ESSENCE BRINGS YOU
GREAT COOKING

MAPLE-BAKED CHICKEN

This no-fuss main dish by Ms. Lula Wilson of Baltimore is always a hit at her family gatherings.

Makes 5 servings.

PER SERVING:

428 calories
33 g protein
21 g fat
24 g carbohydrate
549 mg sodium
106 mg cholesterol

1 3-pound broiler-fryer chicken, cut into 10 serving pieces or 3 pounds drumsticks, thighs, or wings
½ teaspoon fried-chicken seasoning or poultry seasoning
½ teaspoon salt *(optional)*
¼ teaspoon ground black pepper
½ cup maple syrup
¼ cup prepared mustard
2 teaspoons fresh lemon juice
2 tablespoons margarine or butter, cut into small pieces
Optional garnishes: parsley sprigs

Heat oven to 350° F. Remove any visible fat from chicken pieces. Rinse chicken under cold running water; blot dry with paper towels. Rub with seasoning blend, salt (if desired), and pepper. In large baking dish, arrange chicken pieces in single layer. In medium-size bowl, blend syrup, mustard, and lemon juice; pour mixture over chicken. Dot with margarine. Cover with foil; bake 30 minutes. Uncover dish; bake basting occasionally with pan juices, until browned and glazed, about 20 additional minutes. Transfer to serving platter; garnish with parsley.

ZESTY BROILED GARLIC CHICKEN

8 medium-size chicken thighs, skin and visible fat removed
¼ cup olive oil
¼ cup red wine vinegar
2 tablespoons finely chopped fresh parsley
1 tablespoon minced garlic
1 tablespoon chopped fresh rosemary leaves or 1 teaspoon
  dried rosemary

Rinse chicken under cold running water; blot dry with paper towels. On slotted rack of broiler pan, arrange chicken pieces so that they do not touch. In small bowl, combine oil, vinegar, parsley, garlic, and rosemary; beat until blended. Generously brush chicken on all sides with seasoning mixture. Broil 5 inches from heat source about 8 minutes; turn pieces with tongs and brush again with seasoning. Broil 8 additional minutes or until chicken is browned, and when cut to bone, juices are clear. (Avoid overcooking, which makes for dry, tough chicken.)

Makes 4 servings.

PER SERVING:

490 calories
52 g protein
29 g fat
2 g carbohydrate
176 mg sodium
178 mg cholesterol

ESSENCE BRINGS YOU
GREAT COOKING

CHICKEN MARSALA

It may surprise you that a dish this elegant is also low in fat and calories. It's an ideal choice for an intimate, healthful dinner-party entrée.

Makes 4 servings.

PER SERVING:

247 calories
29 g protein
5 g fat
11 g carbohydrate
83 mg sodium
65 mg cholesterol

1 tablespoon olive oil
2 garlic cloves, sliced
4 chicken breast halves, skin and visible fat removed
1 pound sliced mushrooms (try wild mushrooms such as shiitakes or cèpes)
⅔ cup Marsala wine
2 tablespoons minced flat-leaf parsley

In large nonstick skillet, heat oil. Sauté garlic until golden; discard garlic. Add chicken breasts to oil; sauté until nicely browned, about 4 minutes on each side. Add mushrooms to skillet; pour in Marsala. Cover and simmer gently until chicken is fork-tender, about 5 to 8 minutes (depending on thickness). Using slotted spoon, transfer chicken to warm platter or plates. Over high heat, bring liquid to boil, stirring to scrape up any browned bits from bottom of skillet. Cook until liquid is thickened and reduced by half; stir in parsley. Spoon sauce over chicken.

CHICKEN SUCCOTASH

1 2½-pound broiler-fryer chicken
1 teaspoon salt *(optional)*
½ teaspoon paprika
2 tablespoons peanut oil or vegetable oil
1 medium-size onion, chopped
1 rib celery, sliced
Water
1 pound shelled green lima beans, or 1½ cups frozen
2 medium-size tomatoes, chopped
3 ears fresh corn, or 1½ cups frozen (thawed) whole-kernel corn
¼ teaspoon ground black pepper
Optional garnish: chopped parsley, celery leaves

Makes 6 servings.

PER SERVING:

549 calories
43 g protein
19 g fat
52 g carbohydrate
454 mg sodium
88 mg cholesterol

If desired, remove and discard skin from chicken. Cut into serving pieces; remove any visible fat. Rinse chicken under cold running water; blot dry with paper towels. Season with ½ teaspoon salt (if desired) and paprika. In large skillet, heat oil; add chicken pieces and sauté on all sides until nicely browned, about 12 minutes. Remove chicken from skillet; discard all but 2 tablespoons fat. Add onion and celery; sauté until vegetables are limp, about 5 minutes. Add about 1 inch water; over medium heat, bring to boil. Add beans and tomatoes; top with browned chicken. Reduce heat; cover and cook until beans are almost tender, about 20 minutes. Meanwhile, if using ears of corn, with long sharp knife, cut corn from cob; using dull edge, scrape pulp from cob. Stir corn into skillet mixture; sprinkle with remaining salt (if desired) and black pepper. Cook 5 additional minutes or until chicken is cooked through and vegetables are of desired tenderness. Sprinkle with parsley or celery leaves.

AUSTIN LESLIE'S PERFECT CRISPY FRIED CHICKEN

Austin Leslie of the ever-popular Chez Helene in New Orleans has turned frying chicken into a science.

Makes 6 servings.

PER SERVING:

501 calories
32 g protein
35 g fat
11 g carbohydrate
667 mg sodium
136 mg cholesterol

1 2½-pound whole broiler-fryer chicken
1½ teaspoons salt *(optional)*
¼ teaspoon ground black pepper
1 large egg
1 cup evaporated milk
1 cup water
½ cup unbleached all-purpose flour
1¼ cups peanut oil
Optional garnishes: fresh garlic and parsley, minced

Cut chicken into serving pieces. Rinse with cold running water, dry thoroughly. Sprinkle with 1 teaspoon salt (if desired) and ⅛ teaspoon pepper; refrigerate uncovered for at least 1 hour. In large bowl, beat egg, milk, water, remaining salt (if desired), and remaining pepper. Dip chicken into egg mixture, allowing excess to run off; dredge chicken in flour. Place chicken pieces in single layer in pan or dish; refrigerate, uncovered, for at least an hour to allow coating to set. In deep 12-inch skillet, heat oil. (Oil has reached correct temperature for frying when it bubbles after being sprinkled with small amount of flour.) Add chicken pieces; do not crowd. Cook chicken on first side for 15 minutes; turn with tongs. Cook an additional 15 minutes or until crisp, golden, and cooked through. Sprinkle with garlic and parsley, if desired.

ESSENCE BRINGS YOU
GREAT COOKING

HERB OVEN-FRIED CHICKEN

Pack this one for your next picnic.

1 2½-to 3-pound broiler-fryer chicken, cut into 8 to 10 serving pieces
1½ cups cornflake crumbs
2 teaspoons fresh chopped parsley
1 teaspoon dried, crushed thyme or oregano
½ teaspoon paprika
½ teaspoon salt *(optional)*
¼ teaspoon ground black pepper
½ cup buttermilk or milk

Makes 6 servings.

PER SERVING:

278 calories
28 g protein
13 g fat
7 g carbohydrate
355 mg sodium
89 mg cholesterol

Remove any visible fat from chicken. Rinse chicken with cold running water; blot dry with paper towels. Heat oven to 425° F. In medium-size bowl, mix crumbs, herbs, paprika, salt (if desired), and pepper. Into small bowl, pour buttermilk. Dip chicken into buttermilk; roll in cornflake mixture until evenly coated.* Arrange chicken pieces in well-greased 13-by-9-inch pan. Bake uncovered 30 minutes. Turn chicken; bake an additional 20 minutes or until thickest pieces are done. Serve warm or cold.

*To further reduce fat and calories, remove chicken skin before dipping the chicken into buttermilk.

ESSENCE BRINGS YOU
GREAT COOKING

COUNTRY SMOTHERED CHICKEN

Makes 4 servings.

PER SERVING:

542 calories
44 g protein
35 g fat
12 g carbohydrate
144 mg sodium
153 mg cholesterol

1 3-pound broiler-fryer chicken, cut into serving pieces
¼ cup peanut oil
⅓ cup unbleached all-purpose flour
1½ cups water
1 medium onion, chopped
1 teaspoon salt *(optional)*
¼ teaspoon ground black pepper

Remove any visible fat from chicken. Rinse chicken with cold running water; blot dry with paper towels. In large skillet, heat oil. Add chicken pieces; brown on all sides. Sprinkle chicken with flour; turn to coat and brown all sides. Stir in water slowly until blended; add onion, salt (if desired), and pepper. Bring to boil; reduce heat to medium-low. Cover with tight-fitting lid; simmer about 10 minutes. Reduce to low heat; simmer 15 to 20 minutes or until chicken is fork-tender.

ESSENCE BRINGS YOU
GREAT COOKING

CHICKEN AND DUMPLINGS

There were four children in my family. On our birthdays, we could select the meal for dinner. Every year I chose chicken and dumplings. It was my unparalleled favorite. The meat was always so tender, it fell from the bone, the dumplings—not the drop kind, but rolled flat and cut into small rectangles—were chewy and delicious, and covering it all was a lot of richly flavored gravy. Ice cream and cake were the only foods that tasted better. Every December 20 I had it all!

1 2½-to 3-pound broiler-fryer or stewing hen, cut into serving pieces
Water
1 bay leaf
1 onion, chopped
1 celery rib, sliced
1 teaspoon salt *(optional)*
½ teaspoon ground black pepper

DUMPLINGS:
2 cups unbleached all-purpose flour
1½ teaspoons baking powder
½ teaspoon salt *(optional)*
½ cup broth from cooking chicken

Makes 5 servings.

PER SERVING:

596 calories
40 g protein
28 g fat
42 g carbohydrate
285 mg sodium
139 mg cholesterol

Remove any visible fat from chicken. Rinse chicken thoroughly with cold water; blot dry with paper towels. In large pot or Dutch oven, combine chicken, about 3 quarts water, bay leaf, onion, celery, salt (if desired), and pepper. Over medium-high heat, bring to boil; reduce heat to simmer. Cook, partially covered, until chicken is tender and easily pierced with fork, about 45 minutes (longer for stewing hen). Meanwhile prepare dumplings. Into large bowl, sift together flour, baking powder, and salt (if desired). Stir in 1 cup chicken broth until blended. Knead into stiff dough. On floured surface, roll dough out to ⅛ inch thick. Cut into strips about 1½ inches wide and 2 inches long. During last 15 minutes of chicken cooking time, one at a time, drop dumplings into pot. Cover and cook until chicken and dumplings are done.

ESSENCE BRINGS YOU
GREAT COOKING

LEAH'S CHICKEN CREOLE

When in New Orleans, stop in at Dooky Chase and enjoy the superb Creole dishes prepared by chef and co-owner (with her husband) Leah Chase. In the meantime, you can enjoy one of her specialties at home.

Makes 6 servings.

PER SERVING:

413 calories
44 g protein
20 g fat
13 g carbohydrate
884 mg sodium
204 mg cholesterol

1 2½-pound broiler-fryer chicken, cut into 10 pieces, visible fat removed
1 teaspoon salt *(optional)*
¼ teaspoon ground black pepper
2 tablespoons vegetable oil
1 medium-size onion, chopped
1 medium-size green bell pepper, chopped
1 28-ounce can whole tomatoes, coarsely chopped, liquid reserved
1 cup water
2 medium-size garlic cloves, finely chopped
½ teaspoon dried thyme
⅛ teaspoon cayenne pepper
1 pound raw shrimp, peeled, deveined
12 small okra pods, tops removed
2 tablespoons chopped parsley

Rinse chicken with cold running water; blot dry with paper towels. Season chicken with ½ teaspoon salt (if desired) and pepper. In saucepot or Dutch oven with heavy lid, heat oil over medium-low heat. Add chicken; cover and steam about 10 minutes. Remove chicken; set aside. Add onion and green pepper; sauté about 5 minutes until tender. Add tomatoes (with liquid), water, garlic, thyme, remaining ½ teaspoon salt (if desired), and pepper. Cover and cook 5 minutes. Add chicken, shrimp, okra, and parsley; simmer, uncovered, for 10 minutes. Serve over rice.

LATTICE-TOP CHICKEN POT PIE

This classic savory pie is quite rich; serve with a lightly dressed fresh salad of mixed greens for a memorable meal.

Pastry for deep dish double-crust 9-inch pie (see recipe on page 403 or use ready-to-bake crust)

8 pearl onions, peeled

2 large carrots, cut into ½-inch-thick slices

4 tablespoons (½ stick) butter or margarine

4 tablespoons unbleached all-purpose flour

½ cup chicken broth

1 cup milk

½ teaspoon poultry seasoning

¼ teaspoon ground white pepper

¼ cup chopped fresh parsley

2 cups cooked chicken, cubed (about 1 inch)

10 medium-size mushrooms, trimmed, quartered, sautéed

1 cup frozen green peas, thawed

Makes 6 servings.

PER SERVING:

547 calories
21 g protein
32 g fat
41 g carbohydrate
606 mg sodium
67 mg cholesterol

Prepare pastry; chill. In steamer basket over boiling water, steam onions and carrots about 5 minutes; remove and set aside. Heat oven to 375° F. In medium-size saucepan over medium heat, melt butter. Using wire whisk or wooden spoon, blend in flour, making thin paste. Cook until mixture bubbles and lightly browns. Blend in broth and milk. Simmer, stirring constantly, until thick, 5 to 7 minutes. Stir in poultry seasoning, pepper, parsley, chicken, mushrooms, and peas. Divide dough into 2 pieces, one slightly larger than the other. On lightly floured surface, roll out larger piece to form 11-inch circle. Transfer to 9-inch baking dish or pie pan. Roll out remaining dough to ¼-inch thickness; cut into 1-inch-wide strips. Spoon filling into baking dish; arrange dough strips in lattice pattern over filling. Trim dough to form 1-inch overhang; turn under. Flute or crimp edges. Bake 30 to 40 minutes or until crust is nicely browned and filling is bubbling hot.

WEST INDIAN CHICKEN CURRY WITH YELLOW RICE

This boneless chicken curry main dish is exceptionally tasty and elegant.

Makes 6 servings.

PER SERVING
(CHICKEN ONLY):

376 calories
29 g protein
18 g fat
22 g carbohydrate
461 mg sodium
88 mg cholesterol

- 2½-pound chicken, quartered, skin and fat removed
- Water
- 1 small onion, quartered
- 1 celery rib, halved
- 1 bay leaf
- 2 medium-size carrots, peeled diced
- 2 medium-size potatoes, peeled, diced
- 1 rib celery, chopped
- 2 tablespoons olive oil
- 1 tablespoon curry powder, preferably Madras
- 1 tablespoon ground cumin
- 1 tablespoon turmeric
- 1 tablespoon sugar
- 1 teaspoon dried thyme
- 1 teaspoon salt *(optional)*
- 1 medium-size onion, chopped
- 1 cup chicken broth (from chicken cooked in recipe)
- *Optional garnishes:* peanuts, raisins, chutney

Remove any visible fat from chicken. Rinse chicken with cold running water; blot dry with paper towels. In heavy pot, combine 3 quarts water, quartered onion, celery halves, and bay leaf; bring to boil. Add chicken; cover and simmer until very tender (ready to fall off bone), about 1 hour for broiler-fryer or 2½ hours for stewing hen. Meanwhile, in large saucepan with about ½ cup water or in vegetable steamer, briefly steam carrots, potatoes, and chopped celery to partially cook. In Dutch oven, heat olive oil. Add curry, cumin, turmeric, sugar, thyme, and salt (if desired); stir until blended. Add chopped onion; sauté until onion softens, about 5 minutes. When cooked, remove chicken from cooking liquid; bone chicken. Skim any visible fat from chicken broth; strain through fine sieve or double thickness of cheesecloth into bowl (discard seasonings). Stir 1 cup chicken broth into curry-onion mixture (store remaining broth for future use). Add partially cooked vegetables and chicken to sauce; stir to mix well. Over low heat, cover and simmer just until vegetables are of desired tenderness and flavors blend. Serve with Yellow Rice (see following recipe). If desired, garnish with peanuts, raisins, or chutney.

Yellow Rice

This dressed-up rice goes well with curry and Creole dishes.

2 cups water
½ teaspoon turmeric or ⅛ teaspoon saffron
¼ teaspoon ground ginger
¼ teaspoon dry mustard
½ teaspoon cayenne pepper
1 teaspoon salt *(optional)*
2 teaspoons granulated sugar
1 cup long-grain rice

Makes 4 servings.

PER SERVING:

376 calories
29 g protein
18 g fat
22 g carbohydrate
461 mg sodium
88 mg cholesterol

In 3-quart saucepan with tight-fitting lid, over medium-high heat, combine all ingredients; bring to boil. Reduce heat until mixture simmers; using fork, stir mixture 1 or 2 times. Cover pan and simmer, without stirring or lifting lid, until rice is tender and all liquid is absorbed, about 14 minutes.

ESSENCE BRINGS YOU
GREAT COOKING

GROUNDNUT STEW

This peanut-flavored chicken dish from West Africa is eaten in many versions throughout the continent.

Makes 5 servings.

PER SERVING:

669 calories
45 g protein
47 g fat
20 g carbohydrate
717 mg sodium
106 mg cholesterol

1 large broiler-fryer chicken, cut into serving pieces
⅓ cup peanut oil or other cooking oil
2 medium-size onions, sliced ¼-inch thick
2 cups water
¾ cup smooth, no-sugar-added peanut butter
6 medium-size tomatoes, chopped
1-inch piece fresh ginger
1 teaspoon salt *(optional)*
½ teaspoon ground black pepper
1 teaspoon cayenne pepper, or to taste
2 tablespoons chopped fresh parsley

Remove any visible fat from chicken. Rinse chicken thoroughly with cold running water; blot dry with paper towels. In large heavy skillet, heat oil; when moderately hot, sauté chicken until golden brown on all sides. Remove chicken to large saucepan. Discard all but 2 tablespoons fat from skillet; add onions and sauté until slightly limp, then pile atop chicken. Add water; bring to boil. In medium-size bowl, thin peanut butter with some of cooking liquid from chicken; add to pot along with tomatoes, ginger, salt (if desired), and peppers. Reduce heat; simmer until chicken is tender, about 30 to 45 minutes. Remove ginger. Serve over cooked rice; sprinkle with parsley.

GINGER CHICKEN AND CASHEW STIR-FRY

1 whole chicken breast
1 tablespoon cornstarch
½ teaspoon salt *(optional)*
½ teaspoon sugar
2 tablespoons sodium-reduced soy sauce
1 tablespoon grated fresh ginger or 1 teaspoon ground ginger
3 tablespoons vegetable oil
2 medium-size carrots, thinly sliced on diagonal
1 small green bell pepper, seeded, cut into 1-inch pieces
2 cups green cabbage, shredded
¼ cup chicken broth or bouillon
⅓ cup chopped cashew nuts
2 cups cooked brown rice

Makes 4 servings.

PER SERVING:

371 calories
19 g protein
17 g fat
36 g carbohydrate
640 mg sodium
32 mg cholesterol

Remove and discard skin, bones, and visible fat from chicken. Rinse chicken under cold running water; blot dry with paper towels. Cut chicken into 1-inch cubes or ½-inch wide strips. In medium-size bowl, combine cornstarch, salt (if desired), sugar, soy sauce, and ginger; add chicken and stir to mix well. Marinate about 30 minutes. In wok or skillet, heat 2 tablespoons oil. Add chicken and stir-fry until cooked through and lightly browned on all sides, about 8 minutes; remove from pan. Add carrots and stir-fry just until crisp-tender, about 2 to 3 minutes; remove from pan. Add remaining oil, heat briefly and add bell pepper; stir-fry 1 to 2 minutes; remove from pan. Add cabbage and stir-fry until tender, about 5 minutes. Return chicken and vegetables to pan; stir gently to combine. Add chicken broth; stir until sauce is heated and thickened. Sprinkle with cashews. Serve with brown rice.

ESSENCE BRINGS YOU
GREAT COOKING

HAWAIIAN CHICKEN STIR-FRY

This recipe is also a delicious way to recycle leftover chicken. Simply cut the cooked chicken into strips and add according to recipe, cooking just long enough to reheat.

Makes 4 servings.

PER SERVING:

350 calories
32 g protein
9 g fat
34 g carbohydrate
373 mg sodium
65 mg cholesterol

4 chicken breast halves, skin, bones, and visible fat removed
1 15-ounce can pineapple chunks, drained, juice reserved
¼ cup water
2 tablespoons cider vinegar
2 tablespoons sodium-reduced soy sauce
1 tablespoon cornstarch
½ teaspoon crushed red pepper flakes
½ teaspoon ground ginger
2 tablespoons sesame oil or vegetable oil
½ head of broccoli, stem trimmed, cut into spears or florets, blanched
1 small onion, sliced lengthwise
2 cups cooked brown rice

Rinse chicken with cold running water; blot dry with paper towels. Place breasts between 2 sheets of waxed paper; using rolling pin, flatten slightly and evenly. Cut lengthwise into 1-inch-wide strips; set aside. In medium-size bowl, combine pineapple juice, water, vinegar, soy sauce, cornstarch, pepper flakes, and ginger; stir until blended. Set aside. Preheat wok or large skillet over high heat; add oil, then tilt and rotate pan to spread oil over bottom. Add broccoli; stir-fry until crisp-tender, about 3 minutes; remove from pan. Add chicken and onion to pan; stir-fry until chicken is golden and cooked through, about 5 minutes. Push chicken to sides of pan. Stir sauce, then add to center of pan. Cook until thickened, about 2 to 3 minutes. Add pineapple chunks and cooked broccoli; along with chicken and onion, stir into sauce until coated. Serve over rice.

CHICKEN WING DRUMETTES A L'ORANGE

24 chicken wing drumettes (single-boned meaty portion of wing)
1 teaspoon salt *(optional)*
1 teaspoon ground black pepper or ½ teaspoon cayenne pepper
3 tablespoons packed brown sugar
1 tablespoon cornstarch
1 teaspoon ground ginger
½ cup orange juice
¼ cup orange marmalade
1 tablespoon fresh lemon juice
Optional garnishes: orange slices, watercress sprigs

Makes 24 appetizers.

PER DRUMMETTE:

73 calories
8 g protein
2 g fat
5 g carbohydrate
114 mg sodium
25 mg cholesterol

Remove and discard skin from drumettes; rinse wings with cold running water; blot dry with paper towels. Season with salt (if desired) and pepper. In medium-size saucepan, combine remaining ingredients except garnishes. Over medium heat, simmer until sugar dissolves and ingredients blend; remove from heat and let cool. In large food-storage bag or large glass bowl, combine chicken and sauce; cover and marinate in refrigerator, turning occasionally, at least 2 hours. Heat oven to 350° F. Grease large baking pan; arrange drumettes in single layer. Bake, basting with any leftover marinade, until cooked through and crisp, about 45 minutes. Transfer to serving platter; garnish with orange slices and watercress.

ESSENCE BRINGS YOU
GREAT COOKING

GRILLED CHICKEN FAJITAS

This Mexican dish is a delight when served in a warm tortilla.

Makes great party fare.

Makes 16 fajitas.

½ cup fresh lemon or lime juice
¼ cup vegetable oil
1½ teaspoons crushed oregano
½ teaspoon coarsely ground black pepper
4 pounds boneless chicken breasts, visible fat removed
4 medium-size bell peppers (use different colors for added visual
   appeal), seeded, sliced in thin strips
2 large onions, sliced lengthwise
16 7-inch flour tortillas
Assorted fajita condiments: salsas, chopped tomatoes, shredded lettuce,
   sliced or chopped avocados, sour cream

In large 13-by-9-inch baking dish, combine juice, 2 tablespoons oil, oregano, and pepper; mix well. Add chicken, turning in marinade to coat all pieces evenly. Cover and refrigerate at least 2 hours (preferably 8 to 24 hours), turning chicken several times in marinade. Just before cooking chicken, heat remaining oil in large skillet; add peppers and onion; sauté until tender, about 8 minutes. Cover pepper and onion mixture and keep warm. About 1 hour before serving, prepare grill for barbecuing. Arrange chicken on grill over medium-hot coals. Grill until chicken is fork-tender, about 35 minutes. Baste chicken with remaining marinade and turn occasionally while cooking. To broil: Preheat broiler. Arrange chicken on broiler pan rack. Broil about 6 inches from heat source, cooking as above. On cutting board, using sharp knife, cut chicken into strips. Warm tortillas on grill about 30 seconds. To serve fajitas, wrap portion of chicken and pepper-onion mixture in warm tortilla; arrange filled tortillas on large platter. Place condiments in individual bowls for guests to add items of choice to fajitas.

OVEN-BARBECUED CHICKEN WINGS

30 chicken wings, about 5 pounds
2 cups prepared barbecue sauce
¾ cup brown sugar
2 tablespoons fresh lemon juice
⅓ cup vegetable oil

Heat oven to 350° F. Remove pinfeathers from chicken wings. Rinse wings under cold running water; blot dry and set aside. In small mixing bowl, combine barbecue sauce, brown sugar, lemon juice, and oil; stir well to blend. Place wings in 17-by-11-by-2-inch baking pan. Generously brush both sides of wings with sauce mixture. Cover pan with foil; bake 30 minutes, basting wings with sauce every 10 minutes. Turn wings over and spoon on remaining sauce. Cook uncovered for 30 additional minutes, or until wings are deep brown.

Makes 12 to 18 servings.

PER EACH OF 12 SERVINGS:

384 calories
23 g protein
23 g fat
18 g carbohydrate
413 mg sodium
72 mg cholesterol

CHICKEN STOCK

This versatile broth can be used in many ways: Alone, it makes a tasty, low-calorie minimeal. It can also be used as a base for main-dish soups and stews, and as a flavorful seasoning when cooking vegetables, beans, or rice.

Makes about 3 quarts.

PER QUART:

136 calories
13 g protein
8 g fat
0 g carbohydrate
340 mg sodium
28 mg cholesterol

3 pounds chicken wings
3 pounds chicken pieces (backs, necks, or bones remaining from boning breasts and thighs)
Water
2 medium-size carrots, cut in large pieces
2 medium-size onions, cut in large pieces
2 stalks celery, cut in large pieces
4 sprigs fresh parsley
1 bay leaf
1 teaspoon salt *(optional)*
1 teaspoon crushed black peppercorns

To large stockpot, add chicken and enough water to cover. Over medium heat, bring to simmer. Using slotted spoon, remove any foam from surface. Simmer, uncovered, about 30 minutes. Add remaining ingredients. Simmer, partially covered, 2 additional hours, adding more water as needed to keep chicken covered. Through cheesecloth or sieve, strain stock into large bowl; discard solids. Cover and chill. Remove and discard layer of fat that forms on surface. Tightly cover broth and refrigerate up to 3 days or freeze. Reheat to boiling before use.

BARBECUED CORNISH HENS

These little birds taste delightful when grilled. Do not dry out by overcooking.

2 Cornish game hens (about 1 pound each)
½ lemon
½ teaspoon paprika
½ teaspoon ground black pepper
½ teaspoon salt *(optional)*

BARBECUE SAUCE:
1 8-ounce can tomato sauce or 1 cup tomato juice or V-8 juice
¼ cup red-wine vinegar or cider vinegar
2 tablespoons Worcestershire sauce
2 tablespoons grated onion
1 garlic clove, finely minced
1 teaspoon chili powder
1 teaspoon cayenne pepper or to taste
1 bay leaf

Makes 4 servings.

PER SERVING:

321 calories
33 g protein
16 g fat
8 g carbohydrate
812 mg sodium
106 mg cholesterol

Remove giblets (save for future use) and rinse hens with cold running water; blot dry with paper towels. Using kitchen shears or sharp knife, split hens lengthwise; remove and discard any bits of fat. Rub hens with lemon; rub with paprika, pepper, and salt (if desired). In shallow glass dish, arrange hens; cover and refrigerate up to 2 hours. To prepare barbecue sauce, combine sauce ingredients in medium-size saucepan; mix well. Bring to boil; reduce heat to low. Simmer sauce, stirring occasionally, about 10 minutes; set aside. If using charcoal grill, begin fire about 30 minutes before cooking time. Heat coals to medium heat (coals are ready when you can hold your hand just above grid at cooking height about 3 to 4 seconds). Lightly brush grid with oil or spray with cooking spray. Arrange hens skin side down on grid. Grill covered about 15 minutes; baste with sauce. Turn skin side up; baste again. Continue to grill, turning and basting frequently (to prevent overcooking), until hens are tender and all traces of pink are gone from meat when cut near bone, about 20 to 30 additional minutes.

CHUTNEY-GLAZED CORNISH HEN

For an easy one-dish meal, roast your choice of parboiled vegetables such as sweet, white, yellow or red-skinned potatoes, bell peppers, carrots, mushrooms, squash, and turnip bottoms in pan with hen.

Makes 2 servings.

PER SERVING:

385 calories
33 g protein
14 g fat
20 g carbohydrate
368 mg sodium
106 mg cholesterol

1 1-pound Cornish game hen
¼ teaspoon salt *(optional)*
¼ teaspoon ground black pepper
Sprigs of 1 or 2 fresh herbs (such as thyme, parsley, tarragon, sage, and celery leaves)
1 teaspoon vegetable oil, butter, or margarine
¼ cup prepared chutney (marmalade or jelly can be substituted)
Parboiled vegetables

Remove neck and giblets from body cavity of hen (wrap and freeze for future stewing or for use in gravy or stuffing); remove any visible fat from cavity and folds. Rinse bird under cold running water; blot dry with paper towels. Pick off or singe any hairs. Rub cavity and skin with salt (if desired) and pepper. Stuff cavity with herbs. Truss bird by folding wings back and underneath body; tie drumsticks together. Heat oven to 350° F. Rub hen well with oil. On rack in shallow pan, place hen breast side up. Roast, brushing or basting occasionally, with pan drippings, 30 minutes. Brush generously with chutney; add parboiled vegetables to pan. Roast, basting hen and vegetables with pan drippings, until hen is done, about 30 additional minutes or until drumstick moves easily in socket.

Turkey

Don't wait for Thanksgiving to roast a turkey. This big bird gives you a lot of meat for your money, has high-quality protein, and is relatively low in fat. After the first delicious meal, there are diverse spin-offs for leftovers—salads, sandwiches, pot pies, and casseroles. Turkey is now a year-round favorite with almost everyone. Whole turkeys are available in several forms.

ROASTERS—the traditional turkey, ranging from about 10 to 30 pounds. The larger birds are more economical per pound as they have more meat in proportion to bone.

FRYER ROASTERS—small meaty turkey, weighing from 4 to 9 pounds; ideal for singles and small families.

FROZEN SELF-BASTING—injected with oil before freezing, then bastes itself as it cooks.

FROZEN PRESTUFFED—these turkeys go from the freezer to the oven with no thawing. Don't try to duplicate this method at home; safe prestuffing requires special technology.

Sometimes the parts are greater than the whole. If you're cooking for just yourself or for only a few, or if time is tight, it might be more practical for you to buy and prepare a boneless turkey breast, drumsticks, wings, thighs, or cutlets.

ROAST TURKEY

The best leftovers begin with a perfectly roasted bird. Follow these simple steps for a tender, moist, beautiful, golden brown whole turkey.

PER 4 OUNCE-
SERVING (WHITE
MEAT):

153 calories
34 g protein
.83 g fat
0 g carbohydrate
59 mg sodium
94 mg cholesterol

PER 4 OUNCE-
SERVING (DARK
MEAT):

210 calories
33 g protein
8 g fat
0 g carbohydrate
93 mg sodium
100 mg cholesterol

1 8-to-24-pound fresh or frozen turkey
2 tablespoons vegetable oil

If frozen, thaw turkey on tray in refrigerator 3 to 4 days; allow 5 hours per pound of turkey to completely thaw. Or, place wrapped turkey in sink and cover with cold water; allow about ½ hour per pound of turkey to completely thaw. Change water frequently. Do not thaw poultry at room temperature. Remove plastic wrapping from thawed turkey. Remove giblets and neck from body and neck cavities. To remove neck, it may be necessary to release legs from band of skin or wire lock. Rinse turkey inside and out with cool water; blot dry with paper towel. Return legs to wire lock or band of skin, or tie loosely. Tuck tip of wings under back of turkey. Skewer neck skin with poultry pin or round toothpick to back of turkey for neat appearance. Heat oven to 325° F. With turkey on flat rack in shallow roasting pan (about 2 inches deep), insert meat thermometer deep into thickest part of thigh next to body, not touching bone. Brush turkey with vegetable oil to prevent drying. Roast according to chart below. Turkey is done when meat thermometer registers 180° to 185° F and drumstick is soft and moves easily at joint. When skin of turkey is golden brown, shield breast loosely with rectangular piece of foil to prevent overbrowning. See box below for approximate roasting time.

Weight (pounds)	Time (hours*)
8 to 12	3 to 4
12 to 16	3½ to 4½
16 to 20	4 to 5
20 to 24	4½ to 6

*Add 30 minutes cooking time for stuffed turkey

ESSENCE BRINGS YOU
GREAT COOKING

TURKEY BROTH AND GIBLETS

Use to make a rich-tasting dressing or gravy.

Turkey giblets
4 cups water
1 stalk celery, sliced
1 carrot, coarsely sliced
1 onion, sliced
1 bay leaf
2 sprigs parsley
4 peppercorns
½ teaspoon salt *(optional)*

Makes about 4 cups broth; 1½ cups chopped giblets.

PER CUP:

82 calories
12 g protein
3 g fat
2 g carbohydrate
275 mg sodium
165 mg cholesterol

Remove giblets from turkey cavities. (Discard liver if green.) Rinse with cold running water. In large saucepan, combine giblets and 4 cups water or enough water to cover. Add celery, carrot, onion, bay leaf, parsley, peppercorns, and salt (if desired). Over medium-high heat, bring liquid to boil; reduce heat to low. Cover and simmer 15 minutes; remove and set aside cooked liver. Cover and simmer until gizzard is tender, 60 to 90 additional minutes. Remove giblets; set aside. Pour broth through sieve to strain; discard remaining solids. Store broth in covered container in refrigerator until time to use. Remove cooked meat from neckbone; chop together with liver, heart, and gizzard. Store in covered container in refrigerator until time to use.

ESSENCE BRINGS YOU
GREAT COOKING

GRANDMA'S OLD-FASHIONED GIBLET GRAVY

Makes about 5 cups.

PER CUP:

29 calories
3 g protein
1 g fat
.85 g carbohydrate
450 mg sodium
22 mg cholesterol

Turkey giblets and neck
1 stalk celery, cut up
1 small onion, chopped
1 teaspoon salt *(optional)*
½ teaspoon ground black pepper
Water
¼ cup unbleached all-purpose flour

During final hour of roasting turkey, in 3-quart saucepan over medium heat combine giblets, neck, celery, onion, ½ teaspoon salt (if desired), and ¼ teaspoon pepper, and 3 cups water. Bring to boil; reduce heat and simmer; cover about 1 hour and 15 minutes or until giblets are tender. Remove giblets and neck; pour broth through sieve into bowl. Discard celery and onion. Remove meat from neck and chop with giblets; set aside. When turkey is done, remove rack with turkey from roasting pan. Transfer turkey to warm platter; keep warm. Pour pan drippings from roasting pan into 4-quart measure. Let stand several minutes to allow fat to separate from juice. Spoon about 2 tablespoons of fat back into roasting pan; discard any remaining fat. Over medium heat, stir flour into hot fat in roasting pan. Cook, stirring constantly with wooden spoon to loosen bits in pan, about 3 minutes or until flour is cooked and of desired brownness; remove from heat. In large liquid measure, combine giblet broth, pan drippings from turkey, and enough water to equal 4½ cups. Gradually stir liquid mixture into browned flour until well blended. Return to heat and bring to boil; reduce heat and cook about 8 minutes until thickened. Add chopped meat, remaining salt (if desired), and pepper. Cook about 2 minutes to heat giblets. Pour into gravy boat to serve.

TURKEY POT ROAST

Today's new turkey is meatier and cooks more quickly. This change-of-pace, low-fat pot roast provides lots of flavor in less time.

1 uncooked turkey hindquarter or 2 boned turkey thighs
1 teaspoon salt *(optional)*
¼ teaspoon ground black pepper
1 small onion, chopped
2 garlic cloves, peeled, minced
½ teaspoon dried basil, crumbled
¼ teaspoon dried thyme
1 cup fat-skimmed turkey broth or water
3 medium-size potatoes, peeled, halved
4 medium-size carrots, cut into chunks
1 tablespoon cornstarch
¼ cup cold water
Optional garnish: 2 tablespoons chopped fresh parsley

Makes 4 servings.

PER SERVING:

429 calories
41 g protein
14 g fat
33 g carbohydrate
685 mg sodium
117 mg cholesterol

Heat oven to 450° F. Rinse turkey and blot dry with paper towels. Season with salt (if desired) and pepper. In ovenproof, nonstick Dutch oven, place turkey skin side up. Bake 25 minutes until skin is crisp, drain and discard any fat. Add onion, garlic, basil, thyme, and broth. Cover and simmer over low heat (or bake at 375° F) until turkey is nearly tender, about 30 minutes. Add potatoes and carrots. Cover and cook until vegetables are tender, about 20 minutes. Transfer turkey and vegetables to platter; keep warm. Skim any fat from pan juices and discard. In Dutch oven on burner over medium heat, bring to slow simmer. In measuring cup, mix cornstarch and cold water; stir into simmering pan juices. Cook, stirring, until sauce thickens. Pour sauce over or around meat and vegetables. Sprinkle with parsley.

SPICY ORANGE-GLAZED TURKEY DRUMSTICKS

Makes 12 servings.

PER SERVING:

206 calories
30 g protein
8 g fat
2 g carbohydrate
263 mg sodium
74 mg cholesterol

8 medium-size uncooked turkey drumsticks (about 3 to a 2-pound package)
3 tablespoons orange-juice concentrate
2 tablespoons lemon juice
2 tablespoons vegetable oil
½ teaspoon ground ginger
1 teaspoon salt *(optional)*
¼ teaspoon freshly ground black pepper
1 tablespoon orange peel grated
Optional garnishes: kumquats, watercress, arugula, sage leaves, or other greens or herbs

Rinse drumsticks with cold running water; blot dry with paper towels. Remove and discard skin, if desired. Heat oven to 375° F. To make orange sauce, in small mixing bowl, combine all remaining ingredients except garnishes; whisk to blend well. In large, greased baking pan, arrange turkey legs in single layer, keeping them separated. Baste turkey with orange sauce. Bake 70 to 85 minutes, turning once and basting frequently. Drumsticks are thoroughly cooked when meat loses pink color and juices run clear when cut. Transfer to serving platter; garnish with kumquats and greens.

ESSENCE BRINGS YOU
GREAT COOKING

Maple-Baked Chicken, Creole Okra and Tomatoes, and Mixed Greens (with corn).

SAVORY TURKEY STEW

1 pound uncooked turkey breast
¼ cup unbleached all-purpose flour
½ teaspoon salt *(optional)*
¼ teaspoon ground black pepper
¼ cup safflower oil
1 large onion, chopped
1 large garlic clove, minced
2 cups chicken broth
1 cup water
4 medium-size carrots, cut into chunks
4 medium-size potatoes, cubed
1 pint brussels sprouts
½ teaspoon dried thyme leaves
½ teaspoon poultry seasoning
1 bay leaf

Makes 6 servings.

PER SERVING:

311 calories
18 g protein
11 g fat
35 g carbohydrate
497 mg sodium
29 mg cholesterol

Remove skin from turkey; cut meat into 1-inch cubes. On waxed paper combine flour, salt (if desired), and pepper. Coat meat cubes with flour; reserve leftover flour. In 5-quart Dutch oven heat oil; brown meat on all sides, few pieces at a time. Remove turkey as it browns. Reduce heat to medium. Add onion and garlic to drippings in pan. Cook, stirring, about 3 minutes. Stir in reserved flour, cook and stir about 5 minutes until lightly browned. Stir in broth and water; cook until slightly thickened. Add vegetables, seasonings, and turkey. Heat to boil; reduce heat and simmer, covered, 15 to 20 minutes or until vegetables are of desired tenderness. Remove bay leaf; serve immediately. Delicious served over egg noodles.

ESSENCE BRINGS YOU
GREAT COOKING

TURKEY ROLL WITH CONFETTI VEGETABLE STUFFING

This roll has a dramatic look for special occasions.

Makes 12 main-dish servings; slice thin for about 18 appetizer servings.

PER EACH OF 12 SERVINGS:

325 calories
43 g protein
13 g fat
5 g carbohydrate
316 mg sodium
116 mg cholesterol

- 1 10-ounce bag fresh spinach, rinsed
- 1 cup shredded carrots
- 1 cup chopped zucchini
- 1 cup fresh whole corn kernels cut from cob or frozen whole kernels
- 1 small medium-size red bell pepper, seeded, chopped
- ⅓ cup ricotta cheese
- 1 teaspoon salt *(optional)*
- ½ teaspoon ground black pepper
- 1 4-pound uncooked boneless turkey breast
- 2 tablespoons melted butter or margarine

Heat oven to 325° F. Wash spinach in cold water. In large saucepan, steam spinach until completely wilted. Drain spinach, then squeeze dry; chop. In medium-size bowl, mix spinach, carrots, zucchini, corn, bell pepper, ricotta, ½ teaspoon salt (if desired), and pepper. Set aside. Remove skin from turkey; cut skin into 2 pieces through center; set aside. Bone turkey, then separate into 2 breast portions. Place turkey cut side up on cutting board. Through long side of breast, cut horizontally through thickest portion, leaving 1-inch piece intact at far side. Open and "butterfly" breast. With wooden mallet pound turkey to approximately 10-by-8-by-⅓-inch thick. Sprinkle with remaining ½ teaspoon salt (if desired); spread with half of vegetable mixture. Starting at narrow end, roll meat with filling, jelly-roll style. Cover with piece of reserved skin. Tie roll together with kitchen string. Repeat same procedure with other breast. Place rolls skin side up on rack in shallow roasting pan. Brush with butter. Roast until cooked through, about 90 minutes. Let stand 10 minutes; remove string before slicing.

FRUITED TURKEY KABOBS

1 pound uncooked turkey breast

¼ cup lime or lemon juice

2 tablespoons vegetable oil

1 tablespoon molasses or honey

1 teaspoon fresh thyme or rosemary leaves

½ teaspoon salt *(optional)*

¼ teaspoon cayenne or white pepper

¼ teaspoon garlic powder

1 green bell pepper, seeded, cut into 8 chunks

2 small plums, halved

2 1-inch-thick slices fresh pineapple with rind, each cut into 4 wedges

1 orange, cut into 4 wedges

Prepare grill or heat broiler as directed by manufacturer. Cut turkey into 1-inch cubes. In glass bowl combine juice, oil, molasses, herbs, and other seasonings; add turkey. Stir to completely coat turkey; let stand about 15 minutes. Prepare bell pepper and fruit. Arrange turkey, bell pepper and fruit alternately on 8 separate skewers. Grill or broil kabobs about 5 inches from heat source for 15 to 20 minutes, turning once and basting with marinade left in bowl. Serve warm.

Makes 4 servings.

PER SERVING:

230 calories

22 g protein

9 g fat

15 g carbohydrate

314 mg sodium

49 mg cholesterol

TURKEY A LA KING

Makes 4 servings.

PER SERVING:

396 calories
27 g protein
19 g fat
27 g carbohydrate
735 mg sodium
82 mg cholesterol

2 tablespoons butter or margarine
1 cup sliced fresh mushrooms
½ cup chopped onion
3 tablespoons unbleached all-purpose flour
¾ cup milk
½ cup chicken stock
½ teaspoon salt *(optional)*
⅛ teaspoon ground black, white, or cayenne pepper
2 tablespoons chopped fresh parsley
2 cups cubed cooked turkey
1 cup frozen green peas, thawed
¼ cup chopped pimiento
Biscuits, cornbread squares, popovers, toast, or pastry shells
Optional garnish: flat-leaf parsley

In large saucepan, melt butter. Add mushrooms and onion; sauté 5 minutes. Over low heat, stir in flour; cook, stirring constantly, 1 minute. Using whisk, gradually blend in milk and stock; add salt (if desired) and pepper. Cook, constantly stirring until mixture is thick and creamy, about 5 minutes. Add chopped parsley, turkey, peas, and pimiento. Heat to low simmer, then cover and cook about 5 minutes. To serve, place biscuits on 4 plates, spoon turkey mixture over biscuits. Garnish with parsley.

ESSENCE BRINGS YOU
GREAT COOKING

NEW ENGLAND TURKEY CHOWDER

1 tablespoon butter or margarine
1 small onion, chopped
1 stalk celery, chopped
2 cups turkey or chicken broth
2 large potatoes, peeled, diced
½ teaspoon salt *(optional)*
¼ teaspoon ground black or white pepper
Dash hot pepper sauce
2 cups cubed or chopped cooked turkey
2 tablespoons cornstarch
2 cups milk (use low-fat or skim milk to reduce calories and cholesterol)

In large saucepan, melt butter; sauté onion and celery until soft, about 5 minutes. Add broth, potatoes, salt (if desired), pepper, and hot pepper sauce. Over medium heat, bring to boil. Reduce heat; cover and simmer until potatoes are tender, about 10 to 15 minutes. Stir in turkey. In medium-size bowl, blend cornstarch and milk; stir into soup mixture. Cook until thickened, about 2 minutes.

Makes 4 servings.

PER SERVING:

316 calories
29 g protein
11 g fat
34 g carbohydrate
808 mg sodium
77 mg cholesterol

TURKEY HASH

Makes 10 servings.

PER SERVING:

300 calories
29 g protein
9 g fat
25 g carbohydrate
309 mg sodium
69 mg cholesterol

2 tablespoons vegetable oil
1 large onion, coarsely chopped
1 small green bell pepper, seeded, cut into 1-inch chunks or strips
1 teaspoon crushed sage
2 tablespoons unbleached all-purpose flour
¾ teaspoon salt *(optional)*
½ teaspoon ground black pepper
2 pounds diced or chopped roasted turkey
2 pounds boiled, cubed red-skinned potatoes or all-purpose
   white potatoes
1 cup chicken broth or milk
Optional garnishes: sage leaves, flat-leaf parsley sprigs

In large Dutch oven, heat oil. Add onion, bell pepper, and sage; sauté about 3 minutes. Stir in flour, salt (if desired), and black pepper; cook 2 additional minutes. Stir in cooked turkey, potatoes, and broth; mix well. Reduce heat to low; cook uncovered, about 10 minutes.

TURKEY-CITRUS SALAD

1 bunch fresh spinach or 6 cups other leafy greens, thoroughly rinsed
  to remove grit, dried
3 cups fresh grapefruit sections (about 3 grapefruit), drained, juice
  reserved
2 cups fresh orange sections (about 4 oranges), drained, juice reserved
2 cups cooked turkey, sliced, cubed, chopped, or julienned (cut into
  thin strips)
1 tablespoon honey
½ teaspoon dry mustard
½ teaspoon paprika
¼ teaspoon garlic powder
⅓ cup calorie-reduced mayonnaise
½ cup halved or chopped walnuts
Optional garnish: kumquats and fresh currants

Makes 4 servings.

PER SERVING:

402 calories
29 g protein
18 g fat
35 g carbohydrate
117 mg sodium
60 mg cholesterol

On 4 dinner plates, arrange greens. Atop greens, arrange fruit sections in wheel-spoke or other decorative pattern; add turkey. In small bowl, combine ½ cup reserved juices, honey, mustard, paprika, and garlic powder. Stir in mayonnaise; blend well. Drizzle salads with dressing; sprinkle with nuts. Garnish with kumquats and currants.

ESSENCE BRINGS YOU
GREAT COOKING

TURKEY SALAD

This basic turkey salad can be served with lettuce and vegetables such as sliced cucumbers, cherry tomatoes, alfalfa sprouts, and green-pepper rings; or use this salad to make hearty sandwiches.

Makes 6 servings.

PER SERVING:

174 calories
23 g protein
7 g fat
4 g carbohydrate
180 mg sodium
126 mg cholesterol

3 cups diced cooked turkey
1 cup chopped celery
¼ cup chopped sweet pickles
2 hard-boiled eggs, chopped
¾ cup mayonnaise
1 tablespoon fresh lemon juice

In large bowl, combine all ingredients; mix well. Chill.

TURKEY MEATLOAF

Switch and save: Ground turkey has up to 50 percent less saturated fat than other ground meats.

1 tablespoon vegetable oil
1 medium-size onion, chopped
2 scallions, chopped
2 garlic cloves, minced
2 medium-size carrots, diced
1 rib celery, diced
1 small green bell pepper, seeded, diced
2 large egg whites
½ teaspoon salt *(optional)*
½ teaspoon ground black pepper
¼ teaspoon cayenne pepper
½ cup catsup
½ cup skim milk
2 pounds ground turkey
¾ cup dry bread crumbs

Makes 10 servings.

PER SERVING:

189 calories
14 g protein
8 g fat
13 g carbohydrate
354 mg sodium
34 mg cholesterol

In medium-size nonstick skillet, heat oil; add onions, scallions, garlic, carrots, celery, and bell pepper. Sauté about 5 minutes; let vegetable mixture cool. Heat oven to 350° F. In large bowl, combine egg whites, salt (if desired), black and cayenne peppers, ¼ cup catsup, and milk; using whisk or fork, beat until blended. To egg mixture, add turkey, crumbs, and cooked vegetables; using wooden spoon or hands, mix ingredients together just until uniform. Lightly pack mixture into 9-by-5-by-3-inch loaf pan, slightly rounding top. Pour remaining catsup over top. Bake 50 minutes; let stand 15 minutes before slicing.

ESSENCE BRINGS YOU
GREAT COOKING

TURKEY MEATBALLS AND SPAGHETTI WITH BASIC HOMEMADE TOMATO SAUCE

Makes 6 servings.

PER SERVING:

612 calories
25 g protein
17 g fat
88 g carbohydrate
760 mg sodium
64 mg cholesterol

1 pound ground turkey
1 cup dry or fresh bread crumbs
1 teaspoon dried oregano
½ teaspoon salt *(optional)*
½ teaspoon ground black pepper
1 small onion, finely chopped
2 medium-size garlic cloves, minced
1 large egg, beaten slightly

2 tablespoons vegetable oil
2 cups spaghetti sauce, purchased or homemade (see following recipe)
1 16-ounce package spaghetti
Optional garnish: fresh basil leaves

   In large bowl, combine turkey, bread crumbs, spices, and egg; mix well. With hands, shape turkey mixture into 1½- to 2-inch balls. In large skillet, heat oil; tilt and rotate pan to spread oil over bottom. Add meatballs to skillet, cooking in batches to avoid crowding; turn occasionally to brown on all sides. Skim and discard fat from drippings. Add spaghetti sauce. Over medium-low heat, cover and simmer meatballs 8 to 10 minutes. Meanwhile, cook spaghetti according to package directions until tender but firm (al dente). Drain spaghetti; toss with about ¼ cup sauce to coat. Transfer spaghetti to platter; top with remaining sauce and meatballs. Garnish with basil leaves.

Basic Homemade Tomato Sauce

Use this simple and versatile sauce to top pasta, meat loaf, stuffed cabbage, and other favorites. In summer, when fresh tomatoes are flavorful and less expensive, use about 8 medium-size tomatoes as an alternative to canned tomatoes in this recipe.

2 tablespoons vegetable oil or olive oil
1 medium-size yellow onion, chopped
1 small green bell pepper, seeded minced
1 clove garlic, chopped
1 35-ounce can plum tomatoes, chopped
1 6-ounce can tomato paste
1 cup water
2 teaspoons brown sugar
2 tablespoons chopped fresh parsley
1 teaspoon salt (optional)
½ teaspoon ground black pepper
1 bay leaf

Makes 4 cups.

PER CUP:

191 calories
4 g protein
8 g fat
31 g carbohydrate
1,193 mg sodium
0 mg cholesterol

In 3-quart saucepan over medium heat, heat oil; cook onion, bell pepper, and garlic until tender, about 7 minutes. Stir in tomatoes and remaining ingredients. Over high heat, bring to boil. Reduce heat to medium-low; cook, partially covered, about 30 minutes. Discard bay leaf.

TURKEY WITH PUMPKIN TORTELLINI

*Lori Merritt, our Eastern Advertising Sales Manager,
is a fabulous cook as well. One taste of her delicious tortellini, and
I had to have the recipe.*

Makes 4 servings.

ESTIMATED
PER SERVING:

649 calories
33 gm protein
23 gm fat
76 gm carbohydrate
559 mg sodium
144 mg cholesterol

2 tablespoons olive oil
1 large onion, chopped
3 garlic cloves, minced
1 teaspoon crushed hot red pepper
2 bay leaves
½ teaspoon salt *(optional)*
1 pound ground turkey
5 small ripe plum tomatoes, chopped
2 cups ready-made spaghetti sauce with extra mushrooms
1 pound fresh or dried pumpkin tortellini

In large skillet, heat olive oil. Sauté onion, garlic, red pepper, bay leaves, and salt (if desired) about 5 minutes. Crumble turkey and add to skillet; cook, stirring occasionally, until turkey browns, about 10 minutes. Stir in tomatoes; cook about 5 minutes. Stir in spaghetti sauce; cook 30 additional minutes. Prepare tortellini according to package directions; drain well. Spoon meat sauce over pasta.

$\mathcal{M}$eat—

The New Breed

Recipes

COUNTRY POT ROAST WITH GRAVY

ROLLED RUMP ROAST WITH PAN-ROASTED VEGETABLES

BUDGET BEEF BURGUNDY

STEAK FILLETS WITH RED-WINE SAUCE

SKILLET STEAK 'N' POTATOES

GINGER BEEF-VEGETABLE STIR-FRY

BEEF-AND-BROCCOLI STIR-FRY

BEEF-AND-VEGETABLE STEW

TANGY BARBECUED SHORT RIBS OF BEEF

HONEY-GLAZED COUNTRY RIBS

BASIC DRY BARBECUE RUB

ALL-PURPOSE BARBECUE SAUCE

BAKED SHORT RIBS WITH WINE

TEXAS OVEN-BARBECUED BRISKET

WARM BEEF-AND-BLACK-EYED-PEA SALAD

LIME-CHILI VINAIGRETTE

HOME-STYLE BEEF-VEGETABLE SOUP

Recipes

BARBECUED BEEF SANDWICHES

BEEFY TAMALE PIE

PICADILLO

HERBED BEEF PATTIES

BEEF-MACARONI SKILLET SUPPER

CARIBBEAN MEATBALLS WITH PINEAPPLE CHUTNEY

CHILI WITH CORN BREAD DUMPLINGS

VEAL SCALLOPS WITH MUSHROOMS

HERB-BAKED VEAL CHOPS

VEAL PICCATA

ROSEMARY-BAKED RACK OF LAMB

LAMB AND EGGPLANT DINNER

CURRIED LAMB CHOPS AND MUSHROOMS

HEARTY LAMB STEW

GRILLED LAMB-AND-VEGGIE KABOBS

BLUE CHEESE LAMB PATTY

CURRIED GOAT

TIPS TO CONTROL FAT AND CALORIES IN MEAT

1. Choose leaner cuts of meat. For beef: Round tip, top round, eye of round, top loin, tenderloin, and sirloin are the leanest. Brisket, chuck, flank, and ribs are somewhat fattier.

2. Trim all visible fat from meat before cooking and eating. Most beef cuts are now trimmed to ¼ inch. Use a sharp knife to cut away the remaining fat carefully.

3. Use cooking methods that reduce rather than add fat. Broiling, roasting, pan broiling, and grilling require no additional fat.

4. Remove fat from sauces, gravies, broths, soups, stews, and chili by chilling them and skimming the hardened fat from the top.

5. Use ground meat products that are 80 to 90 percent lean.

6. Keep serving sizes small. Three ounces of cooked meat makes a healthful serving. A 3-ounce serving is about the size of a deck of playing cards.

MEAT has gone on a diet. The new breeds of meat have more lean and less fat. The old profile, once prized for its heavy marbling of fat, had started to sag as meat came to be considered out-of-step with new guidelines for healthy eating. Ranchers and butchers, however, responded to our changing dietary habits and now bring to market meat that is a leaner, trimmer version of its former self.

Meat is a significant source of many nutrients that are essential to good health. Beef is one of the best sources of iron, a nutrient often lacking in the diets of women. It contains a high percentage of heme iron, which is more easily absorbed by the body than nonheme iron found in plant sources. Meat also supplies the often missing mineral zinc. The protein in meat is nutritionally complete, containing all the essential amino acids necessary for growth. Beef is also a major source of five of the B-complex vitamins, including thiamin, riboflavin, niacin, and vitamins B^{12} and B^6. Vitamin B^{12} is found naturally only in animal foods.

THE MEAT EATER'S DILEMMA

Meat has been the mainstay of the American diet since colonial times. In the South, it was commonly said that we ate all the parts of the pig except the oink! In many African nations, owning cattle and eating meat are measures of a person's worth in society. Yet we are increasingly aware of health risks associated with saturated fat and cholesterol common in meat. So how can a meat eater adjust to these changing dietary times? With simple moderation. The primary goal is not to cut out red meats per se but to reduce your intake of saturated fats and cholesterol. Pay attention to the frequency with which you eat red meats and the amounts you consume. Make deliberate selections and enjoy their succulent flavors.

BASIC COOKING METHODS

To get the most flavor and the most value for your money, cook meat according to the most suitable method. Don't buy an expensive tender cut of meat such as round, when you plan to cook it for a long time to make stew. For safety's sake, cook meat until well done. Heat kills bacteria, including salmonella. Avoid rare meat, especially ground beef (at home and in restaurants).

Easy Steps to Cooking Meat

BRAISING

1. In heavy-bottomed pot or Dutch oven, brown meat in small amount of oil; pour off fat.
2. Add small amount of liquid to pan—water, stock, bouillon, vegetable juice—and desired seasonings; cover pan tightly.
3. Simmer on top of range or in oven until fork-tender.

BROILING

1. Place meat on rack in broiler pan. Place pan 2 to 5 inches from heat source. The thicker the cut, the farther the meat should be placed from the heating unit so it will cook evenly.
2. Broil one side until browned; season cooked side if desired.
3. Turn meat; cook second side until browned and done. Season second side if desired.

PANFRYING

1. Heat small amount of oil in skillet over medium heat.
2. Add meat; do not cover.
3. Turn occasionally until browned and well done; season as desired.

ROASTING

1. Place meat fat-side-up on rack in shallow roasting pan; season as desired.
2. Insert meat thermometer so tip does not rest in fat or on bone. Do not add water or cover.
3. Roast at 325° F until thermometer reaches 170° F.

BUYING MEAT

The U.S.D.A. round purple stamp indicates that the meat has been inspected and is a mark of wholesomeness. Tender young beef is red and its fat is creamy white. As it gets older, beef darkens and fat yellows.

HOW MUCH TO BUY

The amount to purchase for a meal depends on the amount of bone and fat as well as the intended use. An average serving of cooked boneless meat is 3 to 4 ounces. If the meat is combined in a dish with vegetables, pasta, or grains, you can use even less. For a bone-in roast, allow 1/3 to 1/2 pound per serving. For boneless roast, allow 1/4 to 1/3 pound per serving. It's a money-saving idea to buy larger cuts and plan ahead for leftovers for future meals.

ESSENCE BRINGS YOU
GREAT COOKING

CUTS OF MEAT

There are more than 60 different cuts of beef alone. Meat easily divides, however, into two categories—tender and less tender.

All meat is muscle and toughens with exercise and age. Meat from the legs, neck, shoulder, rump, and flank will be tougher than the less exercised rib and loin sections. Old animals will be tougher than young ones.

VEAL

Considered a delicacy, veal is calf meat. A lean pick, veal has no marbling and little or no outer-fat covering. Depending on the animal's age and diet, its color when raw will range from slightly grey with a suggestion of pinkness (milk fed) to pink (older, grain fed), and even red (grazed). This expensive meat has no poor cuts. Most valued are the thin and tender scallops. Because of the absence of fat, veal should be cooked with moist heat or basted during roasting.

LAMB

Lamb is the meat of a sheep under the age of one year. Baby lamb is 6 to 8 weeks old, and spring lamb, 3 to 5 months old. After a year, sheep is called a yearling mutton; after 2 years, a mutton. Mutton has the most pronounced flavor.

In times past, lamb was traditionally slaughtered in the spring and became known as "spring" lamb. Today it's widely available year-round. Lamb is highly amenable to added flavorings. Some of the seasonings for marinating that best enhance lamb are garlic (make slits in the meat and insert slivers of garlic), curry, rosemary, mild mustard, ginger, barbecue sauce, and the most popular—mint. Plum, red currant, apple, and mint jelly, marmalade, or chutney make superb glazes for lamb roasts.

GOAT

Throughout the Caribbean islands, goats tethered to a post or fence are a common sight. Their ability to thrive with little fuss have made goats an island staple. Not only is a goat's will strong, but so is its flavor. Long, slow stewing or grilling with appetizing seasonings such as curry, make goat a tender, savory delight.

JERK

Jerk is the popular Jamaican method of barbecuing that has caught fire across the islands and the States. Jerk is said to have originated with the Maroons—Jamaican people of African descent who escaped enslavement by British colonists. As they travelled on the run across the hills of Portland, the Maroons caught wild pigs and used hot peppers, spices and slow roasting in earthen pits as a means to preserve and season their meat. Today those same basic techniques are used around the island by home cooks, chefs, and street-food vendors to render pork, chicken, beef, sausage, and seafood into spicy delicacies. Although most Jamaicans have their own variations on the jerk-seasoning theme, the essentials are Scotch Bonnet peppers, Jamaican pimiento (allspice), scallions, thyme, onions, and garlic blended into a dry rub or paste.

The Barbecue

Barbecue is a method of cooking and the term for food cooked by that method, as well as the name of the event where the cooking takes place! It is a near-sacred culinary tradition that also defines our palate. Just the thought of marinated meat cooked over coals real slow to allow the smoke and peppery hot sauce to penetrate, is enough to start gastronomical juices and memories flowing. In backyards, church yards, and local parks; in portable grills, makeshift oil drums, and pits in the ground; from split chickens, to slabs of ribs, to whole pigs; for celebrating, fund-raising, and simple good times, barbecue is without equal. The cooking technique boils down to two things—slow cooking and having a barbecue sauce to boast about!

The genesis of this time-honored cookout can be traced to the Motherland where we began mopping roasting foods with fiery basting sauces. To update your barbecue for healthier and expanded choices, add fish and vegetables to the grill. Even a whole turkey (an economical and tasty way to feed a crowd) can be cooked on a covered grill or in a smoker. Marinating and using naturally flavored wood such as hickory, maple, or mesquite can further enhance grilled flavors.

ESSENCE BRINGS YOU
GREAT COOKING

COUNTRY POT ROAST WITH GRAVY

Instead of fatty meat drippings, this flavorful gravy is made from vegetables cooked with the roast.

Makes 16 servings.

PER SERVING:

159 calories
19 g protein
6 g fat
5 g carbohydrate
229 mg sodium
58 mg cholesterol

1 4-pound lean, boneless round roast
2 garlic cloves, crushed
2 tablespoons unbleached all-purpose flour
2 tablespoons vegetable oil
1 cup tomato juice
2 large carrots, sliced
2 ribs celery, sliced
2 medium-size onions, chopped
1 teaspoon salt *(optional)*
½ teaspoon coarsely ground black pepper
1 teaspoon crushed oregano

Wipe roast with damp paper towels; rub with garlic. On waxed paper, coat roast with flour. In 8-quart Dutch oven, heat oil over high heat. Add roast and cook, turning often, until browned on all sides. Pour off all fat. Add remaining ingredients. Heat until boiling; reduce heat to low. Cover pot and simmer, turning roast occasionally, until meat is fork-tender, about 2½ hours. Transfer meat to serving platter. Spoon off all visible fat; lift vegetables from liquid and place in blender or food processor. Again, remove any visible fat left in pot. Add liquid from pot to blender; do not fill to more than ¾ full. Process until sauce is smooth and well blended. Pour into pot and heat until boiling. Serve with roast.

ROLLED RUMP ROAST WITH PAN-ROASTED VEGETABLES

5-pound rolled beef rump roast
3 tablespoons unbleached all-purpose flour
1 teaspoon salt *(optional)*
1 teaspoon cracked black pepper
1 teaspoon paprika
¼ teaspoon dry mustard
¼ cup vegetable oil
2 ribs celery, cut into 4-inch lengths
1 small onion, quartered
2 garlic cloves, chopped
2 bay leaves
Vegetables for roasting (see following guide)

Makes 18 servings.

PER SERVING:

407 calories
34 g protein
10 g fat
46 g carbohydrate
207 mg sodium
85 mg cholesterol

Heat oven to 325° F. Using damp paper towels, wipe meat. In small bowl, combine flour, salt (if desired), pepper, paprika, and mustard; rub meat all over with seasoning mixture. In large skillet or roasting pan, heat oil; brown meat on all sides. Transfer to roasting pan with rack. Add celery, onion, garlic, and bay leaves. Roast, basting occasionally, about 3 to 3½ hours or until fork-tender. Add vegetables during last 30 to 45 minutes (depending on desired tenderness); turn occasionally. Warm large platter; transfer roast. Discard celery and bay leaves. Arrange vegetables on platter. To make gravy, remove rack; skim and discard fat from pan drippings. To pan, add up to 1 cup water; stir to blend and loosen browned bits on bottom. Bring gravy to boil; strain into small bowl or gravy boat.

Pan-Roasted Vegetables

Small red-skinned potatoes: Allow 2 or 3 2-inch potatoes per person. Scrub well; halve or leave whole and pare band of peel from each potato.
Carrots: Allow 1 medium-size carrot per person. Scrape or peel, if desired, and cut into large chunks.
String beans: Allow 1 pound string beans per 4 servings. Snap off stem ends, removing string. In boiling water, blanch beans 2 to 3 minutes.
Zucchini: Allow ½ medium-size zucchini per person. Trim and discard stem and blossom ends; slice.

ESSENCE BRINGS YOU
GREAT COOKING

BUDGET BEEF BURGUNDY

Makes 8 servings.

PER SERVING:

333 calories
31 g protein
13 g fat
16 g carbohydrate
273 mg sodium
95 mg cholesterol

1 2-pound boneless chuck rump roast
2 tablespoons unbleached all-purpose flour
2 garlic cloves, minced
¼ teaspoon salt *(optional)*
¼ teaspoon ground black pepper
3 tablespoons vegetable oil
1 cup sliced mushrooms
8 small white-skinned onions, peeled
1 cup red Burgundy or other dry red wine
1 13-ounce can beef broth
1 teaspoon dried oregano
1 teaspoon dried basil
1 cup cooked fresh or frozen green peas *(optional)*
12 ounces egg noodles, cooked or 3 cups warm cooked rice
Optional garnish: chopped parsley

Cut roast into 1½-to-2-inch cubes, trimming and discarding visible fat. In brown paper or plastic bag, combine flour, garlic, salt (if desired), and pepper; add meat and shake to coat evenly. In heavy Dutch oven over medium-high heat, heat oil. In batches, brown cubed beef on all sides. As browned, remove meat and set aside. Remove and discard all but 2 tablespoons pan drippings. Add mushrooms and onions; sauté about 5 minutes. Stir in wine, broth, and herbs. Return meat to pot; bring to boil. Reduce heat to low; cover and simmer until meat is fork-tender, about 2 hours. Stir in peas. Delicious served with wide egg noodles or rice. Sprinkle with parsley.

STEAK FILLETS WITH RED-WINE SAUCE

4 boneless beef steaks (about 4 ounces each), use rib-eye, shell or other prime-quality beef
2 tablespoons vegetable oil
1 tablespoon butter or margarine
1 teaspoon salt *(optional)*
½ teaspoon freshly ground black pepper
½ pound mushrooms, rinsed thoroughly in cold water, dried, sliced
2 tablespoons chopped shallots
½ cup low-sodium beef broth
1 tablespoon cornstarch
½ cup red wine
3 tablespoons minced fresh parsley

Makes 4 servings.

PER SERVING:

155 calories
17 g protein
6 g fat
4 g carbohydrate
411 mg sodium
42 mg cholesterol

Set oven at warm or lowest setting; place heatproof platter in oven. Trim any excess fat from steaks. Wipe meat with damp cloth. In 12-inch skillet or 2 medium-size skillets, over medium-high heat, heat butter and oil. Add steaks, arranging them so they do not touch each other. Cook steaks 4 to 5 minutes on each side for medium-rare or longer for desired doneness. Sprinkle with salt (if desired) and pepper. Transfer steaks to warm platter; keep warm in oven while preparing sauce. Remove all but 2 tablespoons fat from skillet (do not remove juices). Over medium heat, add mushrooms and shallots; sauté until tender, about 5 minutes. Stir in beef broth and heat to boiling. In measuring cup or small bowl, blend cornstarch and wine. Into mushroom mixture, gradually stir wine; cook, stirring constantly until thickened, about 2 minutes. Spoon sauce over steaks; sprinkle with parsley. Serve at once.

ESSENCE BRINGS YOU
GREAT COOKING

SKILLET STEAK 'N' POTATOES

Makes 4 servings.

PER SERVING:

372 calories
28 g protein
15 g fat
30 g carbohydrate
684 mg sodium
77 mg cholesterol

4 cube steaks (about 1 pound)
¼ teaspoon ground black pepper
2 tablespoons vegetable oil
6 small potatoes (about 1½ pounds), well scrubbed, sliced
1 1-ounce envelope onion soup mix, mixed with ⅔ cup hot water

Sprinkle steaks with pepper. In large skillet over high heat, heat oil. Add meat; brown quickly, turning once. Remove meat; set aside. Reduce heat under skillet; add potatoes. Sauté about 10 minutes, shaking skillet to prevent sticking. Push potatoes to one side of skillet. Return steaks to skillet. Pour soup mixture over all. Cover and gently simmer 25 minutes, or until meat and potatoes are tender. Delicious served with brussels sprouts.

GINGER BEEF-VEGETABLE STIR-FRY

This recipe uses a small amount of beef for flavor and protein; lean pork, chicken, or tofu can be substituted.

½ pound flank steak, partially frozen for easier slicing
2 tablespoons vegetable oil
2 medium-size garlic cloves, minced
1 stalk celery, sliced
1 small green bell pepper, seeded, cut into thin strips
1 medium-size onion, sliced
4 medium-size carrots, diagonally cut into thin slices
2 cups shredded cabbage
1 tablespoon grated fresh ginger or 1 teaspoon ground ginger
¼ teaspoon cayenne pepper
½ cup beef broth
¼ cup water
1 tablespoon cornstarch
2 tablespoons sodium-reduced soy sauce
2 cups cooked brown rice

Makes 4 servings.

PER SERVING:

350 calories
17 g protein
13 g fat
40 g carbohydrate
438 mg sodium
30 mg cholesterol

Wipe meat with damp paper towels. Using sharp knife, cut meat across grain into very thin slices. In 12-inch skillet, wok, or Dutch oven over medium-high heat, add 1 tablespoon oil. Add beef and garlic; cook, stirring quickly and frequently, about 3 minutes or until beef loses all pink color. Remove to platter. Add remaining tablespoon oil; when hot, add celery, bell pepper, onion, carrots, cabbage, ginger, and pepper. Cook, quickly stirring and tossing, about 5 minutes. Stir in beef, broth, and water; let steam just until all vegetables are tender. In small bowl, blend cornstarch and soy sauce; gradually stir into hot mixture. Cook, stirring constantly until thickened; about 1 minute. Serve over cooked brown rice.

ESSENCE BRINGS YOU
GREAT COOKING

BEEF-AND-BROCCOLI STIR-FRY

Ready in just 30 minutes.

Makes 4 servings.

PER SERVING:

253 calories
18 g protein
16 g fat
10 g carbohydrate
604 mg sodium
84 mg cholesterol

¾ pound flank steak, partially frozen for easier slicing
1 small head broccoli
1 small red bell pepper, seeded, cut into chunks
1 tablespoon cornstarch
2 tablespoons sodium-reduced soy sauce
½ teaspoon crushed red pepper flakes
1 tablespoon rice vinegar
1¼ cups beef broth
2 tablespoons peanut oil
1 large scallion, sliced
1 tablespoon grated fresh ginger

Slice steak across grain into thin slices (about ⅛ inch thick); cut slices into 2-inch-long pieces. Cut florets from broccoli; cut broccoli stem diagonally into ¼-inch-thick pieces, discarding coarse bottom. Seed bell pepper; cut into chunks or thin strips. In small bowl, combine cornstarch, soy sauce, pepper flakes, vinegar, and chicken broth; stir until blended, then set aside. In wok or large frying pan, heat oil over medium-high heat. In small batches, add meat; cook each batch about 2 minutes to brown quickly. Longer cooking will cause meat to lose juices and not brown. Remove meat and set aside. Add scallion, ginger, broccoli, and bell pepper; cook, tossing and stirring, about 1 minute. Add cornstarch mixture. Cook until thickened, about 1 minute; cover wok to steam broccoli about 4 minutes. Stir in beef; cook until meat is heated through, about 1 minute. Serve over brown rice or rice noodles.

BEEF-AND-VEGETABLE STEW

This hearty stew is from the kitchens of Joyce Hatendi, a home-economics teacher in Zimbabwe, and her daughter, Mary Hatendi, director of the Zimbabwe Tourist Office in New York City. In Zimbabwe this traditional dish is served with a cornmeal porridge called sadza; we enjoy it over rice.

1 pound stewing beef, cut into 1-inch cubes
1 teaspoon salt *(optional)*
½ teaspoon ground black pepper
2 tablespoons oil *(optional)*
2 medium-size onions, chopped
2 large garlic cloves, crushed
Water
2 medium-size tomatoes, chopped
½ pound broccoli rabe or mustard greens, rinsed thoroughly to remove grit, thinly shredded
2 cups diced potatoes, turnips, or carrots (these vegetables can be added 20 minutes prior to end of cooking time for more flavorful, heartier stew)

Makes 4 servings.

PER SERVING:

445 calories
28 g protein
22 g fat
34 g carbohydrate
610 mg sodium
74 mg cholesterol

Rinse meat in cold water (do not blot dry); and add beef to Dutch oven. Sprinkle with salt (if desired) and pepper. Over medium heat, partially cover and cook until juices evaporate and only fat rendered from meat remains. Cook meat, turning with wooden spoon, until brown on all sides, about 10 minutes. Add oil as needed to equal about 2 tablespoons. Add onions and garlic; sauté until translucent. Stir in 2 or more tablespoons water (depending on desired thickness of sauce). Add tomatoes, cover, and cook until beef is fork-tender, about 1 hour, adding vegetables, if desired. Serve over rice.

TANGY BARBECUED SHORT RIBS OF BEEF

Makes 4 servings.

3 pounds beef short ribs
½ teaspoon salt *(optional)*
½ teaspoon freshly ground black pepper
1 teaspoon crushed red pepper flakes
4 tablespoons lemon juice

BARBECUE SAUCE:
2 tablespoons butter or margarine
½ cup finely chopped onion
1 small garlic clove, minced
2 tablespoons brown sugar
2 tablespoons vinegar
¼ teaspoon black pepper
½ cup catsup
1 teaspoon Worcestershire sauce
½ cup water
1 beef bouillon cube
Optional garnish: parsley, tomato slices

Trim visible fat from meat. In small bowl, combine salt (if desired), black pepper, red-pepper flakes, and lemon juice. Spoon mixture over meat; marinate in refrigerator 1 hour or overnight. To make barbecue sauce: In medium-size saucepan, melt butter; stir in onion and garlic. Sauté several minutes until golden. Stir in sugar, vinegar, and pepper until sugar dissolves. Add catsup, Worcestershire sauce, water, and bouillon cube. Heat oven to 450° F. Meanwhile, simmer sauce 20 minutes, stirring occasionally. Place ribs in shallow roasting pan; place in oven for 30 minutes, turning ribs once to brown meat and melt excess fat. Decrease oven setting to 300° F. Remove pan from oven and remove meat to platter; pour off fat. Return meat to pan; spoon ribs with about ½ or ¾ of sauce. Return to oven; bake 1½ hours, basting frequently with additional sauce. Serve whole or cut into 1-or 2-bone portions. Garnish serving platter with parsley and tomato slices.

HONEY-GLAZED COUNTRY RIBS

Select rib or chuck cuts for meatier, more tender ribs; the yield will be three servings per pound.

6 pounds beef rib short ribs, cut into ¾- to 1-inch-thick strips, each with
  3 cross-cut bones
Basic Dry Barbecue Rub (see following recipe)
All-Purpose Barbecue Sauce (see following recipe; substitute 1/4 cup
  honey for brown sugar and 1 teaspoon ground ginger for cumin)

Trim all visible fat from beef; season with Basic Dry Barbecue Rub. Wrap meat; refrigerate overnight. Prepare All-Purpose Barbecue Sauce. Prepare grill; adjust grid to 4 inches above medium-hot coals. Grease grid; arrange meat; grill about 5 minutes. Turn meat; brush with barbecue sauce. Grill, turning and basting with sauce, until fork-tender, about 12 more minutes.

Makes 18 servings.

PER SERVING:

186 calories
17 g protein
11 g fat
3 g carbohydrate
156 mg sodium
53 mg cholesterol

ESSENCE BRINGS YOU
GREAT COOKING

BASIC DRY BARBECUE RUB

Create a personal trademark rub by adding your favorite seasonings to this basic dry-marinade recipe.

Makes about ¼ cup.

- 2 tablespoons freshly ground black pepper
- 2 tablespoons paprika
- 1 tablespoon salt *(optional)*
- 1 teaspoon chili powder
- 1 teaspoon cayenne pepper
- 1 teaspoon garlic powder or ground lemon zest (peel)

In small jar with tight-fitting lid, combine all ingredients; vigorously shake to mix well. Rub onto beef, pork, or poultry; wrap meat and refrigerate overnight before cooking.

ALL PURPOSE BARBECUE SAUCE

Makes about 2½ cups.

PER CUP:
286 calories
1 g protein
11 g fat
49 g carbohydrate
1,124 mg sodium
0 mg cholesterol

- 2 tablespoons vegetable oil
- 1 medium-size onion, finely chopped
- 2 medium-size garlic cloves, minced
- 1 teaspoon ground cumin
- ¼ teaspoon cayenne pepper
- 1 cup catsup
- ½ cup cider vinegar
- ½ cup water
- ¼ cup fresh lemon juice
- 2 tablespoons packed brown sugar
- 2 tablespoons Worcestershire sauce

In 2-quart saucepan, heat oil; sauté onion and garlic, about 5 minutes. Stir in remaining ingredients; simmer 20 minutes. Makes about 2½ cups sauce.

ESSENCE BRINGS YOU
GREAT COOKING

BAKED SHORT RIBS WITH WINE

6 pounds short ribs, cut in 2-inch pieces
1 cup unbleached all-purpose flour
⅓ cup vegetable oil
1½ teaspoons crushed thyme leaves
1⅓ teaspoons paprika
1 10½-ounce can beef bouillon
1½ cups red wine

Heat oven to 350° F. Wipe ribs with damp paper towels. Place flour in large paper bag; add ribs. Twist bag to seal and shake well to coat meat. Heat oil in skillet. Remove meat from bag. Several pieces at a time, cook meat until browned. Remove with slotted spoon and place in large baking pan. Sprinkle with thyme and paprika. Combine bouillon and wine; pour over meat. Cover tightly with foil. Bake 1 hour, basting occasionally. Remove cover; bake 30 minutes longer or until meat is fork tender.

Makes 12 to 18 servings.

PER EACH OF 12 SERVINGS:

363 calories
27 g protein
21 g fat
8 g carbohydrate
137 mg sodium
79 mg cholesterol

N O T E
To make gravy, combine 2 tablespoons flour with 4 tablespoons water. Add to pan after removing foil.

ESSENCE BRINGS YOU GREAT COOKING

TEXAS OVEN-BARBECUED BRISKET

Our version of the 24-hour Texas pit-cooked brisket takes only 6 hours. The moist, juicy, and flavorful results are well worth the wait!

Makes 10 servings.

PER SERVING:

382 calories
54 g protein
15 g fat
3 g carbohydrate
525 mg sodium
162 mg cholesterol

1 5-pound lean-beef brisket
1 large garlic clove, peeled, halved lengthwise
1 tablespoon liquid smoke *(optional)*
½ teaspoon celery salt *(optional)*
½ teaspoon onion salt *(optional)*
¼ teaspoon ground black pepper
1 cup barbecue sauce

Wipe brisket with damp cloth. Rub meat with cut side of garlic. Sprinkle with liquid smoke, salts (if desired), and pepper, then rub seasonings into meat. Place meat in large glass baking dish; cover with foil. Refrigerate 4 hours or overnight to marinate. Preheat broiler; broil meat, about 8 minutes, until seared on each side. Heat oven to 275° F. Place meat on large sheet of foil, ; brush both sides of brisket with about ½ cup of barbecue sauce. Wrap in foil, sealing completely. Place in baking pan; bake 5½ to 6 hours. To serve: Remove from foil; thinly slice across grain. Spoon slices with remaining barbecue sauce or pass sauce separately.

WARM BEEF-AND-BLACK-EYED-PEA SALAD

This hearty main-dish salad, which features familiar foods in a unique combination, was the first-place winner in the 1987 National Beef Cook-Off.

1 16-ounce package frozen black-eyed peas
1 cup Lime-Chili Vinaigrette (see following recipe)
1½ pounds top sirloin steak, 1½ inches thick, trimmed of fat
¼ cup red wine vinegar
1 cup diced jicama* (¼-inch cubes)
1 red or green bell pepper, seeded, cut into 1-inch strips or chopped
1 4-ounce can green chilies, drained
½ cup sliced scallions
½ cup sliced black olives
¼ cup chopped cilantro
About 8 lettuce leaves
Optional garnishes: cherry tomatoes, cilantro sprigs

Makes 8 servings.

PER SERVING:

384 calories
25 g protein
23 g fat
19 g carbohydrate
419 mg sodium
57 mg cholesterol

Prepare peas according to package directions; drain and reserve. Prepare Lime-Chili Vinaigrette. Place steak in plastic bag or shallow glass dish. In small bowl, combine ¼ cup vinaigrette and vinegar; pour over steak, turning meat to coat. Close bag securely, place in refrigerator to marinate about 1 hour, turning meat at least once. Remove steak and place on lightly greased broiler rack. Broil, 3 inches from heat source, 6 to 7 minutes on each side or until cooked to personal preference. Meanwhile, in large skillet, combine remaining vinaigrette, cooked black-eyed peas, jicama, bell pepper, chilies, scallions and olives. Cover and simmer over medium-low heat about 5 minutes or until heated through; add cilantro. Line serving dish with lettuce. Spoon pea mixture over lettuce leaves, making a depression in center. Carve steak diagonally into thin slices. Arrange beef in center of pea mixture. Garnish with tomatoes and cilantro sprigs.

*Jicama is a crunchy vegetable, readily available in Hispanic, and specialty food shops.

ESSENCE BRINGS YOU
GREAT COOKING

LIME-CHILI VINAIGRETTE

Makes 8 servings.

PER CUP:

64 calories
0 g protein
7 g fat
1 g carbohydrate
68 mg sodium
0 mg cholesterol

½ cup lime juice
½ cup vegetable oil
1 teaspoon ground cumin
1 teaspoon chili powder
1 teaspoon sugar
½ teaspoon salt *(optional)*
½ teaspoon minced garlic

In medium-size bowl or jar with tight-fitting lid, combine all ingredients. Beat with whisk or shake vigorously until well blended. Makes 1 cup dressing.

HOME-STYLE BEEF-VEGETABLE SOUP

3 tablespoons vegetable oil

1 large onion, chopped

1 medium-size stalk celery, strings removed and sliced

2 medium-size carrots, sliced at least ½-inch thick

1 garlic clove, minced

1 pound boneless chuck (for stewing), cut in ½- to ¾-inch cubes

6 cups water

3 cubes or 3 teaspoons beef bouillon granules

8 black peppercorns

2 whole allspice

1 teaspoon thyme leaves

1 bay leaf

1 large potato, peeled and cubed

1 medium-size turnip, peeled and cubed

1 cup frozen lima beans, partially thawed

1 cup frozen whole-kernel corn, partially thawed

1 large tomato, peeled, seeded, cubed *(optional)*

2 tablespoons chopped parsley

Makes 6 to 8 servings.

PER SERVING:

342 calories
21 g protein
17 g fat
27 g carbohydrate
832 mg sodium
49 mg cholesterol

In large Dutch oven or stockpot over medium heat, heat 2 tablespoons oil. Add onion, celery, carrots, and garlic; sauté until vegetables are tender, about 5 minutes. Remove from pot and cover. Add remaining oil to pot; add beef. Brown on all sides, stirring occasionally. Add water and bouillon. Tie peppercorns, allspice, thyme, and bay leaf in several layers of cheesecloth bouquet garni; add to pot. Bring to simmer; cook about 20 minutes. Add sautéed vegetables, potato, turnip, and lima beans; simmer until meat is fork-tender, about 20 minutes. Stir in corn, tomato, and parsley; cook 10 minutes. Discard bouquet garni.

ESSENCE BRINGS YOU
GREAT COOKING

BARBECUED BEEF SANDWICHES

These hearty dinner sandwiches are a quick and tasty way to serve leftover roast.

Makes 4 servings.

PER SERVING:

508 calories
39 g protein
17 g fat
50 g carbohydrate
925 mg sodium
92 mg cholesterol

¾ cup catsup
2 tablespoons packed brown sugar
2 tablespoons minced onion
1 medium-size garlic clove, minced
½ teaspoon dry mustard
¼ teaspoon cayenne pepper or ½ teaspoon hot pepper sauce
¼ cup water
1 tablespoon vinegar
2 cups shredded or strips of cooked beef
4 sandwich buns, split

In medium-size saucepan over medium heat, combine first 8 ingredients. Bring to boil; reduce heat to low. Simmer, stirring occasionally, about 25 minutes Stir in beef; cover and cook 10 additional minutes. Meanwhile, if desired, toast buns. Spoon beef filling equally between split buns.

BEEFY TAMALE PIE

2 tablespoons light olive oil
1 large onion, chopped
1 garlic clove, minced
1 small green bell pepper, seeded, chopped
1 to 2 tablespoons chili powder
½ teaspoon salt *(optional)*
1 pound lean ground beef
3½ cups canned tomatoes
4 ounces packaged cornbread mix
1 8-ounce can whole-kernel corn, drained
12 pitted ripe (black) olives, halved
Optional garnishes: avocado, bell pepper slices, parsley, or cilantro
sprigs

Makes 6 servings.

PER SERVING:

359 calories
18 g protein
19 g fat
33 g carbohydrate
1,013 mg sodium
44 mg cholesterol

In large heavy skillet, heat oil; sauté onion, garlic, and bell pepper until tender but not brown. Mix chili powder and salt (if desired) with meat; add to skillet. Cook, breaking up large pieces of meat, about 10 minutes or until meat is browned. Add tomatoes; simmer slowly, stirring occasionally, uncovered 20 minutes. Meanwhile, heat oven to 350° F. Prepare cornbread mix according to package directions, omitting egg. In lightly greased 9- or 10-inch pie pan or 2-quart casserole, spread cornbread batter over bottom and sides. Stir corn and olives into meat; spoon filling into pie pan. Bake 30 minutes or until crust is done and filling is steaming hot. Garnish with avocado, bell pepper, and parsley.

PICADILLO

Especially popular in Cuba and Puerto Rico, this hash made with ground beef is uniquely flavored with raisins and capers.

Makes 6 servings.

PER SERVING:

478 calories
34 g protein
30 g fat
18 g carbohydrate
468 mg sodium
123 mg cholesterol

- 2 tablespoons olive or vegetable oil
- 1 large onion, finely chopped
- 1 large green bell pepper, seeded, chopped
- 1 garlic clove, finely chopped
- 1 fresh hot red or green pepper, seeded, chopped
- 2 pounds ground round steak
- 2 large tomatoes, peeled, chopped (about 2 cups)
- ½ teaspoon ground cumin
- ½ teaspoon salt *(optional)*
- ½ teaspoon freshly ground black pepper
- ½ cup seedless raisins
- ¼ cup pimiento-stuffed green olives, sliced
- 1 tablespoon capers

In large skillet, heat oil; sauté onion, bell pepper, garlic, and hot pepper until onion is tender, but not browned, about 5 minutes. Add meat; cook, stirring and breaking up, until it has lost its red color. Add tomatoes, cumin, salt (if desired), black pepper, and raisins; mix thoroughly. Simmer gently, uncovered, until cooked, about 20 minutes. Stir in olives and capers; cook a few minutes longer. Delicious served over rice.

HERBED BEEF PATTIES

Recent tests indicate that blotting cooked patties with white paper towels can reduce the amount of fat up to 9 percent. For light summertime meals, serve with Cucumber-Yogurt Sauce.

½ pound 90-percent lean ground beef
½ teaspoon dried rosemary
½ teaspoon dried thyme
½ teaspoon coarsely ground black pepper
¼ teaspoon salt *(optional)*
2 slices red onion
2 slices tomato
2 hamburger buns, split, lightly toasted

CUCUMBER-YOGURT SAUCE:
¼ cup plain nonfat yogurt
¼ cup finely chopped cucumber
¼ teaspoon dried basil leaves, crushed

In large bowl, combine meat and seasonings; mix thoroughly. Shape into 2 patties, each ½-inch thick. Heat large skillet over medium to medium-high heat until hot, about 5 minutes. Or prepare grill. Add patties; pan broil or grill 7 to 8 minutes, turning once. Remove to large plate lined with 3 layers paper towels. Let sit 1 minute, turning once. Meanwhile, mix ingredients for Cucumber-Yogurt Sauce. On each bun half, place patty; top with onion and tomato slices. Spoon with sauce.

Makes 2 servings.

PER SERVING:

365 calories
25 g protein
17 g fat
26 g carbohydrate
594 mg sodium
70 mg cholesterol

ESSENCE BRINGS YOU
GREAT COOKING

BEEF-MACARONI SKILLET SUPPER

Makes 4 servings.

PER SERVING:

339 calories
19 g protein
16 g fat
30 g carbohydrate
801 mg sodium
51 mg cholesterol

¾ pound lean ground beef
1 tablespoon vegetable oil
½ cup chopped onion
½ cup chopped green pepper
1 garlic clove, minced
2 tablespoons chopped parsley
½ teaspoon salt *(optional)*
½ teaspoon dried basil
1 16-ounce can tomatoes, chopped
1 cup elbow macaroni
1 cup beef broth
⅛ teaspoon hot pepper sauce

Brown beef in hot oil in large skillet, breaking meat into bite-size chunks; do not overcook. Pour off all but 1 tablespoon pan liquid. Add onion, green pepper, garlic, 1 tablespoon parsley, salt (if desired), and basil. Cook until onion is transparent. Stir in tomatoes, macaroni, broth, and pepper sauce. Bring to boil; reduce heat. Cover and simmer 25 minutes or until macaroni is tender. Sprinkle with remaining parsley.

CARIBBEAN MEATBALLS WITH PINEAPPLE CHUTNEY

1 pound ground beef
1 cup soft whole wheat bread crumbs
½ cup minced green bell pepper
2 garlic cloves, finely minced
½ teaspoon salt *(optional)*
1 teaspoon ground ginger
½ teaspoon allspice
1 large egg, lightly beaten
½ cup skim milk
Pineapple Chutney (see following recipe)

Makes about 24 meatballs.

PER MEATBALL:

66 calories
4 g protein
3 g fat
6 g carbohydrates
91 mg sodium
20 mg cholesterol

Heat oven to 400° F. In large mixing bowl, combine all ingredients except chutney; mix well. Gently shape mixture into 1-inch meatballs. In large baking pan, arrange meatballs in single layer. Into small bowl, spoon about ¼ cup chutney; brush meatballs with chutney. (To avoid salmonella contamination, do not use brush or chutney that has come in contact with raw meat at table.) Bake, rotating balls once or twice, until cooked through and brown, 15 to 20 minutes. Arrange on serving platter; insert wooden picks, if desired. Spoon remaining chutney into serving bowl or pineapple shell. Set aside for table use.

ESSENCE BRINGS YOU
GREAT COOKING

Pineapple Chutney

Makes about 1 pint.

1 medium-size pineapple or 16-ounce can crushed pineapple in juice (reserve juice)
⅓ cup packed brown sugar
¼ cup cider vinegar
1 tablespoon minced onion
¼ teaspoon salt *(optional)*
⅛ teaspoon ground cinnamon
⅛ teaspoon ground cloves
¼ cup raisins *(optional)*

With long knife, cut off crown and stem end of pineapple. Stand pineapple upright and cut downward to remove rind; cut out eyes. Cut flesh into small cubes. In large saucepan, combine pineapple with remaining ingredients. Over low heat, cook, covered, about 10 minutes. Uncover and cook, stirring occasionally, until thickened, about 10 additional minutes. Let cool; cover and refrigerate. Delicious served with meat, poultry, or fish.

N O T E

To serve chutney in pineapple shell, cut pineapple in half lengthwise or crosswise, then run knife between rind and flesh, close to rind. Remove flesh, leaving shell intact.

CHILI WITH CORN BREAD DUMPLINGS

2 tablespoons butter or margarine
1 cup chopped onion
1 cup diced celery
¼ cup diced green pepper
2 pounds lean ground beef
2 16-ounce cans salt-free, whole tomatoes, chopped
6-ounce can unsalted tomato paste
1 cup water
1 teaspoon salt *(optional)*
2 tablespoons chili powder
1 teaspoon hot pepper sauce
2 16-ounce cans kidney or pinto beans, drained, rinsed

Heat butter in large Dutch oven. Add onion, celery, and green pepper. Sauté and stir 5 minutes; do not brown. Add beef and continue cooking until meat is no longer red. Add tomatoes, tomato paste, salt (if desired), chili powder, and hot-pepper sauce. Let simmer uncovered 45 minutes, stirring often to prevent sticking. Add beans and heat thoroughly, about 10 minutes. Pour chili into 4-quart casserole dish and prepare dumplings.

Makes 8 to 10 servings.

PER EACH OF 8 SERVINGS:

429 calories
25 g protein
23 g fat
31 g carbohydrate
591 mg sodium
86 mg cholesterol

Corn Bread Dumplings

¾ cup yellow cornmeal
¼ cup flour
½ teaspoon salt *(optional)*
1½ teaspoon baking powder
1 large egg
½ cup milk
¼ cup shortening at room temperature
1 tablespoon finely chopped fresh parsley
¼ cup grated Parmesan cheese

Heat oven to 425° F. In medium-size mixing bowl sift together cornmeal, flour, salt (if desired), and baking powder. Add egg, milk, and shortening. Beat with wooden spoon until smooth, about 1 minute; do not overbeat. Stir in parsley. Drop rounded tablespoons of mixture around edge of casserole dish of chili. Sprinkle with Parmesan cheese. Bake 20 minutes or until golden brown.

ESSENCE BRINGS YOU GREAT COOKING

VEAL SCALLOPS WITH MUSHROOMS

Ed Bradley, the famed newscaster, is also a creative cook. He picked up cooking skills from his father and Uncle Lewis. His foray into the culinary arts was further honed during the years he spent in France as a foreign correspondent. This is his recipe for what he calls, "a nice easy meal."

Makes 6 servings.

PER SERVING:

280 calories
31 g protein
8 g fat
15 g carbohydrate
257 mg sodium
97 mg cholesterol

- 2 ounces dried porcini mushrooms
- 1½ cups lukewarm water
- 1 garlic clove, sliced
- 1 bunch flat-leaf parsley, stems removed
- 1½ pounds veal scallops
- ½ cup unbleached all-purpose flour
- ¼ cup olive oil
- 1 tablespoon butter or margarine
- Freshly ground black pepper to taste
- ½ teaspoon salt *(optional)*
- ½ cup dry red wine
- 1 tablespoon tomato paste

In medium-size bowl, combine mushrooms and water; soak 30 minutes. Meanwhile, chop together garlic and half parsley. Place veal between sheets of waxed paper; pound to ⅛-inch thickness. Dredge in flour, shaking off excess. In 12-inch skillet, over medium heat, heat oil and butter. Add chopped parsley and garlic; sauté 1 minute. Add veal in single layer; sauté 2 minutes on each side. Sprinkle with pepper and salt (if desired); remove from skillet. Spoon off excess fat; save juices. Add wine and tomato paste to skillet; stir, scraping bottom to loosen browned bits. Over low heat, reduce sauce, about 15 minutes. Drain mushrooms, pouring liquid through cheesecloth to strain. Add mushrooms and liquid to skillet; simmer 15 minutes. Taste and adjust seasonings. Return veal to skillet; cook 5 minutes. Chop remaining parsley. Transfer veal to warm serving dish, spoon with sauce; sprinkle with parsley.

ESSENCE BRINGS YOU
GREAT COOKING

378

HERB-BAKED VEAL CHOPS

2 veal rib chops
½ teaspoon ground sage
¼ teaspoon salt *(optional)*
⅛ teaspoon ground black pepper
2 tablespoons unbleached all-purpose flour
1 egg white
1 tablespoon water
4 tablespoons dry bread crumbs

Heat oven to 350° F. Wipe chops with damp paper towels; trim excess fat. Season meat on both sides with sage, salt (if desired), and pepper. Dredge chops with flour. In plate with rim, beat egg white and water. Dip chops into egg mixture, then into bread crumbs. In large greased ovenproof skillet or baking dish, arrange chops in single layer. Cover and bake 30 minutes; turn chops over and bake uncovered 15 additional minutes, or until golden brown. To test for doneness, cut into chop close to bone. Meat should not look rare or feel soft, but juice should be slightly pink.

Makes 2 servings.

PER SERVING:

235 calories
26 g protein
7 g fat
15 g carbohydrate
468 mg sodium
97 mg cholesterol

ESSENCE BRINGS YOU
GREAT COOKING

VEAL PICCATA

Makes 4 servings.

PER SERVING:

327 calories
32 g protein
17 g fat
7 g carbohydrate
326 mg sodium
131 mg cholesterol

¼ cup unbleached all-purpose flour

1 pound leg of veal, sliced very thin into 3-by-4-inch pieces to form veal scallops

2 tablespoons vegetable oil

2 tablespoons unsalted butter

Juice of 1 lemon

⅓ cup dry white wine

1 lemon

½ teaspoon salt *(optional)*

¼ teaspoon ground black pepper

Lightly flour veal on both sides. In large heavy skillet, heat oil and butter. Add as many scallops as will fit in one layer. Keeping heat as hot as possible without allowing fat to burn, sauté scallops until lightly browned and firm to touch, about 2 to 3 minutes per side. When veal is nearly cooked, sprinkle with lemon juice. Remove veal from pan and keep warm. Cook remaining scallops in same manner. To deglaze, over high heat, stirring constantly and loosening any browned-on bits, add wine to pan. Reduce liquid by half. Add juices that have accumulated around scallops and reduce to about 3 tablespoons. Pour sauce over veal. Slice lemon paper thin and put slice on each veal scallop. Sprinkle with salt (if desired) and pepper.

ROSEMARY-BAKED RACK OF LAMB

1 small 7-rib rack of lamb (2 pounds or less); have butcher cut away heavy, bony section from meaty end
¼ teaspoon garlic powder
¼ teaspoon salt *(optional)*
⅛ teaspoon black pepper
3 tablespoons apricot preserves
1 tablespoon chopped fresh rosemary

Heat oven to 400° F. Cut skin and most fat away from meaty side of rack. To French (expose ends of bones) with sharp knife, trim away an inch or more of fat and flesh from ribs. If desired, cover ribs with foil to prevent burning. Rub garlic powder, salt (if desired), and pepper into roast. Score remaining thin outer layer of fat in diamond pattern. In roasting pan, place roast rib side down. Cook 15 minutes. Meanwhile, in small saucepan melt preserves; stir in rosemary. Brush roast with herb glaze. Reduce heat to 375° F; continue roasting for 35 minutes, basting occasionally, until done. To test, pierce meaty portion with tip of sharp knife. If juices run pink, roast is medium rare; if clear, roast is well done. Let stand 10 minutes before slicing between ribs. Serve mature red wine such as Bordeaux.

Makes 3 servings.

PER SERVING:
385 calories
37 g protein
18 g fat
14 g carbohydrate
295 mg sodium
123 mg cholesterol

ESSENCE BRINGS YOU
GREAT COOKING

LAMB AND EGGPLANT DINNER

Makes 4 servings.

PER SERVING:

376 calories
27 g protein
23 g fat
17 g carbohydrate
1,090 mg sodium
90 mg cholesterol

2 tablespoons olive oil
1 pound ground lean lamb
1 onion, chopped
1 small green bell pepper, seeded, chopped
1 garlic clove, minced
1 small eggplant, cut into 1-inch cubes
1 16-ounce jar tomato or spaghetti sauce
½ teaspoon salt *(optional)*
¼ teaspoon ground black pepper
1 teaspoon crushed basil
1 teaspoon dried oregano
½ cup shredded part-skim mozzarella cheese

In Dutch oven, heat oil; add lamb and cook, stirring and breaking meat into chunks until it loses pink color. Push meat to one side. Spoon off all but 2 tablespoons fat. Add onion, bell pepper, and garlic to cleared side of Dutch oven; sauté about 3 minutes or until onion is clear. Stir in eggplant, tomato sauce, salt (if desired), pepper, basil, and oregano. Partially cover pot; simmer over low heat about 20 minutes or until eggplant is tender. Sprinkle with cheese; cover and cook about 2 minutes or just until cheese melts slightly.

CURRIED LAMB CHOPS AND MUSHROOMS

2 tablespoons butter or margarine

4 shoulder or rib lamb chops, about 1 inch thick, trimmed of excess fat

1 cup sliced mushrooms

1 small onion, chopped

1 cup beef broth or 1 beef bouillon cube in 1 cup water

1 tablespoon curry, or to taste

¼ teaspoon ground cinnamon

¼ teaspoon salt *(optional)*

¼ teaspoon ground black pepper

Optional garnishes: tomato wedges, chopped parsley

Makes 4 servings.

PER SERVING:

209 calories
17 g protein
13 g fat
4 g carbohydrate
438 mg sodium
67 mg cholesterol

In heavy 12-inch skillet over moderately high heat, warm butter. When foaming stops, add chops; cook uncovered, about 3 minutes on each side or until well browned. Remove from skillet. Add mushrooms and onion to skillet; cook about 5 minutes. Stir in broth, curry, cinnamon, salt (if desired), and pepper, scraping up any browned bits stuck to skillet. Bring to boil; reduce heat to medium low. Add chops to skillet; spoon sauce and mushrooms over them. Simmer about 10 minutes. Garnish with tomato wedges sprinkled with chopped parsley. Delicious served with green peas and rice pilaf or mashed potatoes.

HEARTY LAMB STEW

Makes 6 servings.

PER SERVING:

281 calories
22 g protein
13 g fat
19 g carbohydrate
708 mg sodium
66 mg cholesterol

1 teaspoon salt *(optional)*
½ teaspoon ground black pepper
½ teaspoon bouquet garni (mixture of dried thyme, parsley, and a
   bay leaf)
¼ teaspoon ground celery seed
2 tablespoons peanut oil
1½ pounds lamb shoulder, cut into 1-inch cubes
2 cups beef bouillon
6 small potatoes, peeled
6 small white turnips, peeled
4 carrots, scraped, and cut into halves
6 small onions, peeled
1 cup fresh green beans, ends trimmed, cut into halves

In small bowl, mix salt (if desired), pepper, bouquet garni, and celery seed; rub over lamb pieces. In Dutch oven over medium heat, heat oil. Add meat; stirring occasionally, brown meat lightly on all sides. Stir in bouillon. Cover and simmer 45 minutes, stirring occasionally. Add vegetables; cover and cook until tender, about 30 additional minutes.

ESSENCE BRINGS YOU
GREAT COOKING

GRILLED LAMB-AND-VEGGIE KABOBS

½ cup olive oil or vegetable oil
¼ cup red-wine vinegar
2 tablespoons chopped mint leaves
1 garlic clove, minced
½ teaspoon salt *(optional)*
1 pound lamb, cut into 1-inch cubes
2 small zucchini, cut into 1-inch rounds
2 small yellow summer squash, cut into 1-inch rounds
1 green bell pepper, seeded, cut into 8 pieces
1 red bell pepper, seeded, cut into 8 pieces
4 scallions, green portion trimmed to 1½ inches
Optional garnish: mint leaves

In glass baking dish, combine oil, vinegar, mint leaves, garlic, and salt (if desired). Add lamb; toss to coat. Cover and refrigerate overnight or several hours, turning occasionally. Prepare outdoor grill for cooking or preheat broiler. Reserve lamb marinade. On 4 12-inch skewers, alternate lamb with zucchini, squash, bell peppers, and scallions. Place skewers on grill or broiler rack; baste kabobs with marinade. Cook 20 minutes or until lamb is of desired doneness. Brush kabobs with marinade several times during cooking; turn once. Delicious served with rice. Garnish with mint.

Makes 4 servings.

PER SERVING:

318 calories
25 g protein
22 g fat
6 g carbohydrate
333 mg sodium
78 mg cholesterol

BLUE CHEESE LAMB PATTY

Enjoy this patty plain with vegetables or a salad, or with all the trimmings on a bun or in a pita bread.

Makes 1 serving.

PER SERVING:

317 calories
25 g protein
21 g fat
5 g carbohydrate
473 mg sodium
95 mg cholesterol

¼ pound ground lean lamb
1 teaspoon finely chopped onion
1 tablespoon catsup
¼ teaspoon Worcestershire sauce
Dash of ground black pepper
2 tablespoons crumbled blue cheese

On waxed paper, combine lamb, onion, catsup, Worcestershire sauce, and pepper. Shape lamb into 2 thin patties. Top 1 patty with half cheese; cover with remaining patty and press edges together to seal. Place patty on broiler rack, 3 to 4 inches from heat. Broil 6 minutes or until browned on top; turn over and broil an additional 3 minutes. Top with remaining cheese.

CURRIED GOAT

2½ pounds goat meat, cut into 1-inch cubes
1 small fresh hot green pepper, chopped
2 tablespoons curry powder or to taste
3 garlic cloves, finely minced
1 teaspoon salt *(optional)*
½ teaspoon ground black pepper
2 scallions, thinly sliced
2 cups water
1 tablespoon oil
1 large onion, chopped

Rinse meat briefly with cold water; blot dry with paper towels. In large bowl, combine hot pepper, 1 tablespoon curry powder, garlic, salt (if desired), and black pepper. Dredge meat in seasonings; sprinkle with scallions. Cover and let stand 30 minutes. Scrape seasonings off meat back into bowl. In Dutch oven heat oil. Lightly brown meat. Add water and seasonings from bowl. Cook over medium heat 45 minutes or until meat is fork-tender. Add remaining curry powder, butter, and onion; cook 10 minutes. Serve over rice.

Makes 6 servings.

PER SERVING:

241 calories
40 g protein
7 g fat
4 g carbohydrate
532 mg sodium
113 mg cholesterol

CHAPTER NINE

You Sweet Thing

Recipes

AMBROSIA PLATTER

TROPICAL FRUIT SALAD

FRESH PEACHES AND BERRIES IN TORTILLA SHELLS

FRESH PEAR SAUCE

BAKED BANANAS

BANANA FRITTERS

FRESH WINTER FRUIT BOWL

BAKED PRUNE COMPOTE

BASIC PIECRUST

BASIC DOUBLE PIECRUST

FRESH PEACH OPEN-FACED PIE

NO-BAKE BLUEBERRY-MANGO PIE

THREE-BERRY LATTICE-TOPPED PIE

FRESH STRAWBERRY TART

LEMON MERINGUE PIE

NO-SUGAR-ADDED APPLE-RAISIN PIE

MAPLE-PEAR CRISP

FLUFFY FROZEN PEANUT BUTTER PIE

DAVID'S FAVORITE SWEET POTATO PIE

SWEET POTATO–ORANGE CHIFFON PIE

SWEET POTATO–APPLE CRISP

PECAN PIE

DEEP-DISH APPLE COBBLER

COCONUT LAYER CAKE

BOILED WHITE FROSTING

APRICOT-BRANDY POUND CAKE

Recipes

We have an emotional attachment to sweets. Our use of "Honey," "Sweetness," and "Sweetheart" as names of endearment for our loved ones indicates the special link between our feelings and this taste sensation.

Our favorite desserts are loaded with tradition; they are also often loaded with calories and fat. Enjoy a taste of the past by keeping portions small (this is the hard part), or by replacing lard, butter, cream, and whole eggs with margarine, skim milk, and egg whites. The rich flavor and aroma of homemade desserts and the fond memories they may stir make them worth the effort.

CHOOSING YOUR GRAND FINALE

There are two basic things to consider when selecting the dessert to complete a menu. The first rule of thumb is the richer the main course, the lighter the dessert. Season is the second factor—cool, light desserts are refreshing choices for summer, while warm and hearty desserts add enjoyment to cold-weather meals.

What's Best When

SPRING
A fresh crop is sprung.
Strawberries.

SUMMER
The sky is the limit when it comes to summer fruits.
Apricots, berries, cherries, currants, melons, nectarines, peaches, plums, and watermelons.

FALL
There is an autumn cornucopia of choices.
Apples, pears, pomegranates, persimmons, and Tokay grapes.

WINTER
Citrus provides sunny flavor during cold weather
Carambolas, cranberries, kumquats, oranges, persimmons, tangerines.

YEAR-ROUND
Bananas, pineapples.

ESSENCE BRINGS YOU
GREAT COOKING

Tropical

Tropical fruits, with strange shapes and peels, are appearing Stateside more and more frequently. More than a curiosity, these luscious, exotic fruits can be the basis of a new realm of desserts. Coconut, one of the most versatile of the tropical fruits—providing food, drink, and oil for Islanders—is enjoyed there in its fresh form. In this country, we usually turn the familiar dried and grated coconut into glorious cakes. Bananas—another staple of the islands—can be found in American lunch boxes and in banana cream pie and the classic banana pudding.

Following are some of the less familiar tropical fruits you should get to know.

BREADFRUIT—Before it is ripe, this fruit is boiled, roasted, or baked like a vegetable. When it turns yellow and brown, it is made into a dessert.

CARAMBOLA—Otherwise known as star fruit. Does not require peeling. Add to fruit salads, fruit tarts, and beverages.

CHERIMOYA—The taste and texture resembles banana-flavored custard.

CUSTARD APPLE—Also called a sweetsop. The interior has soft, creamy pulp.

GUAVA—Popular as juice, nectar, jams, and jellies. Roselike aroma.

JACKFRUIT—This fruit with its warty, dark-green skin can weigh up to seventy pounds. It is eaten raw as a fruit or cooked as a vegetable.

MANGO—Simply the best! Ranges in color from green to gold and rosy red.

PAPAYA—This sweet, succulent, orange-yellow fleshed fruit is called paw-paw on some islands. Color ranges from pale gold to pink, orange-yellow to red-orange.

PASSION FRUIT—Named for its flower, which symbolizes the passion of Christ. Dark and wrinkled skin. Strain juice from pulp and use to flavor punches, tea, and sherbets.

INSTANT DESSERT SAUCE

Fresh fruits such as berries, apricots, and papaya can be quickly pureed in a blender or pressed through a sieve to make a rich-tasting sauce to serve with cakes, ice creams, puddings, or other desserts.

DRIED FRUIT

Prunes (dried plums) and other dried fruits are rich sources of fiber. They also contain important vitamins and minerals, and are naturally low in fat.

HONEY

A truly amazing food—more than five hundred bees must gather nectar from more than two million flowers to produce a single pound of honey! The flavor, aroma, and consistency of honey vary according to the type of flower from which the nectar is gathered. Every plant imparts a distinctive flavor to its honey. Clover, wildflower, orange blossom, and buckwheat (considered the healthiest) are popular flavors. As a rule, the light-colored honeys are mild in flavor, and the dark are stronger. Honey has long been thought to have medicinal value. Factually, honey contains sixty-four calories per tablespoon; that's more than sugar. Yet the fructose is sweeter, so you can use less. Some honey comes with a cut comb in the jar; the comb is edible. Substituting honey for granulated sugar is not an exact science—you must experiment. Generally, use ⅓ to ¾ cup honey (depending on desired sweetness) to 1 cup sugar. Reduce oven temperature by twenty-five degrees. It is recommended that honey not be fed to a child under one year of age, because of the bacteria it may contain.

MOLASSES

The dark, thick syrup left after most of the water used in processing sugarcane and sugar beets has been boiled off. Molasses contains trace amounts of iron, potassium, and calcium. Unsulfured molasses is the superior form. Count on sixty calories per tablespoon.

AMBROSIA PLATTER

Ambrosia is a mythological term that means "food of the gods."
It also means something extremely pleasing to taste or smell. All this and it is
so easy to make.

2 carambolas (star fruit), sliced
6 navel oranges, pared, sliced into rounds or sectioned, seeded
2 grapefruits, pared, sectioned, seeded
2 kiwi fruit, pared, sliced
1 pineapple, pared, cut into spears
1 16-ounce jar stewed prunes, drained
3 tablespoons honey
¼ cup orange juice
1 cup unsweetened coconut, plain, or toasted
Optional garnish: lettuce leaves

On empty or lettuce-lined platter, arrange fruit in visually appealing pattern. In small bowl, blend honey and juice; drizzle over fruit. Sprinkle with coconut.

Makes 10 servings.

PER SERVING:

190 calories
1 g protein
3 g fat
43 g carbohydrate
5 mg sodium
0 mg cholesterol

TROPICAL FRUIT SALAD

This is a lovely and light meal with an array of wonderful flavors. Perfect for a summer luncheon.

Makes 4 servings.

PER SERVING:

318 calories
18 g protein
11 g fat
43 g carbohydrate
307 mg sodium
30 mg cholesterol

- 1 small ripe pineapple
- 2 medium-size ripe papayas
- 8 ounces plain or herb goat cheese, part-skim-milk mozzarella, or Jarlsberg cheese
- 8 small lettuce leaves or 1 cup alfalfa sprouts
- 1 cup fresh blackberries
- 4 large fresh strawberries (stems attached for aesthetic appeal)
- 8 dried dates *(optional)*
- *Optional garnish:* edible flowers (available in gourmet-food shops—not from florists)

Using long sharp knife, quarter pineapple lengthwise. Slice pulp from rind. Leaving pulp on rind and wedge intact, cut pulp into bite-size pieces. Halve papayas lengthwise; using spoon, remove and discard seeds. Slice crosswise. Divide cheese into 4 pieces. On each of 4 dinner plates, arrange bed of lettuce; top with pineapple wedge, ½ papaya, cheese, blackberries, strawberry, dates, and flowers. Delicious served with nut bread.

FRESH PEACHES AND BERRIES IN TORTILLA SHELLS

3 ripe peaches, sliced
1 cup fresh raspberries
1 cup fresh blueberries or blackberries
2 tablespoons granulated sugar
6 6-inch flour tortillas
½ teaspoon ground cinnamon
¼ cup melted margarine

Makes 6 servings.

PER SERVING:

136 calories
1 g protein
8 g fat
17 g carbohydrate
91 mg sodium
0 mg cholesterol

Heat oven to 400° F. In large bowl, combine peaches and berries; sprinkle with bit of the sugar. Cover and refrigerate fruit mixture to chill. Meanwhile, wrap flour tortillas in foil; place in oven about 5 minutes to soften. In small bowl, mix remaining sugar and ground cinnamon. Brush one side of each warm tortilla with melted margarine; lightly sprinkle with cinnamon-sugar mixture. Turn tortillas and repeat procedure. Gently ease tortillas into each of 6 10-ounce custard cups; place 6-ounce custard cup in center of each tortilla to shape tortilla into bowl. Place custard cups on baking sheet; bake about 5 minutes. Remove 10-ounce cups. Turn tortillas upside down, fanning out tops, on baking sheet. Bake until lightly browned and crisp, about 5 additional minutes. Remove 6-ounce cups. Transfer to wire racks to cool completely. Place tortilla shell on each of 6 plates. Fill each shell with fruit mixture.

ESSENCE BRINGS YOU
GREAT COOKING

FRESH PEAR SAUCE

Serve this delicious sauce over waffles, pancakes, or French toast, or as a side dish. Leftovers can be refrigerated and enjoyed chilled or reheated.

Makes 4 servings.

PER SERVING:

126 calories
1 g protein
1 g fat
32 g carbohydrate
trace sodium
0 mg cholesterol

4 medium-size ripe pears
Juice of ½ lemon
⅓ cup water or apple juice
2 tablespoons sugar or honey
½ teaspoon ground allspice, ginger, or coriander
Optional garnish: fresh mint leaves

Rinse pears with cold water. Using sharp knife, halve and core pears; peel if desired, then chop or dice. In small saucepan, combine all ingredients except mint; over medium heat, bring to boil. Reduce heat to low; cover and simmer 5 to 8 minutes until pears are tender. If desired, coarsely mash cooked pears; stir to mix. Garnish with fresh mint leaves.

BAKED BANANAS

This versatile recipe makes a delicious side dish or desert.

4 medium-size ripe yet firm bananas
¼ cup packed brown sugar
1 teaspoon grated lemon or orange peel
½ cup orange juice or rum
1 tablespoon butter or margarine, cut into small pieces

Heat oven to 350° F. Peel bananas; halve lengthwise (quarter, if desired). Arrange bananas in lightly greased baking dish; sprinkle with sugar, lemon peel, and juice. Dot with butter. Bake, basting occasionally with accumulated syrup from dish, 15 to 20 minutes.

Makes 4 servings.

PER SERVING:

195 calories
1 g protein
4 g fat
43 g carbohydrate
36 mg sodium
8 mg cholesterol

ESSENCE BRINGS YOU
GREAT COOKING

BANANA FRITTERS

Delicately yet distinctively flavored, these delicious fritters are popular throughout the tropical islands. Serve as a side dish or dessert.

Makes about 20 fritters.

PER FRITTER:

82 calories
1 g protein
5 g fat
10 g carbohydrate
26 mg sodium
29 mg cholesterol

2 large eggs
¾ cup unbleached all-purpose flour
1 tablespoon fine or granulated sugar
½ teaspoon baking powder
⅛ teaspoon salt *(optional)*
1 cup milk
5 firm ripe bananas
½ cup vegetable oil

In large mixing bowl, using wire whisk, beat eggs, flour, sugar, baking powder, salt (if desired), and milk until blended. Cover and refrigerate at least one hour. Using small knife, thinly slice bananas and fold into chilled batter. In large skillet, heat oil. When hot enough to sizzle drop of water, add batter by large spoonful (about ¼ cup) for each fritter, allowing space between them for turning. Cook several minutes until golden brown on bottom, then turn fritters over and brown other side. In batches, add remaining batter to skillet. Serve warm. Fritters are delicious sprinkled with sugar and lemon juice or served with cream.

FRESH WINTER FRUIT BOWL

Feel free to substitute your favorite of the best fresh fruits from the market to make this refreshing honey-sweetened salad.

2 cups seedless green grapes
2 cups seedless red grapes
3 oranges, peeled, sliced crosswise
2 grapefruit, peeled, cut into segments
3 kiwi fruit, peeled, sliced crosswise
1 pomegranate, peeled, separated into seeds
¼ cup honey
1 cup orange juice

Makes about 20 ½-cup servings.

PER SERVING:

64 calories
trace protein
trace fat
15 g carbohydrate
2 mg sodium
0 mg cholesterol

In large bowl, combine all fruit except half of pomegranate seeds; mix well. In small saucepan, over low heat, combine honey and orange juice; heat and stir just until honey blends. Let cool; drizzle over fruit mixture. Gently mix fruit; sprinkle with remaining pomegranate seeds.

ESSENCE BRINGS YOU GREAT COOKING

BAKED PRUNE COMPOTE

Makes 4 servings.

1 cup applesauce
1 cup apple juice
3 tablespoons lemon juice
1 tablespoon pure vanilla extract
½ teaspoon ground cinnamon
¼ teaspoon ground ginger
¼ teaspoon grated nutmeg
½ cup dried apricot halves (preferably sulfur-free)
½ cup pitted prunes
12 dried figs, halved
1 pear, thinly sliced
1 cup plain yogurt

Heat oven to 300° F. In 2-quart casserole, blend applesauce, apple juice, lemon juice, vanilla, cinnamon, ginger, and nutmeg. Stir in dried apricots, prunes, figs, and pear. Cover and bake 1½ hours. Serve warm or cold. Top each serving with dollop of yogurt.

BASIC PIECRUST

1¼ cups sifted flour
½ teaspoon salt *(optional)*
⅓ cup solid vegetable shortening, chilled
¼ cup ice water

In medium-size bowl, sprinkle flour with salt (if desired). Using pastry blender, cut in shortening until mixture resembles coarse meal. Sprinkle water over surface, 1 tablespoon at a time, mixing in lightly and quickly with fork, just until pastry holds together. Shape into ball; dust lightly with flour. Flatten ball; wrap and chill. On lightly floured surface, roll dough into circle about 3 inches larger than pan size. To transfer pastry, lay rolling pin across center of pastry circle, fold half of pastry over pin and ease into pan. Press gently into bottom and sides of pan. Trim dough to even edges. Tuck edges under to form rim; flute or crimp as desired.

Makes 1 8-inch or 9-inch piecrust.

PER SERVING:

140 calories
2 g protein
8 g fat
14 g carbohydrate
.35 mg sodium
0 mg cholesterol

BASIC DOUBLE PIECRUST

This flaky pastry contains no cholesterol.

2⅓ cups unbleached all-purpose flour
½ teaspoon salt *(optional)*
½ cup plus 1 tablespoon vegetable oil
4 tablespoons ice water

Into large bowl, sift flour and salt (if desired). In small bowl, using fork, beat oil and water until sightly thickened and creamy; pour all at once over flour mixture. Toss with fork to blend. Gather pastry together (if too dry, add a few drops of oil and mix again). Shape into ball; chill before using.

Makes 1 8-inch or 9-inch piecrust.

PER SERVING:

248 calories
4 g protein
14 g fat
27 g carbohydrate
137 mg sodium
0 mg cholesterol

ESSENCE BRINGS YOU
GREAT COOKING

FRESH PEACH OPEN-FACED PIE

Makes 8 servings.

PER SERVING:

218 calories
3 g protein
12 g fat
29 g carbohydrate
222 mg sodium
0 mg cholesterol

1 unbaked 9-inch Basic Piecrust (recipe on page 403)
4 cups peeled or unpeeled, sliced, ripe peaches
1 tablespoon uncooked quick-cooking tapioca
3 tablespoons sugar
½ teaspoon ground cinnamon
⅛ teaspoon mace
2 tablespoons cold unsalted butter or margarine, cut into small pieces
2 tablespoons lemon juice
2 tablespoons no-sugar-added apricot preserves (optional)
Low-Cal Whipped Topping (optional; recipe on page 437)

Heat oven to 400° F. Fill piecrust with sliced peaches. In small bowl, mix tapioca, sugar, cinnamon, and mace; sprinkle over peaches. Dot with butter; sprinkle with lemon juice. Bake 25 minutes. Reduce temperature setting to 350° F. Bake 20 minutes more, or until crust is golden brown and juices are bubbling. Meanwhile, if desired, prepare whipped topping. Brush peaches with preserves, if desired. Let pie cool on rack until warm or room temperature. Serve with whipped topping.

NO-BAKE BLUEBERRY-MANGO PIE

Naturally sweet and rich with vitamins, minerals, and fiber, this exquisite dessert created by Aris LaTham, of Sun-Fired Foods of Takoma Park, is actually good for you.

1 cup almonds
½ cup pecans
Water
1 cup chopped pitted dates
1½ cups fresh blueberries
1 teaspoon five-spice seasoning or ¾ teaspoon ground cinnamon and
   pinch ground nutmeg
3 large ripe mangoes
Optional garnishes: blueberries, star-fruit slices, fresh figs, mint leaves

Makes 1 9-inch pie;
12 servings.

PER SERVING:

181 calories
2 g protein
9 g fat
26 g carbohydrate
3 mg sodium
0 mg cholesterol

In separate medium-size bowls, soak almonds and pecans in enough water to cover for 12 hours; drain and rinse. In food processor, using S blade or manual grinder, grind almonds to consistency of moist meal; transfer to medium-size bowl. Grind pecans in same manner; add to almond meal. In food processor, blend ⅓ cup dates and 3 tablespoons water until smooth. Stir date mixture into nut mixture; mix until thoroughly blended. Shape dough into ball; place on 12-inch length of waxed paper. Top with another 12-inch length of paper. Flatten ball with palm of hand. Using rolling pin, roll out dough to 11-inch diameter. Carefully remove top sheet of paper. Invert pie crust into lightly oiled 9- inch pie plate; press gently into plate (patch if it tears). Trim excess crust, press gently with fingertips to even edges of dough. Place crust in dehydrator set at 125° F for 2 hours, or heat conventional oven to 250° F; place crust in oven. Immediately turn off heat; let crust sit in oven with door closed 30 minutes or until it is dry and set. Meanwhile, in food processor, combine 1 cup blueberries (set aside best looking berries for garnish), remaining ⅓ cup dates and five-spice seasoning; process until of smooth, jam-like consistency. Using sharp paring knife, peel mangoes; in large pieces, cut pulp from seed. With broad sides down, cut mango pieces into thin slices. On bottom of prepared pie shell, fan ½ the mango slices into spoke-like spiral or other pattern. Spread with ½ blueberry jam in even layer. Top jam with remaining mango slices fanned into spiral or chosen pattern. Spread with remaining jam. Garnish with whole blueberries, star fruit, figs, or mint leaves.

ESSENCE BRINGS YOU
GREAT COOKING

THREE-BERRY LATTICE-TOPPED PIE

Makes 10 servings.

PER SERVING:

311 calories
3 g protein
14 g fat
40 g carbohydrate
165 mg sodium
trace mg cholesterol

Pastry for double-crust 10-inch pie (recipe on page 427)
6 cups fresh berries (2 cups each raspberries, blackberries, and blueberries, or combination)
1¼ cups sugar
¼ cup unbleached all-purpose flour
⅛ teaspoon salt *(optional)*
2 teaspoons grated orange or lemon zest (peel)
2 tablespoons butter or margarine, cut into pieces
2 tablespoons milk

Prepare pie pastry. Roll ⅔ of pastry into 12-inch circle. Transfer to 10-inch pie plate; do not trim edge. Refrigerate while preparing filling. Heat oven to 425° F. Remove stems and hulls from berries; rinse with cold water. Dry berries on paper toweling. In large bowl, sprinkle berries with 1 cup sugar, flour, salt (if desired), and orange zest; toss lightly to combine and coat berries. Taste berries for sweetness; if too tart, add small amount additional sugar. Spoon into pie shell; dot with butter. Roll remaining pastry into 10-inch circle; cut into 1½-inch-wide strips. Top filling with pastry strips arranged in woven lattice pattern. Fold bottom crust over edge of strips; form raised edge and crimp. Brush crust with milk; sprinkle with remaining ¼ cup sugar. Place on middle oven rack. (Place sheet of foil on lower rack of oven to catch spills.) Bake until crust is golden and filling bubbly, about 40 to 45 minutes. Cool slightly before slicing. Delicious served with cream or ice cream.

"A pie man named Santiago blew a bugle to attract customers as he walked down the street with his big basket of pies on his arm. He could swing it too (play the music well), and so could the waffle man who drove around town in a big wagon fitted out with a kitchen. When he blew his mess all the customers came running."

—Satchmo

ESSENCE BRINGS YOU
GREAT COOKING

FRESH STRAWBERRY TART

Fresh fruit tarts are the dessert gems of summer. For variety, you can use any other lush, ripe, in-season fruit or berry.

CRUST:

1 cup unbleached all-purpose flour

1 tablespoon sugar

½ cup (1 stick) butter or margarine, cut into 8 pieces

2 to 3 tablespoons ice water

FILLING:

¼ cup sugar

2 tablespoons cornstarch

1 cup milk

1 large egg

1 teaspoon vanilla extract

GLAZE:

⅓ cup red-currant jelly

1 tablespoon water

1½ pints fresh, unblemished strawberries, stems removed, rinsed, blotted dry

Makes 1 8-inch tart; 6 to 8 servings.

PER EACH OF 6 SERVINGS:

267 calories

4 g protein

13 g fat

34 g carbohydrate

158 mg sodium

38 mg cholesterol

To make pastry: In mixing bowl, combine flour and sugar; using pastry cutter or 2 table knives, cut butter into flour until mixture resembles coarse crumbs. In small amounts, add ice water, stirring until dough forms ball. Remove; flatten slightly. Wrap in plastic wrap or waxed paper; refrigerate 1 hour. Let dough stand at room temperature just until malleable. Heat oven to 350° F. On lightly floured surface, roll out dough to form 10-inch circle. Roll dough onto rolling pin; carefully transfer to lightly greased 8-inch round tart pan with removable rim. Gently press dough into pan; trim, leaving overhang. Fold overhang under, forming edge about ¼ inch higher than pan rim. Prick pastry all over. Place in oven on lowest rack. Bake until golden brown, about 25 to 35 minutes (check periodically for bubbles; prick with wooden pick).

(cont. on p. 408)

ESSENCE BRINGS YOU
GREAT COOKING

Cool pastry completely in pan on wire rack. Meanwhile, prepare filling: In medium- size saucepan, mix sugar and cornstarch; stir in milk until smooth. Over medium heat, cook, constantly stirring, until mixture reaches boil and thickens; cook 1 more minute. In small bowl, using fork, beat egg; stir in small amount of hot milk mixture. While stirring rapidly (to prevent lumps), slowly pour in egg mixture. Stir and cook just until thickened (do not boil); stir in vanilla. Cover and refrigerate until chilled, about 40 minutes. Meanwhile, prepare glaze: In small saucepan, over low heat, stir jelly and water until jelly melts; set aside. Remove tart ring, leaving shell on base, or slide pastry onto serving dish. Spoon filling into shell; spread evenly. Beginning at outer edge and working toward center, arrange strawberries, stem end down, in filling. Carefully brush strawberries with glaze. Refrigerate to set glaze and store until time to serve or pack.

Fresh fruit platter with Nutty Banana Bread.

LEMON MERINGUE PIE

1½ cups sugar
½ cup cornstarch
¼ teaspoon salt *(optional)*
1½ cups water
4 large eggs, separated
½ cup fresh lemon juice
1 tablespoon grated lemon rind
2 tablespoons butter or margarine
1 9-inch baked Basic Piecrust (recipe on page 403)

(recipe on page 403)

MAKES 8
SERVINGS.

PER SERVING:

345 calories
5 g protein
14 g fat
53 g carbohydrate
353 mg sodium
145 mg cholesterol

In 2-quart saucepan, combine 1¼ cups of sugar, cornstarch and ⅛ teaspoon of salt (if desired); mix well. Stir in water until blended. Over medium heat, cook and stir, until mixture boils and thickens. Remove from heat. In small bowl, lightly beat egg yolks; stir in small amount of hot mixture. Slowly pour egg mixture into remaining hot mixture, stirring vigorously to prevent lumps. Over very low heat, cook and stir until mixture is thick, about 2 minutes. Add lemon juice, lemon rind, and butter; stir until blended. Pour lemon filling into baked piecrust. Heat oven to 400° F. Meanwhile, to prepare meringue: In small, clean bowl, with clean beaters (mixer or rotary), beat room-temperature egg whites and remaining ⅛ teaspoon salt just until soft peaks form. Sprinkle in remaining ¼ cup sugar, about 1 tablespoon at a time, beating well after each addition. Beat until stiff and shiny. Spread meringue to cover lemon filling. Swirl meringue to make decorative top. Bake until meringue has golden-brown touches, about 12 minutes. Let pie cool completely before slicing.

ESSENCE BRINGS YOU
GREAT COOKING

NO-SUGAR-ADDED APPLE-RAISIN PIE

Makes 8 servings.

PER SERVING:

398 calories
4 g protein
19 g fat
54 g carbohydrate
164 mg sodium
8 mg cholesterol

5 to 6 cups cored, thinly sliced cooking apples such as Cortland, Rome Beauty, Newtown Pippin, McIntosh
½ cup frozen apple juice concentrate, thawed
2½ tablespoons quick-cooking tapioca, uncooked
1 teaspoon ground cinnamon
¼ teaspoon ground nutmeg
½ cup chopped raisins
Pastry dough for 2-crust pie (recipe on page 403)
2 tablespoons butter or margarine

Heat oven to 425° F. In large bowl, combine apples and juice. Sprinkle with tapioca and spices; lightly toss to mix. Stir in raisins. On lightly floured surface, using lightly floured rolling pin, roll out half the dough into 12-inch circle. Carefully fold dough over rolling pin and transfer to 9-inch pie plate. Unfold pastry and carefully fit into plate. Fill with apple mixture; dot with butter. Roll out pastry for top crust into 10-inch circle; cut into ½-inch-wide strips. Moisten top edge of bottom crust with water. Place strips about ¾ inch apart across filling. Lay equal number of pastry strips at right angles, diagonally, or woven through bottom strips. Trim strips even with bottom pastry overhang. Pinch edges to seal; fold under to form high edge. Using thumb and forefinger, flute edge all around. Bake 10 minutes; reduce heat to 375° F. Bake 30 additional minutes, or until filling is bubbly and crust golden.

MAPLE-PEAR CRISP

6 firm ripe pears, cored, peeled, and sliced or chopped
2 tablespoons maple syrup
1 teaspoon ground cinnamon
2 tablespoons water
½ cup quick-cooking rolled oats (uncooked)
1 tablespoon unbleached all-purpose flour
⅓ cup maple sugar or date sugar*
3 tablespoons butter, margarine, or dairy-free margarine

Preheat oven to 375° F. Grease 1-quart baking dish; set aside. In large bowl, combine pears, syrup, half the cinnamon, and water. Transfer to prepared baking dish. In same bowl, combine oats, flour, maple sugar, remaining cinnamon, and butter; using pastry blender or fork, mix until crumbly. Sprinkle topping mixture evenly over pears. Bake until top is golden brown and fruit is tender, about 30 to 35 minutes.

*Available in health-food stores.

Makes 8 servings.

PER SERVING:

174 calories
1 g protein
5 g fat
35 g carbohydrate
50 mg sodium
12 mg cholesterol

FLUFFY FROZEN PEANUT BUTTER PIE

This treat is so rich, all you'll need is a sliver.

Makes 12 to 16 slices.

PER SLICE:

225 calories
5 g protein
18 g fat
20 g carbohydrate
226 mg sodium
19 mg cholesterol

1 9-inch baked Basic Piecrust (recipe on page 403)
1 8-ounce package cream cheese, at room temperature
1 cup confectioners' sugar
½ cup creamy peanut butter, at room temperature
½ cup milk
1 teaspoon vanilla extract or 1 tablespoon rum
2 cups whipped cream or whipped topping
Optional garnishes: chocolate shavings (or other chocolate decoration),
 ¼ cup chopped peanuts

Cool pie pastry on rack. In large mixing bowl, beat together cheese, sugar, and peanut butter, until light and fluffy. Gradually blend in milk and vanilla. Fold in 1 cup of whipped cream; blend well. (Refrigerate remaining cream.) Into cooled piecrust, spoon filling; freeze until firm, about 3 hours. If not served same day, after pie is frozen, wrap in airtight freezer wrap. When ready to serve, decorate with remaining whipped cream; sprinkle with chocolate and nuts.

DAVID'S FAVORITE SWEET POTATO PIE

This spicy pie with its spirited topping was rated tops by Venezula Newborn's* husband, David.

2 pounds (about 6 medium-size) sweet potatoes or yams
Water
½ cup (1 stick) butter or margarine
1½ cups sugar
1 teaspoon ground cinnamon
½ teaspoon ground nutmeg
3 large eggs, lightly beaten
1 cup half-and-half or light cream
1 teaspoon pure vanilla extract
1 9-inch unbaked Basic Piecrust (recipe on page 403)

WHIPPED CREAM TOPPING:
1 cup heavy cream
1 tablespoon cognac or brandy
1 teaspoon pure vanilla extract
Optional garnish: pecan halves

Makes 12 servings.

PER SERVING:

334 calories
5 g protein
17 g fat
44 g carbohydrate
255 mg sodium
95 mg cholesterol

In 4-quart saucepan with lid, place sweet potatoes and enough cold water to cover. Over high heat, partially cover and bring to boil. Reduce heat; simmer potatoes until fork-tender, about 45 minutes. Heat oven to 350° F. Drain potatoes; when cool enough to handle, peel and remove blemishes. In large bowl, using potato masher or fork, mash potatoes. To remove lumps or string, press potatoes through large sieve back into bowl. Add butter, 1¼ cups sugar, spices, eggs, half-and-half, and vanilla. Using wooden spoon, beat until smooth. Into prepared piecrust, pour filling. Bake 60 minutes or until knife inserted into center comes out clean. Meanwhile, prepare Whipped Cream Topping: In medium-size, well-chilled bowl, beat cream until thickened, about 5 minutes. Gradually add remaining ¼ cup sugar, cognac, and vanilla. Continue beating until stiff peaks form. Refrigerate until ready to serve. Serve pie warm or chilled; garnish with whipped cream topping and pecans.

*Former Essence food editor.

ESSENCE BRINGS YOU
GREAT COOKING

SWEET POTATO–ORANGE CHIFFON PIE

Makes 10 servings.

- 1 baked 9-inch Basic Piecrust (recipe on page 403)
- 1 envelope unflavored gelatin
- ¾ teaspoon ground cinnamon
- ½ teaspoon ground ginger
- ½ teaspoon ground nutmeg
- ¾ cup packed brown sugar
- 3 large eggs, separated
- 2 tablespoons maple syrup
- ½ cup evaporated skim milk
- ½ cup orange juice
- 1 tablespoon grated orange peel
- 1¼ cups cooked sweet potatoes, mashed
- Low-Cal Whipped Topping (recipe on page 437)
- *Optional garnish:* orange slices or segments

Prepare piecrust. In 1-quart saucepan, mix gelatin, cinnamon, ginger, nutmeg, and ½ cup sugar; set aside. In small bowl, using wire whisk, beat egg yolks with syrup, milk, orange juice, and orange peel. Stir egg mixture into gelatin mixture. Stir in sweet potatoes, blending well. Over medium-low heat, cook and stir until mixture thickens; remove saucepan from heat. Let mixture cool. In large bowl, using electric or rotary beater, beat egg whites until soft peaks form. Gradually sprinkle in remaining sugar, beating until sugar is dissolved and stiff peaks form. With rubber spatula, gently fold sweet-potato mixture into egg whites until blended. Spoon mixture into prepared piecrust. Refrigerate until filling is set. To serve, spoon or pipe Low-Cal Whipped Topping around pie edge; garnish with orange slices.

SWEET POTATO–APPLE CRISP

Mary Medlock of Joliet, Illinois, was a winner in the 1986 Homecookin'
Cookfest for this creative dessert recipe.

FILLING:

3 cups mashed, cooked sweet potatoes, or 3 1-pound cans sweet
    potatoes, drained, mashed
¾ cup packed brown sugar
1 cup granulated sugar (add less if using canned sweet potatoes
    packed in syrup)
3 large eggs, lightly beaten
½ cup (1 stick) margarine, melted
1 tablespoon pure vanilla extract
1 cup unbleached all-purpose flour
1 tablespoon baking powder
1 teaspoon ground cinnamon
½ teaspoon ground nutmeg
¼ teaspoon salt *(optional)*
1 cup evaporated milk
1 20-ounce can apple pie filling

TOPPING:

¼ cup (½ stick) butter or margarine
¼ cup packed brown sugar
¼ cup unbleached all-purpose flour
½ cup quick-cooking rolled oats (uncooked oatmeal)
½ cup chopped pecans

Makes 16 servings.

PER SERVING:

333 calories
4 g protein
13 g fat
51 g carbohydrate
184 mg sodium
56 mg cholesterol

In large bowl using electric or rotary mixer, beat sweet potatoes and
sugars. Add eggs, margarine, and vanilla, beating until smooth. In
medium-size bowl, combine flour, baking powder, cinnamon, nutmeg,
and salt (if desired). Alternately add flour mixture and milk to sweet-
potato mixture. At medium speed, beat until blended. Heat oven to
375° F. Pour mixture into greased 13-by-9-by-2-inch baking dish.
Spread apple-pie filling over sweet-potato mixture. In medium-size
bowl, combine topping ingredients; sprinkle over apples. Bake 50 to 60
minutes. Cool; serve with whipped cream, if desired.

ESSENCE BRINGS YOU
GREAT COOKING

415

PECAN PIE

This time-honored Southern desert makes a memorable gift for a hostess.

Makes 8 servings.

PER SERVING:

478 calories
5 g protein
25 g fat
63 g carbohydrate
331 mg sodium
117 mg cholesterol

Dough for 9-inch Basic Piecrust (recipe on page 403)
3 large eggs
1 cup light or dark corn syrup
½ cup packed light or brown sugar
¼ cup (½ stick) butter or margarine, melted
1 teaspoon pure vanilla extract
1 cup pecan halves or coarsely chopped

Preheat oven to 350° F. Roll dough into ⅛-inch-thick circle. Roll pastry onto rolling pin; transfer to 9-inch pie tin. Unroll, easing into bottom and side of tin. With kitchen scissors or sharp knife, trim pastry edges, leaving 1-inch overhang. Fold overhang under; pinch to form high edge. For decorative edge of cutouts, trim pastry even with outer rim of pie tin. Shape scraps of dough into ball; roll again. Using 1-inch star or other shaped cutter, cut shapes from dough. Refrigerate pastry and cutouts until time to fill. In medium-size bowl, using fork or wire whisk, beat eggs lightly until blended. Beat in corn syrup, brown sugar, butter, and vanilla until blended. Arrange pecans in bottom of piecrust; carefully pour egg mixture over them. If using decorative pastry trim, arrange overlapping cutouts around edge of pie tin (if necessary help cutouts to adhere with beaten egg white). Bake until knife inserted 1 inch from edge comes out clean, about 50 minutes. Cool on rack.

DEEP-DISH APPLE COBBLER

CRUST:
½ cup (1 stick) lightly salted butter
1½ cups unbleached all-purpose flour
4 tablespoons ice water

FILLING:
12 medium-size Newton Pippin or Granny Smith apples
1 cup granulated sugar
1 tablespoon grated orange rind
1 teaspoon ground cinnamon
1 teaspoon nutmeg
¼ teaspoon ground allspice
½ cup flour
4 tablespoons butter, melted

Makes 12 servings.

PER SERVING:

486 calories
3 g protein
24 g fat
69 g carbohydrate
234 mg sodium
61 mg cholesterol

To prepare crust: Cut butter into small cubes; place in medium-size mixing bowl. Sift flour into butter; using pastry blender or fingertips, work until mixture resembles coarse meal. Sprinkle with ice water, 1 tablespoon at a time; mix until dough is formed (adding additional water if needed). Form into ball; dust lightly with flour. Slightly flatten ball and wrap in plastic or waxed paper; refrigerate 30 minutes.

To prepare filling: Peel and core apples; cut into eighths. In large bowl, combine remaining ingredients; mix well. Add apples; toss to mix thoroughly. Spoon filling evenly into lightly greased 13-by-9-by-2-inch baking dish. On lightly floured surface, roll pastry into oblong large enough to cover dish with an inch of overhang all around. Cover apples with pastry; trim overhang evenly. Turn excess dough under, forming rim. Crimp edges to seal tight. Cut several slits in pastry to allow steam to escape; if desired, decorate with design cut from pastry scraps. Refrigerate 15 minutes. Meanwhile, heat oven to 400° F. Bake until crust is nicely browned, about 1 hour. (Place baking sheet or aluminum foil on rack beneath pie to catch drippings.) Remove from oven; let rest 30 minutes before serving.

ESSENCE BRINGS YOU
GREAT COOKING

417

COCONUT LAYER CAKE

This time-honored cake is from <u>The Taste of Country Cooking</u> *by Edna Lewis. Toasting the coconut adds a new and delightful dimension to its taste. Also consider a Fresh Lemon Filling (see recipe on page 422).*

Makes 12 servings.

PER SERVING:

360 calories
6 g protein
14 g fat
57 g carbohydrate
199 mg sodium
57 mg cholesterol

2 cups sifted unbleached all-purpose flour (sift before measuring)
¼ teaspoon salt *(optional)*
3 teaspoons baking powder
½ cup (1 stick) butter or margarine
1¼ cups finely granulated sugar
2 large egg yolks, lightly beaten
2 teaspoons pure vanilla extract
2 teaspoons fresh lemon juice
1 cup milk, at room temperature
3 large egg whites
Boiled White Frosting (see following recipe)
2 cups freshly grated coconut or packaged flaked coconut (plain or lightly toasted)

Into medium-size mixing bowl, sift flour again; add salt (if desired) and baking powder to sifted flour. Set aside. In large mixing bowl, stir butter with wooden spoon until shiny. Add sugar in quarters, stirring well after each addition. When mixture becomes light and graininess diminishes, add egg yolks, mix well. Stir in vanilla and lemon juice. Add ½ cup flour mixture and ¼ cup milk, stirring until batter is smooth. Alternate flour and milk (ending with flour) until all ingredients are used. Beat egg whites to soft peaks; carefully fold into batter. Heat oven to 375° F. Lightly grease 2 9-inch layer-cake pans; dust bottoms with flour. Spoon an equal amount of batter into prepared pans. Place on middle rack of oven; bake until cakes shrink from side of pans, about 30 minutes. (Or pick up pans and listen for quiet noises in cake; if you hear faint sounds, remove from oven.) Turn cakes out onto wire cake rack. Let sit 10 minutes, then cover with light, clean cloth until ready to frost (to prevent drying out). Brush loose crumbs from cake. Place first layer on serving plate; spread generously with frosting, leaving enough for top and sides of cake. Add second layer evenly; spoon rest of frosting onto center of cake and quickly spread over top and sides. Sprinkle grated coconut all over, patting lightly with hand. Then sprinkle with remaining coconut for fluffy appearance.

Boiled White Frosting

1 cup plus 2 tablespoons sugar
¼ cup cold water
3 egg whites (medium to large eggs)
1 teaspoon fresh lemon juice or extract

In quart-size saucepan, combine sugar and water; let sit until water is absorbed, about 15 minutes. Cook over medium-high heat (watch carefully and stir frequently to avoid burning) until syrup spins a thread when it falls from spoon. Meanwhile, beat egg whites. As soon as syrup threads, remove from heat. Quickly finish beating egg whites until they hold their shape, then slowly pour hot syrup into beaten egg whites. Continue to beat until frosting holds its shape. Add lemon juice; let cool briefly before frosting cake.

"That Takes the Cake"

The cakewalk was an international dance fad. There were hundreds of cakewalk contests throughout the country. The winners received a cake as the grand prize—thus the expression "that takes the cake." The cakewalk, which made fun of the dancing and manners of southern White folks, originated on the plantation and grew into a turn-of-the-century rage.

"The marketplaces of West Africa were enlivened by the voices of women calling out the praises of the cakes they baked for sale. They also sold candies made out of sugarcane, which they pulled and boiled to extract the syrupy liquid. When it was fairly thick, the cook added coconut or chopped fruit. Later, many of these women, both slave and free, earned a tidy sum of money selling pralines, as these candies were called, in the streets of Brazil and the United States."
—African Heritage Cooking

APRICOT-BRANDY POUND CAKE

Makes 12 servings.

PER SERVING:

549 calories
7 g protein
7 g fat
77 g carbohydrate
290 mg sodium
187 mg cholesterol

1 cup butter or margarine, at room temperature
3 cups granulated sugar
6 large eggs, at room temperature
3 cups unbleached all-purpose flour
¼ teaspoon baking powder
½ teaspoon salt *(optional)*
1 cup sour cream or low-fat sour cream
1 teaspoon rum extract
1 teaspoon orange extract
1 teaspoon pure vanilla extract
½ teaspoon lemon extract
¼ teaspoon almond extract
½ cup apricot brandy
Optional garnishes: apricot slices, lemon leaves

Heat oven to 325° F. Grease and lightly flour 10-inch tube pan or 16-cup (4-quart) baking mold; set aside. In large mixing bowl, cream butter and sugar until light and fluffy. Add eggs, one at a time, beating well after each addition. Into medium-size bowl or onto waxed paper, sift together flour, baking soda, and salt (if desired); set aside. In medium-size bowl, blend together sour cream, extracts, and brandy. Alternately add flour and sour-cream mixtures to sugar mixture, beating well after each addition until ingredients are blended. Into prepared pan, pour batter. Bake approximately 70 minutes or until wooden pick inserted into center comes out clean. Remove cake from oven; cool in pan on rack 5 minutes. Remove cake from pan; cool completely. Garnish with apricot slices and lemon leaves.

LEMON ROLL CAKE

¾ cup unbleached all-purpose flour
1 teaspoon double acting baking powder
½ teaspoon salt *(optional)*
4 large eggs at room temperature, separated
⅔ cup granulated sugar
1 teaspoon pure vanilla extract
⅓ cup confectioners' sugar
1½ cups Fresh Lemon Filling (recipe follows)
Optional garnish: lemon slices

Makes 10 servings.

211 calories
4 g protein
4 g fat
40 g carbohydrate
251 mg sodium
130 mg cholesterol

Preheat oven to 375° F. Grease 15-by10-inch jellyroll pan; line with waxed paper. In small bowl, combine flour, baking powder, and salt (if desired); set aside. In another small bowl, beat egg whites until soft peaks form; sprinkle in ⅓ cup granulated sugar and continue beating until stiff peaks form. In large bowl, beat egg yolks until thick and lemon yellow; beat in remaining ⅓ cup granulated sugar. Stir in vanilla until blended. Gently stir in flour mixture. With rubber spatula, fold in beaten egg whites until blended. Spread batter evenly in prepared pan. Bake 15 minutes or until cake pulls from edge of pan and springs back when touched with fingertips. While cake bakes, sprinkle clean cotton towel with ¼ cup confectioners' sugar. Quickly turn hot cake onto towel; peel off waxed paper. Without waiting, carefully roll cake with towel, jelly-roll fashion. Cool cake on rack. Gently unroll and spread with Fresh Lemon Filling. Re-roll without towel; sprinkle with remaining confectioners' sugar and garnish with lemon slices, if desired.

"All food, especially cake, must be stirred clockwise if you want it to turn out well."
—Folk Saying

Fresh Lemon Filling

Makes filling for
8-inch layer cake or
jelly-roll cake.

½ cup sugar

2½ tablespoons cornstarch

¼ teaspoon salt *(optional)*

½ cup water

3 tablespoons freshly squeezed lemon juice

1 tablespoon grated lemon peel

2 large egg yolks

1 tablespoon butter or margarine

   In double boiler over hot, not boiling, water or in heavy 2-quart saucepan over low heat, combine sugar, cornstarch, and salt (if desired). Stir in water, juice, peel, and egg yolks; add butter. Cook about 15 minutes, stirring constantly, until mixture is thick and coats the back of a spoon. Cover and refrigerate until chilled.

RICH CHOCOLATE CAKE

This basic cake is tender and moist. The recipe yields two 9-inch layers, one 12-inch round layer, or one 9-by-13-inch sheet cake. Double the recipe for larger cakes or more layers. Keep ingredients at room temperature for about an hour before mixing.

2 cups sugar
2 large eggs
1 cup milk
1 cup cocoa powder
1 cup solid vegetable shortening
1 teaspoon salt *(optional)*
2 teaspoons baking powder
1 teaspoon baking soda
1 teaspoon pure vanilla extract
1 teaspoon almond extract
3 cups all-purpose unbleached flour
1 cup very hot, strong coffee

Makes 12 servings.

PER SERVING:

470 calories
7 g protein
18 g fat
73 g carbohydrate
295 mg sodium
50 mg cholesterol

Heat oven to 325° F. Grease, then flour cake pans. Into large bowl, measure and add all ingredients, except coffee. With mixer at low speed, beat until well mixed, occasionally scraping bowl with rubber spatula. Add coffee. Increase speed to medium; beat about 5 minutes, occasionally scraping bowl. Pour batter into prepared pans, smoothing mixture with rubber spatula. Shake pans back and forth on level surface to even mixture and disperse large air bubbles. Bake 30 minutes or until wooden toothpick inserted into center comes out clean. Cool in pans on racks for 10 minutes, then remove from pans and cool completely on racks. Meanwhile, prepare frosting. When layers are completely cool, frost and decorate cake.

ESSENCE BRINGS YOU
GREAT COOKING

SPICE CAKE WITH BUTTER-CREAM FROSTING

This lively tasting butter cake goes well with any occasion and can be baked in three 8- or 9-inch round layers, one 6-inch and one 10-inch square, or one 12-inch square.

Makes 14 servings.

PER SERVING:

557 calories
4 g protein
28 g fat
74 g carbohydrate
321 mg sodium
132 mg cholesterol

- 2¼ cups cake flour
- 1 teaspoon baking powder
- ½ teaspoon baking soda
- 2 teaspoons ground cinnamon
- 1 teaspoon ground allspice
- ½ teaspoon ground ginger
- ½ teaspoon ground cloves
- 4 large eggs
- 2 cups sugar
- 1 cup (2 sticks) butter or margarine
- 1¼ cups buttermilk
- 2 teaspoons pure vanilla extract

Heat oven to 350° F. Grease, then flour cake pans. In medium-size mixing bowl, combine flour, baking powder, baking soda, cinnamon, allspice, ginger, and cloves; mix well and set aside. Separate eggs, placing yolks in large (4-quart) mixing bowl and egg whites in a medium-size mixing bowl. Set whites aside. Add sugar and butter to yolks; using an electric mixer, beat at medium-high speed about 5 minutes until light and fluffy. Do not overmix. Add about ⅓ flour mixture; to combine, beat at low speed for few seconds. Add half of milk and all vanilla, mixing in same manner. Alternate remaining flour and remaining milk, beating just a few seconds after each addition. (Overbeating makes cake heavy.) With mixer at low speed, beat egg whites until frothy; increase to medium speed and beat until soft peaks form. Beat at high speed until whites are shiny and stand in high peaks when beaters are raised. Using rubber spatula, gently and thoroughly fold beaten whites into cake batter. Pour batter into prepared pans and bake according to following times: Bake 6-inch layers 25 to 30 minutes; 8-, 9-, and 10-inch layers 35 to 40 minutes; 12-inch layers 40 to 45 minutes. Different-size layers can be placed in staggered positions on two racks in middle of oven. Remove smaller cakes when done. Test by inserting wooden pick into center. Cake is done when pick comes out clean. Cool in pans racks 10 minutes, then carefully remove from pans and cool completely on racks. Cakes can now be filled, assembled, frosted, and decorated.

Butter-Cream Frosting

This all-purpose frosting can be prepared in advance and stored in a tightly covered container. This recipe makes enough frosting for a two-layer cake, 12-inch round cake, or 13-by-9-inch sheet cake.

½ cup (1 stick) unsalted butter or margarine
½ cup solid vegetable shortening
1 teaspoon pure vanilla extract
1 16-ounce package confectioners' sugar (4 cups)
2 to 2½ tablespoons milk or half-and-half

In large bowl, using spoon or mixer at medium speed, beat butter and shortening until blended and creamy. Blend in vanilla. Gradually add sugar, one cup at a time, beating well at medium speed after each addition (scrape sides and bottom of bowl often). Mixture will appear dry. Add milk and beat at high speed until light and fluffy. Keep frosting covered with damp cloth until you are ready to use it and while working with it to prevent it from drying. Frosting may be made up to a week in advance; return to room temperature before using.

Makes about 3 cups frosting.

PER ¼ CUP SERVING:

284 calories
trace protein
15g fat
21 g carbohydrate
168 mg sodium
21 mg cholesterol

ESSENCE BRINGS YOU
GREAT COOKING

425

NUTTY BANANA BREAD

This bread's flavor intensifies overnight. Serve with a main dish, as a snack, or for dessert.

Makes 1 loaf, 12 slices.

PER SLICE:

303 calories
6 g protein
17 g fat
35 g carbohydrate
109 mg sodium
46 mg cholesterol

2 cups unbleached all-purpose flour
1 teaspoon baking soda
½ teaspoon salt *(optional)*
½ teaspoon ground cinnamon
¼ teaspoon ground nutmeg
½ cup butter or margarine, softened
¾ cup sugar
2 large eggs
1 teaspoon pure vanilla extract
2 medium-size ripe bananas, mashed
¼ cup cold water
1⅓ cups finely chopped walnuts

Heat oven to 350° F. In medium-size bowl, mix dry ingredients; set aside. In large bowl, cream butter and sugar; beat in eggs until light and fluffy. Beat in vanilla and bananas. Add flour mixture; beat just until blended. Add water; beat just to blend. Stir in walnuts. Add batter to greased 9-by-5-inch loaf pan. Bake 1 hour and 10 minutes, or until wooden pick inserted in center comes out clean. Cool in pan on rack 5 minutes; turn out onto rack to cool completely.

PINEAPPLE-CARROT LOAVES WITH CREAM CHEESE FROSTING

These mini tea cakes make great gifts year-round.

3 cups unbleached all-purpose flour (or use half all-purpose flour and
   half whole wheat flour; add ¼ cup milk)
2 cups sugar
3 large eggs
1¼ cups vegetable oil
1 cup chopped nuts
2½ teaspoons baking soda
2½ teaspoons ground cinnamon
1 teaspoon salt *(optional)*
2 cups (about 4 medium-size) shredded carrots
2 teaspoons pure vanilla extract
1 8-ounce can crushed pineapple in juice, undrained
Cream Cheese Frosting (see following recipe)
Optional garnishes: chopped nuts, shredded carrots, orange rind
   (sprinkle before baking or after frosting)

Heat oven to 350° F. Grease and flour 3 6-by-3-inch loaf pans; set aside. In large bowl, combine all ingredients. With mixer at low speed, or by hand, beat, scraping bowl with rubber spatula, just until blended. With mixer at high speed, beat 3 minutes, occasionally scraping bowl with spatula; by hand briskly beat about 6 minutes. Pour batter into prepared pans; sprinkle with chopped nuts, if desired. Bake until wooden pick inserted in center of cake comes out clean, about 25 minutes. Remove from oven; cool in pan on rack. Frost, if desired.

Makes 3 loaves;
8 slices per cake.

PER SLICE:

378 calories
4 g protein
18 g fat
52 g carbohydrate
48 mg sodium
45 mg cholesterol

Cream Cheese Frosting

Makes 2½ cups frosting; frosts 4 6-inch loaves, 13-by-9-inch cake.

1 8-ounce package cream cheese, softened
2 tablespoons milk, pineapple juice, or orange juice
1 teaspoon pure vanilla extract
1 16-ounce box confectioners' sugar

In medium-size bowl, combine cream cheese, milk, and vanilla; on low speed, beat until blended. Gradually beat in powdered sugar, 1 cup at a time, until smooth and of spreading consistency.

Cutting and hauling sugarcane on an island plantation.

WALNUT-SHERRY CAKE

This elegantly flavored sweet treat by Ireneta Burns of Simi Valley, California, is made with all the ease of a cake mix.

1 18-ounce box yellow cake mix
1 3-ounce package vanilla pudding
1 teaspoon ground or freshly grated nutmeg
4 large eggs
¾ cup vegetable oil
¾ cup sherry
½ cup chopped walnuts
Optional garnish: confectioners' sugar

Makes 12 servings.

PER SERVING:

423 calories
5 g protein
23 g fat
43 g carbohydrate
328 mg sodium
91 mg cholesterol

Heat oven to 350° F. Lightly grease and flour 10-inch Bundt or tube pan; set aside. Into large mixing bowl, measure all ingredients except nuts and sugar. With mixer at low speed, beat just until well mixed, constantly scraping bowl with rubber spatula. Beat at higher speed 2 minutes; stir in nuts. Pour batter into pan. Bake until wooden pick inserted in center comes out clean, about 55 to 60 minutes. On wire rack, cool cake in pan about 10 minutes. Remove cake from pan and cool completely on rack. To garnish: Just before serving, sprinkle confectioners' sugar through sieve over top of cake. To create design on top of tube- or loaf-shaped cake: Invert cake on plate; cover top with paper doily. Sprinkle with confectioners' sugar; remove doily by lifting straight up (pattern will remain on cake).

PUMPKIN SPICE CHEESECAKE

Start with all ingredients at room temperature.

Makes 14 servings.

PER SERVING:

319 calories
4 g protein
22 g fat
26 g carbohydrate
199 mg sodium
120 mg cholesterol

2 tablespoons melted butter
½ cup graham-cracker crumbs
1½ pounds cream cheese (3 8-ounce packages)
1½ cups sugar
1 vanilla bean
3 large eggs
1 cup mashed pumpkin
1 teaspoon pumpkin-pie spice
½ cup sour cream or low-fat sour cream
Optional garnishes: whipped cream, ground cinnamon

Brush 9-inch springform pan with butter, dust with cracker crumbs; set aside. Heat oven to 325° F. In large mixing bowl, combine softened cream cheese and sugar. Open vanilla bean, scrape inside with tip of knife; add to bowl. Using mixer at medium speed, beat until light and fluffy. Add eggs, one at a time, beating about 2 minutes after each addition. Stir in pumpkin, spice, and sour cream; mix well. Pour into prepared pan. Place cake pan in larger pan; fill outer pan with water halfway up sides of cake. Bake until center is set and wooden pick inserted in center comes out clean, about 1 hour. Remove from oven; remove cake pan from water. Cool cake in pan on rack. Remove side of pan; refrigerate until ready to serve. Garnish, if desired, with whipped cream; dust with cinnamon.

ESSENCE BRINGS YOU
GREAT COOKING

BREAD PUDDING WITH BOURBON SAUCE

1 loaf stale French bread
1 quart milk
3 large eggs
¾ cup sugar
1 tablespoon pure vanilla extract
¼ teaspoon ground or freshly grated nutmeg
¾ cup raisins
2 tablespoons butter or margarine, cut into small pieces

Makes 8 servings.

PER SERVING:

646 calories
13 g protein
29 g fat
85 g carbohydrate
571 mg sodium
192 mg cholesterol

Heat oven to 350° F. In large bowl, place bread torn or cut into 1-inch pieces. Pour milk over bread; let bread soak. Meanwhile, in medium-size bowl, beat eggs, sugar, vanilla, and nutmeg. Add to milk-soaked bread. Stir to mix well. Add raisins and butter; stir to mix well. Pour mixture into well-buttered 13-by-9-inch baking dish. Bake for 1 hour. Serve warm or cool with Bourbon Sauce.

Bourbon Sauce

½ cup (1 stick) butter or margarine
¾ cup sugar
1 large egg, lightly beaten
¼ cup bourbon whiskey, or to taste
½ cup pecan halves (optional)

In top of double boiler or in saucepan placed over a pan of boiling water, melt butter. Stir in sugar; heat until sugar dissolves. Add egg, stirring constantly, until mixture thickens. Stir in bourbon and pecans; let cool.

ESSENCE BRINGS YOU
GREAT COOKING

RICE PUDDING

This version of the traditional southern dessert is a quick and tasty way to recycle leftover rice.

Makes 10 servings.

PER SERVING:

148 calories
4 g protein
5 g fat
22 g carbohydrate
62 mg sodium
68 mg cholesterol

2 cups milk
⅓ cup sugar
2 tablespoons butter or margarine
1½ cups cooked rice
2 large eggs, lightly beaten
½ cup raisins
1 teaspoon pure vanilla extract
1 teaspoon ground cinnamon

Heat oven to 350° F. In medium-size saucepan over low heat, heat milk, sugar, and butter to just below simmer. Remove from heat. Stir in rice, eggs, raisins, vanilla, and cinnamon; mix well. Pour into ungreased 1½-quart casserole. Place filled casserole into baking pan with about 1 inch hot water. Bake until custard is set, about 40 to 50 minutes.

SWEET POTATO PUDDING

2 pounds sweet potatoes, peeled, finely shredded

1 cup brown sugar

2 tablespoons butter or margarine, melted

1 teaspoon ground cinnamon

1 teaspoon ground ginger

¼ teaspoon ground or freshly grated nutmeg

2½ cups coconut milk

1 large egg, lightly beaten

2 teaspoons pure vanilla extract

⅓ cup raisins

Heat oven to 350° F. In large bowl, combine all ingredients. Stir until thoroughly mixed. If too thick, add more water for desired consistency. Spoon into greased 2-quart baking dish. Bake about 1½ hours until set. Let cool before serving.

Makes 10 servings.

PER SERVING:

394 calories
5 g protein
15 g fat
63 g carbohydrate
59 mg sodium
27 mg cholesterol

ESSENCE BRINGS YOU
GREAT COOKING

COCONUT-NOODLE PUDDING

Makes about 6 to 8 servings.

PER SERVING:

326 calories
8 g protein
9 g fat
52 g carbohydrate
81 mg sodium
128 mg cholesterol

1 8-ounce package (about 5 cups) wide egg noodles
2 large eggs
2 cups ricotta cheese
½ cup firmly packed light-brown sugar
1 cup milk
½ cup flaked coconut
½ cup raisins
1 teaspoon pure vanilla extract
½ teaspoon ground cinnamon
⅛ teaspoon ground nutmeg
2 tablespoons butter or margarine
Optional garnish: berries or other fresh fruit

Grease 2-quart baking dish; set aside. Heat oven to 350° F. Cook noodles according to package directions. Meanwhile, in medium-size bowl, lightly beat eggs, cheese, and sugar until blended; stir in milk, coconut, raisins, vanilla, and spices. Drain noodles; toss with butter. Add noodles to coconut mixture; mix well. Pour into baking dish; cover with foil. Bake 40 to 45 minutes; to brown top lightly, remove foil during last 20 minutes. Serve warm or chilled. Garnish each serving with berries or other fruit.

ESSENCE BRINGS YOU
GREAT COOKING

GRAND MARNIER SOUFFLÉ

¼ cup butter or margarine

⅓ cup unbleached all-purpose flour

⅛ teaspoon salt *(optional)*

1½ cups milk

½ cup sugar

4 large egg yolks

⅓ cup Grand Marnier or other orange liqueur

1 tablespoon grated orange peel

6 large egg whites, at room temperature

¼ teaspoon cream of tartar

Makes 6 servings.

PER SERVING:

269 calories

8 g protein

14 g fat

26 g carbohydrate

168 mg sodium

209 mg cholesterol

Butter 2-quart soufflé dish or round casserole. Lightly sprinkle with sugar; tap out any excess. In 3-quart saucepan, over low heat, melt butter. Stir in flour and salt (if desired) until mixture has thickened. Remove pan from heat. Add milk; using whisk, beat vigorously until blended. Beat 2 tablespoons sugar into milk mixture. Rapidly beat in egg yolks all at once. Stir in liqueur and orange peel; set aside. Heat oven to 375° F. In large bowl with mixer at high speed, beat egg whites and cream of tartar until stiff peaks form. Using rubber spatula, gently fold egg-yolk mixture, about ⅓ at a time, into egg whites until blended. Pour mixture into soufflé dish, using the back of a spoon, about 1 inch from edge of dish, make 1-inch indentation all around. Bake 30 to 35 minutes until soufflé is well risen above top of dish and golden brown. Using 2 large spoons, serve immediately.

SLIM-LINE CHOCOLATE MOUSSE

Makes 8 servings.

PER SERVING:

120 calories
6 g protein
3 g fat
22 g carbohydrate
112 mg sodium
70 mg cholesterol

1 envelope unflavored gelatin
1 cup skim milk
2 large egg yolks
¼ cup sugar
⅓ cup cocoa powder
½ teaspoon instant-coffee granules
4 egg whites, at room temperature
½ teaspoon cream of tartar
2 tablespoons sugar
Optional garnishes: Low-Cal Whipped Topping, candied or fresh edible flowers, stemmed strawberries, or cherries

In medium-size saucepan, combine gelatin and ¾ cup milk; let stand 1 minute. Over medium heat, cook, stirring constantly, until gelatin completely dissolves, about 2 minutes; remove from heat. In small bowl, beat remaining ¼ cup milk, egg yolks, and sugar; stir into gelatin mixture. Stir in cocoa and coffee. Over medium heat, cook, stirring constantly, until smooth and thickened, about 6 to 8 minutes. Let cool, stirring occasionally, until mixture mounds slightly when dropped from spoon. In medium-size bowl, beat egg whites with cream of tartar until soft peaks form; gradually add remaining 2 tablespoons sugar, beating until stiff peaks form. Using rubber spatula or spoon, gently fold chocolate mixture into egg whites. Spoon mousse into 8 dessert dishes or 1-quart serving dish or mold. Chill at least 2 hours, 4 hours if molding. Garnish as desired.

LOW-CAL WHIPPED TOPPING I

This delicious low-calorie whipped topping is just what you need for holiday desserts. Per serving, it has less than one-third the calories of regular whipped cream!

1 16-ounce can evaporated skim milk
2 tablespoons frozen unsweetened apple-juice concentrate
¼ teaspoon pure vanilla extract

Place pair of beaters in freezer for at least an hour to chill. When ready, pour milk into narrow, deep bowl and beat at high speed for 3 minutes, or until soft peaks form. Add apple-juice concentrate and vanilla; beat until stiff.

Makes about 3 cups.

PER ¼ CUP TOPPING:

43 calories
3 g protein
.16 g fat
7 g carbohydrate
49 mg sodium
1.5 mg cholesterol

LOW-CAL WHIPPED TOPPING II

For a higher-volume topping, chill bowl and beaters in freezer before starting.

3 tablespoons ice water
3 tablespoons nonfat dry milk powder
2 teaspoons lemon juice
2 tablespoons granulated sugar
½ teaspoon pure vanilla or almond extract

Into deep, medium-size bowl, pour water; sprinkle with powdered milk. Beat with rotary or electric beater until soft peaks form. Add lemon juice; sprinkle with sugar. Add extract; beat until stiff peaks form. Serve at once.

Makes 1 cup.

PER 2 TABLESPOON SERVING:

19 calories
.5 g protein
4 g carbohydrate
9 mg sodium
.3 mg cholesterol

FRUITY DATE-NUT BARS

Enjoy the natural flavors of these tasty bars made with no added sugar.

Makes 36 bars.

PER BAR:

84 calories
1 g protein
4 g fat
11 g carbohydrate
5 mg sodium
15 mg cholesterol

2 cups chopped pitted dates
1 cup chopped walnuts
1 cup whole wheat pastry flour
¼ cup corn oil
1 tablespoon pure vanilla extract
¼ teaspoon salt *(optional)*
2 large eggs, lightly beaten
1 16-ounce can unsweetened crushed pineapple, drained

Heat oven to 350° F. In large bowl, combine dates, ¾ cup of walnuts, and the flour; mix well. In medium-size bowl beat oil, vanilla, salt (if desired), eggs, and pineapple. Pour pineapple mixture into date mixture; mix well. Spoon batter into lightly greased 8-by-10-inch baking dish; sprinkle with remaining nuts. Bake 30 to 35 minutes. Cool dish on wire rack; cut into 36 small bars or squares.

THE BEST PEANUT BUTTER COOKIES

¼ cup solid vegetable shortening, at room temperature
¼ cup unsalted butter or magarine, at room temperature
½ cup chunky peanut butter
¼ cup granulated sugar
¼ cup firmly packed light-brown sugar
1 large egg, at room temperature
1 teaspoon vanilla extract
1¼ cups unbleached all-purpose flour
½ teaspoon baking powder
¾ teaspoon baking soda
¼ teaspoon salt *(optional)*
¼ cup chopped, unsalted roasted peanuts

In large bowl, combine first 7 ingredients; beat until creamed and fluffy. Into medium-size bowl or onto waxed paper, sift together flour, baking powder, baking soda, and salt (if desired); stir into peanut-butter mixture. Add nuts, stir until well mixed; chill batter. When ready to bake, heat oven to 375° F. By hand, shape into 1-inch balls; on ungreased baking sheet, arrange about 2 inches apart. Using fork tines, gently press down on each ball, making crisscross pattern. Bake until golden, about 8 to 10 minutes.

Makes about 24 cookies.

PER SERVING:

172 calories
3 g protein
13 g fat
10 g carbohydrate
129 mg sodium
16 mg cholesterol

GINGER RUM BALLS

These no-bake, easy-to-prepare confections make ideal last-minute holiday and hostess gifts.

Makes about 2½ dozen cookies.

PER SERVING:

70 calories
1 g protein
3 g fat
10 g carbohydrate
17 mg sodium
trace mg cholesterol

2 cups fine gingersnap crumbs (vanilla-wafer crumbs and 1 teaspoon ground ginger may be substituted)

1 cup finely ground walnuts or pecans (use food grinder, blender, or food processor)

1 cup confectioners' sugar

1 tablespoon unsweetened cocoa powder

3 tablespoons light corn syrup or honey

¼ cup dark or light rum

Optional garnishes: chopped nuts, plain or toasted shredded coconut, cocoa powder, confectioners' sugar, chocolate sprinkles

In large bowl, combine all ingredients except garnishes; using wooden spoon or your hand, mix well. With wet hands, shape mixture into about 1-inch balls. Roll in chopped nuts or other garnish. These confections will keep well up to 10 days stored in airtight canisters.

Watermelon Sorbet.

WATERMELON SORBET

You can double or triple this recipe as needed. If using an ice-cream maker, freeze in batches according to the capacity of machine.

½ cup granulated sugar
½ cup light corn syrup
½ cup water
2 tablespoons fresh lemon juice
1 9-pound watermelon or 2 quarts watermelon cubes, seeded
Optional garnish: strawberries, mint leaves

To prepare sorbet: In small saucepan over medium heat, combine sugar, corn syrup, and water; cook, stirring until mixture boils. Boil 5 minutes without stirring. Stir in lemon juice; cool to room temperature. In blender, food processor, or food mill, pureé seeded watermelon. Add cooled syrup; pureé until blended.

Electric or manual ice-cream maker: Pour sorbet mixture into freezer can and freeze according to manufacturer's directions. If sorbet is still soft after churning, remove dasher and using large spoon, pack down in container; cover with foil and container lid. Return to machine; pack with ice or place in freezer about 2 to 3 hours before serving.

Freezer method: Pour sorbet mixture into 9-inch square baking pan; cover with foil or plastic wrap and place in freezer, stirring once, until frozen around edges but still slushy in center, 1 to 3 hours (depending on freezer temperature). Spoon into large bowl; with mixer at medium speed, beat until smooth but still frozen. Return sorbet to pan; cover and freeze until firm.

Makes 8 servings.

Makes 1 quart; 8 half cup servings.

PARTY SORBET BALLS: Prescooped sorbet will melt more slowly. Into shallow baking pan lined with waxed paper, arrange scoops of sorbet in single layer. Cover with foil or plastic wrap; freeze until serving time. Arrange scoops in chilled serving bowl; garnish as desired.

PER ½ CUP SERVING:
160 calories
1 g protein
1 g fat
39 g carbohydrate
13 mg sodium
0 mg cholesterol

> "When the pregnant woman began to show, they would rub her belly to determine whether it was a boy or a girl. Boys sat in the belly like watermelons, girls sat round like pumpkins."
>
> —*Jambalaya*

ESSENCE BRINGS YOU
GREAT COOKING

441

BANANA SORBET

This frozen confection tastes like a refreshing breeze from the tropics.

Makes 12 servings.

3 large firm bananas, sliced
2 tablespoons apple brandy
Optional garnishes: mint sprigs, banana slices

Place bananas in plastic bag; freeze until bananas are solid (about 1 hour). In food-processor bowl with metal blade, or in blender, combine bananas and brandy; process until smooth. Into medium-size bowl, scrape banana mixture. Cover tightly and freeze for several hours before serving. To serve, place scoop of sorbet into 12 sherbet glasses or shallow bowls; garnish with mint sprigs and banana slices.

MANGO SORBET WITH BERRIES

3 large ripe mangoes
¼ cup sugar
2 tablespoons fresh lemon juice
1 cup fresh raspberries
1 cup fresh blueberries
Optional garnish: mint sprigs

With sharp knife, carefully peel skin from mangoes. Cut flesh into lengthwise slices; discard seed. Chop to make about 3 cups. In covered blender or food-processor container at low speed, blend mangoes, sugar, and lemon juice until mixture is smooth. Pour into 8-inch square baking pan; cover with foil or plastic wrap. Place in freezer until partially frozen, about 2 hours. Into chilled large bowl, spoon mango mixture. With mixer at high speed, beat until fluffy. Return mixture to baking pan and freeze until firm, about 1 hour. To serve, remove mango sorbet from freezer and let stand at room temperature 10 minutes for easier scooping. Scoop sorbet into serving dish or bowls. Cover with spoonfuls of raspberries and blueberries; garnish with mint sprigs if desired.

Makes 6 servings.

PER SERVING:

127 calories
1 g protein
1 g fat
31 g carbohydrate
5 mg sodium
0 mg cholesterol

CINNAMON-CHOCOLATE ICE CREAM

This delightful dessert is the easy version of a made-from-scratch recipe from San Diego caterer Jerry Strom.

Makes 12 servings.

PER SERVING:

234 calories
3 g protein
16 g fat
21 g carbohydrate
12 mg sodium
58 mg cholesterol

½ gallon chocolate ice cream
1 tablespoon ground cinnamon
Optional garnish: mint leaves

Place ice cream in refrigerator until slightly softened, about 40 minutes. Spoon ice cream into large bowl; sprinkle with cinnamon. With wooden spoon or rubber spatula, blend ice cream and cinnamon; cover bowl and place in freezer until ice cream is firm. Line baking sheet or shallow, large pan with waxed paper. With ice-cream scooper or large spoon, scoop ice cream into balls and place on paper-lined sheet. Place in freezer until ice-cream balls are frozen. In large, chilled bowl or on platter, arrange scoops of ice cream. Garnish with mint sprigs. Serve immediately.

MERRIE'S GINGER TEA

Especially on wintry days, sipping a cup of her hot, spicy brew reminds Merrie Jones, who now lives in Brooklyn, of her sunny native isle of Trinidad.

One 2-inch-long piece gingerroot
2 cups water
2 whole cloves
Honey or sugar to taste *(optional)*

Scrub the gingerroot well. Peel or let skin remain; cut crosswise into thin slices. In small saucepan, combine ginger, water, and cloves. Bring to boil; cover and let steep from 1 to 5 minutes, depending upon desired strength of taste. Pour into teapot or strain into cups. Sweeten to taste.

Makes 2 cups.

SPIRITED CRANBERRY PUNCH

Makes 28 ½-cup servings.

PER SERVING:

84 calories
0 g protein
.07 g fat
12 g carbohydrate
3 mg sodium
0 mg cholesterol

2 quarts cranberry juice cocktail, chilled
2 cups vodka
2 cups ginger ale, chilled
2 cups sparkling mineral water, seltzer, or club soda

In large punch bowl, combine all ingredients, mixing well. Add ice cubes or ice ring.

APRICOT SPICE EGGNOG

3 1-quart cartons or cans eggnog, chilled
3 cups apricot nectar, chilled
½ teaspoon ground cinnamon
¼ teaspoon ground nutmeg

In large punch bowl, combine eggnog and nectar; mix well. Sprinkle with spices; chill. Refrigerate any leftovers.

Makes about 28 ½-cup servings.

PER SERVING:

70 calories
2 g protein
3 g fat
9 g carbohydrate
23 mg sodium
24 mg cholesterol

N O T E
Raw eggs used in preparing homemade eggnog can carry a risk of salmonella poisoning; pasteurized commercial products are a safer choice.

ESSENCE BRINGS YOU
GREAT COOKING

CITRUS SPRITZERS

Makes 16 ½ cup
servings.

1 6-ounce can frozen grapefruit juice concentrate
1 6-ounce can frozen orange juice concentrate
¼ cup fresh lemon or lime juice
3 cups cold water
24 ounces ginger ale, chilled
Optional garnishes: citrus slices, citrus peel cutouts, lemon leaves (without added chemicals)

In large punch bowl, thaw juice concentrates. Stir in lemon juice, cold water, and ginger ale, mixing well. Add ice cubes or ice ring; garnish as desired.

Bibliography

Armstrong, Louis. *Satchmo, My Life in New Orleans*, New York: DaCapo Press, 1954.

Bennet, Lerone, Jr.. *Before the Mayflower: A History of Black America*, New York: Penguin USA, 1988.

Blount, Roy. *One Fell Soup*, Boston: Little, Brown and Company, 1982.

Butler, Cleora. *Cleora's Kitchens: The Memoir of a Cook and Eight Decades of Great American Food*, Tulsa: Council Oak Books, 1990.

Charles, Ray. *Brother Ray*, New York: Warner Books, 1978.

Chase, Leah. *The Dooky Chase Cookbook*, Gretna: Pelican Publishing Co. 1990.

Courlander, Harold. *A Treasury of Afro-American Folklore*, New York: Crown Publishers Inc., 1976.

Darden, Norma Jean and Carole: *Spoonbread and Strawberry Wine*, New York: Fawcett Books, 1978.

Ellison, Ralph. *Invisible Man*, New York: Signet Books, 1952.

Harris, Jessica, B.. *Iron Pots and Wooden Spoons*, New York: Atheneum, 1989.

Herbst, Sharon Tyler. *Food Lover's Companion*, Hauppauge: Barron's Educational Service, Inc., 1990.

Holder, Geoffrey: *The Caribbean Cookbook*, New York: Viking Penguin, 1973.

Lester, Julius. *Black Folktales*: New York: Grove Weidenfeld, 1970.

Lewis, Edna. *The Taste of Country Cooking*, New York: Alfred A. Knopf, 1976.

Mendes, Helen: *The African Heritage Cookbook*, New York: Macmillan Publishing Co., 1971.

National Council of Negro Women, Inc.: *Historical Cookbook of the American Negro*, Washington, D.C.: National Council of Negro Women, Inc., 1958.

Paige, Howard. *Aspects of Afro-American Cookery*, Southfield: Aspects Publishing, 1987.

Pinderhughes, John. *Family of the Spirit Cookbook*, New York: Simon & Schuster, Inc., 1990.

Teish, Luisah, *Jambalaya*, New York: Harper & Row, 1985.

ESSENCE BRINGS YOU
GREAT COOKING

Photography Credits

Chapter One
Root Vegetables, Steven Mark Needham
Akkra, Christophene Salad, Ratatouille, Steven Mark Needham
Vegetable Cheese Pie, Alan Richardson
Vegetarian Kabobs, Marcus Tullis
"Field of Greens," Meredith Nemirov
Picking Greens, The Bettmann Archive

Chapter Two
Black Bean Soup, Robert Tardio
"Girl with Peanuts," The Bettmann Archive
"Vendor with Beans," The Bettmann Archive

Chapter Three
Rice Ring, Marian Tripp Communications
Aris's Kush Tabuleh, David Bishop

Chapter Four
Cheese-Herb Bread, Tom Eckerle
Orange Peanut Muffins, Steven Mark Needham
Banana Bran Pancakes, Steven Mark Needham
Dressing step-by-step, Tom Eckerle
"Aunt Jemima," The Bettmann Archive

Chapter Five
Creamy Scrambled Eggs, Steven Mark Needham
Cheese-and-Vegetable Quiche, Tom Eckerle
Turkey Hash with Baked Eggs, Mark Ferri
Sunrise Health Shake, John Uher

Chapter Six
Catfish Fingers, Steven Mark Needham
Caldo de Peixe, Steven Mark Needham
Island Codfish and Peppers, Rita Maas

Chapter Seven
Roast Chicken with Garden Vegetables, Steven Mark Needham
Barbecued Cornish Hens, Eugene Knowles
Maple-Glazed Chicken, Eric Jacobson
Chicken Succotash, Cynthia Brown
Turkey Meatloaf, Steven Mark Needham
Spicy Orange-Glazed Turkey Drumsticks, Rita Maas
Maple Baked Chicken, Eric Jacobson

Chapter Eight
Rolled Rump Roast with Pan-Roasted Vegetables, Cynthia Brown

Chapter Nine
Watermelon Sorbet, James Kozyra
Assorted Baked Goods, Rita Maas
Deep-Dish Apple Cobbler, Tom Eckerle
Fresh Fruit Platter with Cheese and Nut Bread, Tom Eckerle
Fresh Peach Open-Faced Pie, Tom Eckerle

Index

ESSENCE BRINGS YOU
GREAT COOKING

ESSENCE BRINGS YOU
GREAT COOKING

ESSENCE BRINGS YOU
GREAT COOKING

ESSENCE BRINGS YOU
GREAT COOKING

ESSENCE BRINGS YOU
GREAT COOKING

ESSENCE BRINGS YOU
GREAT COOKING